HULL LIBRARIES

5 4072 10153301 0

STUART WOMEN PLAYWRIGHTS, 1613–1713

General Editor's Preface
Helen Ostovich, McMaster University

Performance assumes a string of creative, analytical, and collaborative acts that, in defiance of theatrical ephemerality, live on through records, manuscripts, and printed books. The monographs and essay collections in this series offer original research which addresses theatre histories and performance histories in the context of the sixteenth and seventeenth century life. Of especial interest are studies in which women's activities are a central feature of discussion as financial or technical supporters (patrons, musicians, dancers, seamstresses, wigmakers, or 'gatherers'), if not authors or performers per se. Welcome too are critiques of early modern drama that not only take into account the production values of the plays, but also speculate on how intellectual advances or popular culture affect the theatre.

The series logo, selected by my colleague Mary V. Silcox, derives from Thomas Combe's duodecimo volume, *The Theater of Fine Devices* (London, 1592), Emblem VI, sig. B. The emblem of four masks has a verse which makes claims for the increasing complexity of early modern experience, a complexity that makes interpretation difficult. Hence the corresponding perhaps uneasy rise in sophistication:

> Masks will be more hereafter in request,
> And grow more deare than they did heretofore.

No longer simply signs of performance 'in play and jest', the mask has become the 'double face' worn 'in earnest' even by 'the best' of people, in order to manipulate or profit from the world around them. The books stamped with this design attempt to understand the complications of performance produced on stage and interpreted by the audience, whose experiences outside the theatre may reflect the emblem's argument:

> Most men do use some colour'd shift
> For to conceal their craftie drift.

Centuries after their first presentations, the possible performance choices and meanings they engender still stir the imaginations of actors, audiences, and readers of early plays. The products of scholarly creativity in this series, I hope, will also stir imaginations to new ways of thinking about performance.

Stuart Women Playwrights, 1613–1713

PILAR CUDER-DOMÍNGUEZ
University of Huelva, Spain

ASHGATE

© Pilar Cuder-Domínguez 2011

All rights reserved. No part of this publication may be reproduced, stored in a retrieval system or transmitted in any form or by any means, electronic, mechanical, photocopying, recording or otherwise without the prior permission of the publisher.

Pilar Cuder-Domínguez has asserted her right under the Copyright, Designs and Patents Act, 1988, to be identified as the author of this work.

Published by
Ashgate Publishing Limited
Wey Court East
Union Road
Farnham
Surrey, GU9 7PT
England

Ashgate Publishing Company
Suite 420
101 Cherry Street
Burlington
VT 05401-4405
USA

www.ashgate.com

British Library Cataloguing in Publication Data
Cuder-Domínguez, Pilar.
 Stuart women playwrights, 1613–1713. – (Studies in performance and early modern drama)
 1. English drama – 17th century – History and criticism. 2. English drama – Women authors – History and criticism. 3. Women dramatists, English – Early modern, 1500–1700. 4. Women in the theater – England – History – 17th century. I. Title II. Series
 822.4'099287-dc22

Library of Congress Cataloging-in-Publication Data
Cuder-Domínguez, Pilar.
 Stuart women playwrights, 1613–1713 / by Pilar Cuder-Domínguez.
  p. cm. — (Studies in performance and early modern drama)
 Includes index.
 ISBN 978-0-7546-6713-1 (hardback: alk. paper) ISBN 978-1-4094-2464-2 (ebook)
 1. English drama—Women authors—History and criticism. 2. English drama—17th century—History and criticism. 3. Women and literature—Great Britain—History—17th century. I. Title.
 PR113.C83 2011
 822'.4099282—dc22

2010027219

ISBN: 9780754667131 (hbk)
ISBN: 9781409424642 (ebk)

Printed and bound in Great Britain by the
MPG Books Group, UK

To Juan Antonio

Contents

Acknowledgements		*ix*
1	Re-Crafting Tragedy: Gender and Genre in Seventeenth-Century Drama	1
2	Early Stuart Women Writers: Elizabeth Cary	15
3	The Interregnum: Margaret Cavendish's Dramatic Experiments	35
4	The Restoration Commercial Stage: Frances Boothby and Aphra Behn	55
5	Late Stuart Writers I: Mary Pix and Delarivier Manley	81
6	Late Stuart Writers II: Catharine Trotter and the Historical Tragedy	103
7	The Last of the Stuarts: Jane Wiseman and Anne Finch	121
Works Cited		*129*
Index		*143*

Acknowledgements

Support for much of the research for this project was provided by the Spanish Ministry of Education's research programme (Project ID HUM2006–09252). I owe a debt of gratitude to many people. Deirdre Finnerty read the first rough copy of this manuscript and helped with proofreading. My thanks to Cambridge University Library, to the English Faculty Library and to St. Edmund's College, Cambridge, for their hospitality and assistance during my research visits over the years. I can truly say that this book would never have been completed without their help. To fellow Aphra Behn Europe Society members, particularly Janet Todd and Derek Hughes, my gratitude for encouraging my research. S.E.D.E.R.I. conferences have often provided a forum for my work and I cannot thank the Society's members in Spain and Portugal enough for their support. My friends and colleagues at the University of Huelva (Zenón Luis-Martínez, Sonia Villegas-López, Mar Gallego, Beatriz Domínguez-García and Auxiliadora Pérez-Vides) and at the University of Seville (Manuel J. Gómez-Lara, María José Mora, and especially Rafael Portillo, who early on encouraged my interest in the theatre) have always patiently listened to my arguments and offered helpful comments on them. Their friendship has made and continues to make a world of difference to me. Finally, my family and particularly my husband have suffered the most and are therefore owed the largest thanks.

Earlier drafts of some sections of the book have been presented at conferences or published before. Chapters Two and Six are based on my articles 'Female Monstrosity, Besieged Masculinity, and the Bounds of Race in Elizabeth Cary's *The Tragedy of Mariam* (1613),' *The Grove* 13 (2006), pp. 57–71, and 'Reason vs. Passion: Catharine Trotter's Deployment of the Historical Tragedy,' in *The Female Wits: Women and Gender in Restoration Literature and Culture*, ed. Pilar Cuder-Domínguez, Zenón Luis-Martínez, and Juan A. Prieto-Pablos, Huelva: Servicio de Publicaciones de la Universidad de Huelva, 2006, pp. 99–114. My discussions of *Bell in Campo* and *The Widdow Ranter* update my essay 'Re-Crafting the Heroic, Constructing a Female Hero: Margaret Cavendish and Aphra Behn,' *Sederi* 17 (2007), pp. 27–45. Some of my arguments on *Abdelazer* were first developed for "Of Spain, Moors, and Women: The Tragedies of Aphra Behn and Mary Pix,' in *(Re)Shaping the Genres: Restoration Women Writers*, ed. Zenón Luis Martínez and Jorge Figueroa Dorrego, Bern: Peter Lang, 2003, pp. 157–73 as well as in 'Iberian State Politics in Aphra Behn's Writing,' in *Aphra Behn (1640–1689): Le Modèle Européen,* ed. Mary Ann O'Donnell and Bernard Dhuicq, Paris: Bilingua GA Editions, 2005, pp. 45–51. I would like to thank the audience and readers on each occasion for their kind interest and feedback.

Chapter 1
Re-Crafting Tragedy:
Gender and Genre in
Seventeenth-Century Drama

Stuart Women Playwrights, 1613–1713 contends that the contribution of female playwrights to the development of drama in England has remained substantially unacknowledged, particularly as regards the field of tragedy. In the last few decades, our image of seventeenth-century English literature has shifted substantially, mostly but not exclusively due to the inclusion of women-authored texts into the canon. Women's authorship of works in prose and verse has been widely acknowledged. In fiction, texts such as Aphra Behn's *Oroonoko* or Margaret Cavendish's *Blazing World* are now the subject of monographic study and collections of essays, with the occasional discussion even at undergraduate level.[1] Other genres so far considered outside the field of literature proper, like diaries, letters, or autobiographies, have entered the scope of much academic debate since Elaine Hobby's pioneering venture in that direction with *Virtue of Necessity* in 1988.[2] In the field of drama, women participated not only as spectators or readers but, more and more, as patronesses, as dramatists, and later on as actresses and managers.[3] Women's role

---

[1] In the last ten years, Margaret Cavendish has been the subject of two monographs, Anna Battigelli's *Margaret Cavendish and the Exiles of the Mind* (Lexington: The University Press of Kentucky, 1998) and Emma L. E. Rees's *Margaret Cavendish: Gender, Genre, Exile* (Manchester: Manchester University Press, 2003) and three further collections of essays, *A Princely Brave Woman: Essays on Margaret Cavendish, Duchess of Newcastle*, ed. Stephen Clucas (Aldershot: Ashgate, 2003), *Authorial Conquests: Essays on Genre in the Writings of Margaret Cavendish*, ed. Line Cottegnies and Nancy Weitz (Madison: Fairleigh Dickinson University Press, 2003), and *Cavendish and Shakespeare, Interconnections*, ed. Katherine Romack and James Fitzmaurice (Aldershot: Ashgate, 2006). In roughly the same period, Aphra Behn has merited at least three collections of essays: *Rereading Aphra Behn; History, Theory, and Criticism*, ed. Heidi Hutner (Charlottesville: University Press of Virginia, 1993), *Aphra Behn Studies*, ed. Janet Todd (Cambridge: Cambridge University Press, 1996), and more recently the *Cambridge Companion to Aphra Behn*, ed. Derek Hughes and Janet Todd (Cambridge: Cambridge University Press, 2004). See also Derek Hughes's monograph *The Theatre of Aphra Behn* (London: Palgrave, 2001).

[2] Elaine Hobby, *Virtue of Necessity: English Women's Writing 1646–1688* (London: Virago, 1988).

[3] David Roberts has charted some of this territory in *The Ladies: Female Patronage of Restoration Drama* (Oxford: Clarendon, 1989). Despite the many discontinuities throughout the century, he reports notable instances of female patronage of the stage in the Restoration period, such as the play *Calisto*, commissioned from John Crown in 1674 by seven ladies at court, including the Princesses Mary and Anne (pp. 102ff).

has been made more visible in this area by the increasing availability of their texts for contemporary readership in scholarly editions.[4] Another valuable approach has successfully challenged the alleged unstageability of women-authored plays, even to the extent of producing so-far unperformed ones, thereby countering the claim that they were not true dramatic pieces.[5]

Despite these worthy efforts, women's works have not been in print in the last few decades, and they still appear to be in the periphery of all major studies of seventeenth-century drama. Perhaps the main exception is Aphra Behn, but due to the fact that Behn's works are mostly comedies, she has entered the canon as a comedy writer, with her fame resting squarely on the remarkable dramatic achievement of *The Rover*. This explains the relatively more neglected area of the contribution of female dramatists to tragedy and its sister genre, tragicomedy, in which no major woman playwright has so far been recognized. Such is also the chosen area for this research project, which builds on recent developments in the field of English drama but stakes out its own fairly unexplored terrain.

Judging solely from the production of a writer such as Behn, female authors of tragedy would seem to be few, or even exceptional. This is far from the truth. As *Stuart Women Playwrights, 1613–1713* aims to prove, many women dramatists of the century tried their hand at tragedy at some point of their writing careers, and since early on, women were translators of tragedies. For instance, Lady Jane Lumley translated Euripides' *Iphigenia at Aulis* around 1550, while Mary Sidney closely adapted Robert Garnier in her *Tragedy of Antonie* in 1592, thus turning it into the first play by an Englishwoman to be published.[6] Katherine Phillips followed her example with Corneille's tragedies *Pompey* and *Horace*. The former was performed in London in 1663, again becoming another landmark of the development of women's drama in the seventeenth century, for it was the first play penned by a woman to be staged in the commercial theatre. Moreover, the first original play written by an Englishwoman, Elizabeth Cary's *The Tragedy of Mariam* (published in 1613), was a tragedy. Some writers wrote mostly tragedies rather than comedies, for example Catharine Trotter and Delarivier Manley. Others, such as Mary Pix, wrote an equal number of both.

One might wonder what kind of appeal tragedies held for women. Tragedy has by far been the more prestigious of the two dramatic genres, and, in dealing with

---

[4] Listing all currently available editions of women-authored play texts is beyond the scope of this work. However, as an example of the changes that have taken place, it is worth noting that, while Catherine Belsey rightly complained in *The Subject of Tragedy* (1985) that there were no editions of Elizabeth Cary's *The Tragedy of Mariam*, the decade 1994–2003 hailed the publication of six.

[5] Perhaps the best example of this productive area is the book *Women and Dramatic Production 1550–1700* (Harlow: Pearson, 2000), by Alison Findlay and Stephanie Hodgson-Wright with Gweno Williams.

[6] Penguin's collection of three of these early tragedies (Lumley's, Sidney's, and Elizabeth Cary's *The Tragedy of Mariam*) has made them available to a wide readership. See Diane Purkiss, ed., *Three Tragedies by Renaissance Women* (London: Penguin, 1998).

high-minded characters, it must have more adequately met the preoccupations and activities of the higher circles of seventeenth-century England. It was in these circles, often among the upper aristocracy of the kingdom, that we find many of the early women playwrights. But the appeal of the form surely went beyond aristocratic concerns, and had something to do with the challenge that such a prestigious form posed for those women who were seeking the admiration and acceptance of fellow writers and intellectuals.

The definition of tragedy inherited by Renaissance writers came from Aristotle's *Poetics* via several medieval theorists and practitioners within and outside of England.[7] According to Reiss, knowledge of the Aristotelian precepts was primarily transmitted via Horace's mediation, and traversed the fourth century in Donatus's writings, the seventh in Saint Isidore of Seville's, to finally reach the Renaissance in Giambattista Cinthio's and Robert Garnier's knowledgeable works. From there it soon crossed the English Channel.[8] The earliest formulation of the theory of tragedy in England came from Sir Philip Sidney, but no doubt the practice of the genre by such major playwrights as Marlowe, Shakespeare, and others soon came to exert quite as much influence, if not more. Bushnell warns that English Renaissance tragedy is 'a mongrel genre, compounded of multiple traditions. But scholars continue to argue about the relative value and influence of the vernacular traditions and new forms of classicism in England.'[9]

Sidney, however, was instrumental in passing on what would be crucial characteristics of the dramatic genre in its English version, when in his *Defence of Poesy* he proclaimed the excellencies of tragedy,

> that openeth the greatest wounds, and showeth forth the ulcers that are covered with tissue; that maketh kings fear to be tyrants, and tyrants manifest their tyrannical humours; that, with stirring the affects of admiration of commiseration, teacheth the uncertainty of this world, and upon how weak foundations gilden roofs are built; that maketh us know, 'Qui sceptra saevus duro imperio regit, / Timet timentes, metus in auctorem redit.'[10]

As a result, the main tragic concept developed by English Renaissance playwrights was that of the fall of princes and its three interrelated themes: 'the fall from a prosperous or "high" condition to a wretched or low one; the role

---

[7] Rita Felski has rehearsed more general questions concerning the definition of tragedy as a genre and as a mode in her introduction to *Rethinking Tragedy* (Baltimore: The Johns Hopkins University Press, 2008), pp. 1–25.

[8] Timothy J. Reiss, 'Renaissance Theatre and the Theory of Tragedy,' in *The Cambridge History of Literary Criticism vol. 3: the Renaissance*, ed. Glyn P. Norton (Cambridge: Cambridge University Press, 1999), pp. 229–47.

[9] Rebecca Bushnell, 'The Fall of Princes: the Classical and Medieval Roots of English Renaissance Tragedy,' in *A Companion to Tragedy*, ed. Rebecca Bushnell (Oxford: Blackwell, 2005), p. 289.

[10] Sir Philip Sydney, 'The Defence of Poesy,' in *Selected Writings*, ed. Richard Dutton (Manchester: Carcanet, 1987), p. 124.

of "Fortune" in causing that fall; and the idea that the tragedies only happen to "mighty men"—kings, conquerors, and those of "great nobility" and not common people.'[11] Emphasis on a tragedy of state made the genre rather forbidding for women, since this was a social milieu in which despite the aristocratic origin of many of these early playwrights, women's participation had traditionally been extremely restricted, and thus an area in which their authorship and speaking up might have been even less warmly received. This may explain why earlier feminist approaches to the genre of the period have focused on male-authored texts and neglected women's authorship. In these early studies, tragedy was considered a 'masculine' form, and therefore the aim was to analyze in male-authored works the construction of women through their absence and their silence, or else to examine the split subjectivity that patriarchal codes enforced on women.[12] More recent criticism has occasionally adopted a more inclusive method, looking into topics such as the rise of a strong female hero in male- and female-authored tragedies of the early seventeenth century.[13]

Nevertheless, as the seventeenth century wore on, the theory and practice of tragedy—and indeed, of all drama—in England underwent considerable transformation. French theorists and practitioners such as Corneille contributed to rethink the themes and conventions of tragedy, with Dryden aiming to reformulate the field in England. Most critical studies perceive Restoration tragedy as evolving from the heroic tragedy of early Stuart rhymed plays to the pathetic or affective tragedy of late Stuart blank verse she-tragedies. This evolution is often understood in fact as a perversion of the form, a decline of the 'pure' tragic form until it fades away into the sentimental drama of the eighteenth century. Already in 1929, Bonamy Dobrée estimated that 'the materials used in Restoration tragedy degenerated into sentimentality (…). The playwrights ceased to desire heroism so greatly as to believe in it, but they went on writing as though they still did believe in it. The result is a too obvious softness.'[14] Nearly forty years later, Ann Righter continued to lament the demise of the heroic mode.[15] Both critics thus identify a 'feminization' of drama that results in its decline. Since this is a period during which women playwrights have entered the public stage and become professionalized,

---

[11] Bushnell, 'The Fall of Princes,' pp. 292–3.

[12] Dympna Callaghan's *Woman and Gender in Renaissance Tragedy* (New York: Harvester Wheatsheaf, 1989) deployed the former approach in its study of Shakespeare's and Webster's tragedies, while Ania Loomba's *Gender, Race, Renaissance Drama* (Oxford: Oxford University Press, 1989) used the latter to discuss Shakespeare, Middleton, and Webster.

[13] Such is the case of Lisa Hopkins's *The Female Hero in English Renaissance Tragedy* (London: Macmillan Palgrave, 2002).

[14] Bonamy Dobrée, *Restoration Tragedy, 1660–1720* (Oxford, Clarendon Press, 1929), p. 43.

[15] Ann Righter, 'Heroic Tragedy,' in *Restoration Theatre*, ed. John Russell Brown and Bernard Harris (New York: Capricorn Books, 1967), p. 155.

'feminization' appears to equal in some critics' minds a loss of prestige and an impoverishment in style that lead to the decline and even demise, of the genre.

Another influential theory was maintained by Laura Brown, who established an evolution in three stages: the social forms of the period 1660–1677, characterized by the popularity of heroic action; a transitional period dating from 1677 to 1707, when the heroic is superseded by affective tragedy; and a final stage when dramatic moral action triumphs, 1700–1760.[16] Brown's study contemplates Restoration tragedy as moving in form and ideology from the aristocratic to the bourgeois, and thus towards the sentimental and the realistic. This theory brings drama closer to the privileged eighteenth-century form, the bourgeois novel, making its way backwards in order to superimpose on drama the novel's own pattern of development.

The last few decades have witnessed unprecedented interest in the Restoration period from a gendered perspective, although not without its contradictions. While serious attention has been paid to the particulars of women's involvement as actresses, managers, playwrights, and audience, one area has remained largely untouched by these critical probings.[17] Theories of Restoration tragedy have traditionally been built on the work of so-called major playwrights, such as John Dryden, Thomas Otway, and Nathaniel Lee, and only very recently have these theories been informed by insights gained from the works of women playwrights. Women writers are generally seen as taking their cue from the men and being alert enough to adopt their innovations. This perspective, however, seems to be now on the wane. In her study of Mary Pix's first play, *Ibrahim, Thirteenth Emperor of the Turks* (1696), Jean I. Marsden states that '[w]hile she-tragedy can be said to have received its start with Otway, most she-tragedies were written in 1698 or later. Rather than following a formula in writing *Ibrahim*, then, *Pix is helping to create a formula that would soon become familiar.*'[18] Other critical works published in the late 1990s bear out this shift in the appreciation of the role of women writers. For instance, Wheatley's overview of Restoration tragedy in *The Cambridge Companion to English Restoration Theatre* invokes Catherine Trotter's *Fatal*

---

[16] Laura Brown, *English Dramatic Form, 1660–1760* (New Haven: Yale University Press, 1981).

[17] Some classic sources produced in the last few years for the study of this field are among others: Jacqueline Pearson, *The Prostituted Muse* (New York: St. Martin's Press, 1988); Elizabeth Howe, *The First English Actresses* (Cambridge: Cambridge University Press; 1992); Isobel Grundy and Susan Wiseman, eds., *Women, Writing, History 1640–1740* (Athens: University of Georgia Press, 1992); Clare Brant and Diane Purkiss, eds., *Women, Texts and Histories 1575–1760* (London: Routledge, 1992); Katherine M. Quinsey, ed., *Broken Boundaries* (Lexington: The University Press of Kentucky, 1996); Helen Wilcox, ed., *Women and Literature in Britain 1500–1700* (Cambridge: Cambridge University Press, 1996); and Margarete Rubik, *Early Women Dramatists 1550–1800* (London: Macmillan, 1998).

[18] Jean I. Marsden, 'Mary Pix's *Ibrahim*: the Woman Writer as Commercial Playwright,' *Studies in the Literary Imagination* 32.2 (1999), p. 35. My emphasis.

Friendship (1698) as the paradigm for what he terms 'the completed movement to private tragedy.'[19] Building on the work of Robert Hume, J. Douglas Canfield has admitted the large variety of Restoration 'serious drama,' which so often resists attempts at categorisation. Like Brown, he perceives several stages in the transformation from aristocratic to bourgeois forms and ideology. However, he has posited a model of sudden rather than gradual transformation taking place around the key date of 1688: 'It is as if, right up to the Glorious Revolution, an aristocratic force field holds the elements of official discourse together; afterward, we can detect a new, bourgeois configuration of discursive elements.'[20] This theorization opens up a space for the re-assessment of the contribution of women playwrights, since this happened mostly during the period of the main shift, which he names 'Revolutionary' (1689–1714). Interestingly, like Wheatley, Canfield constructed his arguments not only on the work of male writers; instead, and this has been extremely uncommon so far, he included among his sources two tragedies written by women (Manley's *Lucius* and Trotter's *Fatal Friendship*).

Nevertheless, fractures and inconsistencies concerning the related areas of gender and dramatic genre can be found every inch of the way. As General Editor of *The Broadway Anthology of Restoration and Early 18th-Century Drama* (2000), Canfield compiled forty-one plays, seven of them women-authored. Though it might seem so, this is not an inconsiderable amount if compared to similar anthologies. What is more striking, in my opinion, is that only one of those seven is a tragedy, Manley's *Lucius* (1717), a play that did not merit a very positive opinion in Canfield's study of the same year.[21] Undergraduate students using such materials would thus get the wrong impression that women simply did not write tragedies at the time. And yet, there is hardly a study of Restoration drama that does not mention at some point the popularity of 'she-tragedies,' so the paradox remains that Restoration tragedy appears to be essentially feminocentric, while its critique often denies women's role in its making. This paradox becomes even more intricate in a historical context, i.e., when we take into account the decline of tragedy as a vital dramatic form as the eighteenth century wears on. Depending on the politics of the critic, the phenomenon may be hailed as a gradual 'perversion' of the form, taken over by the feminizing forces of sentimentalism and melodrama; or else welcomed as the triumph of the bourgeois over the old aristocratic *Weltanschauung*. Some critics go further and favor the term 'serious

---

[19] Christopher J Wheatley, "Tragedy,' in *The Cambridge Companion to English Restoration Theatre*, ed. Deborah Payne Fisk (Cambridge: Cambridge University Press, 2000), p. 79.

[20] J. Douglas Canfield, 'Shifting Tropes of Ideology in English Serious Drama, Late Stuart to Early Georgian,' *Cultural Readings of Restoration and 18th-Century English Theater*, ed. J. Douglas Canfield and Deborah C. Payne (Atlanta: University of Georgia Press, 1995), p. 195.

[21] Canfield, *Heroes and States: on the ideology of Restoration Tragedy* (Lexington: The University Press of Kentucky, 2000), p. 150.

drama' for tragedies written after 1660, since the 'mongrel genre' of Bushnell's definition above became even more hybrid after that date, in a period that also involved the rise of forms of entertainment such as opera.[22]

However, in providing a comprehensive account of women's deployment of the tragic form throughout the seventeenth century, one should look beyond the limits of 'tragedy' proper. Wickham has argued that the basic form of English medieval drama was tragicomedy and that, though the Reformation made it advisable to separate the tragic and the comic according to classical rules, there remained an inherent instability within the core of English tragedy, evidenced for instance in how in 1575 Gascoine subtitled his play *The Glass of Government* 'a Tragicall Comedie.'[23] The juxtaposition of tragic and comic elements was indeed considered 'natural' or life-like for those who might disagree with Aristotelian taxonomies. However, the specific combinations may change. For Maguire, although the basic form of tragicomedy consists of a tragic plot with a happy resolution—the 'tragedie miste' described by Cinthio—this slippery form can also adopt a structure that alternates comic and tragic plots, as occurs in Fletcher's *The Loyal Subject* (1618).[24]

Interest in tragedy's sister genre tragicomedy seems to have developed in sixteenth-century Italy, where Giambattista Guarini's play *Il Pastor Fido* (pub. 1590) soon became extremely influential. In France, tragicomedies were more popular than tragedies during the first half of the seventeenth century, while in England the form is practiced throughout the century, so that critics maintain that it is 'the single most important dramatic genre of the period 1610–1650,'[25] as well as 'the only viable serious genre after 1660,'[26] even though tragicomedy, like tragedy, declines in the eighteenth century. The theorization of tragicomedy started in England with John Fletcher, who composed a short piece of prose addressed 'To the Reader' for the publication of his play *The Faithful Shepherdess* (1609/1610) after its stage failure.[27] Cohen has detailed three successive phases for the period 1576–1642:

---

[22] A case is point is Davenant's *The Siege of Rhodes*, whose original performance in 1656 involved several entertainments, and because of its usage of music has been described as a blend of heroic play and opera.

[23] Glynne Wickham, 'English Tragedy from its origins to 1575,' in *Early English Stages, 1300 to 1660* (vol. 3, London: Routledge, 1981), pp. 219–53.

[24] Nancy Klein Maguire, 'Tragicomedy,' in *The Cambridge Companion to English Restoration Theatre*, ed. Deborah Payne Fisk (Cambridge: Cambridge University Press, 2000), pp. 89–91. On this subject, see also Verna A. Foster, *The Name and Nature of Tragicomedy* (Aldershot: Ashgate, 2004).

[25] Gordon McMullan and Jonathan Hope, eds., *The Politics of Tragicomedy: Shakespeare and After* (London: Routledge, 1992), p. 1.

[26] Nancy Klein Maguire, 'Tragicomedy,' p. 97.

[27] On this subject, see Eugene Waith, *The Pattern of Tragicomedy in Beaumont and Fletcher* (North Haven: Archon Books, 1969).

[Th]e romantic, non-classicist plays of the late sixteenth century, ... the mixed tragicomedy of the opening years of the seventeenth century composed primarily by Marston and Shakespeare; and the more united tragicomedy that emerges in 1608, indebted to Italian neo-classical dramatic theory and practice, and associated above all with Beaumont and Fletcher.[28]

Despite the instability of the term and the aesthetics of the genre, Potter has stated that tragicomedy became increasingly associated with royalist politics, so that '[w]hat it meant, above all, was a play whose source might be Greek romance or Italian pastoral, but whose immediate context was the court and its circle of gentlemen amateurs,' pastoral being, after all, 'a familiar source for analogies between landscape and kingdom.'[29] After the Restoration, tragicomedy managed to hold its ground even if it diversified into two subgenres, divided tragicomedy and the rhymed heroic play.[30]

Like tragedy, tragicomedy seems to have appealed to women as a dramatic form. Margaret Cavendish turned to it during her Interregnum exile in Antwerp, and after the Restoration both Frances Boothby and Aphra Behn devised examples of the genre for the commercial stage. Because part of the reason for such appeal may lie in the royalist politics of tragicomedy that Potter first established, recent feminist criticism has identified here a new and productive venue for interrogation, particularly in relation to Margaret Cavendish's works.[31] The imbrication of tragedy and tragicomedy throughout the seventeenth century, together with the fact of women playwrights' recurrent use of these two forms, support the claim that one should look at both forms of the tragic mode together and not separately.

Consequently, *Stuart Women Playwrights, 1613–1713* aims to establish the importance of these two dramatic genres (tragedy and tragicomedy) in the context of women's coming to voice in seventeenth-century England and, in so doing, at tracing a full genealogy of women-authored works. In a review published in 2000 in the journal *The Eighteenth Century*, Kathryn R. King reflected: 'Feminist literary history traffics, inevitably, in invented traditions. How could it be otherwise? To reclaim a hitherto submerged past one *must* invent.'[32] King

---

[28] Walter Cohen, 'Prerevolutionary Drama,' *The Politics of Tragicomedy: Shakespeare and After*, ed. Gordon McMullan and Jonathan Hope (London: Routledge, 1992), p. 126.

[29] Lois Potter, '"True Tragicomedies" of the Civil War and Commonwealth,' in *Renaissance Tragicomedy: Explorations in Genre and Politics*, ed. Nancy Klein Maguire (New York: AMS Press, 1987), pp. 197 & 201.

[30] See on this subject Nancy Klein Maguire, '"The Whole Truth" of Restoration Tragicomedy,' in *Renaissance Tragicomedy: Explorations in Genre and Politics*, ed. Nancy Klein Maguire (New York: AMS Press, 1987), pp. 218–39.

[31] See, for example, Hero Chalmers, *Royalist Women Writers 1650–1689* (Oxford: Clarendon Press, 2004), and Sophie Tomlinson, *Women on Stage in Stuart Drama* (Cambridge: Cambridge University Press, 2005).

[32] Kathryn P. King, 'Essay Review: Female Agency and Feminocentric Romance,' *The Eighteenth Century* 41.1 (2000), p. 56.

further pondered the uses of such female traditions: 'They confer legitimacy on writing that has been little regarded; organize a mass of still largely uncharted authors, texts, literary relationships, and lines of influence; and provide materials for narratives of resistance.'[33] If King is right, then one such so-far un-invented female tradition exists for women and the tragic mode in the seventeenth century that needs investigation.

This book examines some twenty tragedies and tragicomedies published by English women in the seventeenth century, specifically between 1613 and 1713. These are the publication dates of the first and last tragedies written by a Stuart woman playwright, Elizabeth Cary's *The Tragedy of Mariam* (1613) and Anne Finch's *Aristomenes* (1713). In examining the whole of the century from a gendered perspective, this project breaks away from conventional approaches to the subject that tend to establish an unbridgeable gap between the early Stuart period and the Restoration. However, as the continued practice of tragicomedy attests to, and as recent accounts of the Civil War and Interregnum period have proved, there are inescapable continuities between both periods.[34] Bringing these early writers on board as pioneers feeling their way into the conventions of a dramatic mode enhances and completes our knowledge and understanding of the whole history of English drama, leads to a productive reassessment of current critical theories about the evolution of these dramatic genres throughout the seventeenth century, and opens up the canon of seventeenth-century English drama to women's voices.

A further advantage of this chronology is that it helps trace major changes in dramatic form and ideology in women's tragedies. Neglected questions may be now pursued, such as the so-far unperceived connections between the Senecan tragedy as practiced by Elizabeth Cary at the beginning of the century and the Stoic ethos of Catharine Trotter's towards its end. Through discussion of a corpus of women-authored plays I hope to identify a typology of tragedies and tragicomedies written by Stuart women playwrights, analyzing their main features and comparing them to those of similar plays of the period. All in all, this book may help bring about a major overhaul of current theories of the evolution of English drama as well as an unprecedented reconstruction of the genealogy of seventeenth-century women playwrights.

As mentioned above, all the works chosen for this study were published between 1613 and 1713. This may merit some explanation. 1613, the date of publication of the first original tragedy written by an Englishwoman, is perhaps a fairly obvious point of departure for a study of seventeenth-century drama by women. 1713, the date of the folio edition of Anne Finch's works, roughly coincides not only with the end of the Stuart dynasty in England but also with the end of a period in the history of drama, since the 1720s brought about material transformations

---

[33] Kathryn P. King, 'Essay Review,' p. 56.

[34] See, for instance, Susan Wiseman, *Drama and Politics in the English Civil War* (Cambridge: Cambridge University Press, 1998), for a revisionist account of the period's drama.

in the production of plays in England due to new legislation on that subject. By encompassing the whole of the seventeenth century I am also by-passing the 'considerable fragmentation in the presentation and representation of early modern women's writing' that Salzman has described as being caused by the 'artificial dividing line that is drawn at 1660' and which results in a distortion of women's contribution during the upheavals of the middle years of the century.[35] Within those boundaries of 1613 and 1713, the Stuart monarchy undoubtedly endows the period with a relative ideological continuity in contents, themes, and concerns.

By opting for dates of publication I may seem to be favoring printed works over manuscripts. This is not meant to belittle the importance of manuscripts in the study of Renaissance literature, but it is indicative of the fact that they need to be studied separately, because they involve a completely different set of ideological implications and relations to the audience. Moreover, as the seventeenth century wore on, manuscript circulation gave way to publication as the preferred kind of dissemination, to the extent that by the end of the period, practically all plays, whether they had been hits or flops, were printed and widely distributed, often achieving a 'second life' beyond the stage. Opting for published plays also does away with the problem of so-called 'closet' drama. *Stuart Women Playwrights, 1613–1713* examines plays both staged and unstaged in the commercial playhouses as long as they were published, which would entail their author's will to let their works enter the public sphere in which they would become part of a tradition of women's writing. Finally, this book discusses only original works by women. Once more, this is slippery ground when dealing with early modern writing, since the concept of originality is a much more recent construction. However, it seems to me that close adaptations or translations of continental authors such as those made by Jane Lumley and Mary Sidney in the sixteenth century and Katherine Phillips in the seventeenth, in spite of being important, raise questions that differ widely from those in the rest of the works under discussion, and therefore would need to be analyzed separately. In the context of this book they will be acknowledged only briefly in relation to other works and authors.

The critical approach of *Stuart Women Playwrights, 1613–1713* is indebted to three crucial academic movements of the last few decades: new historicism and cultural materialism, feminism, and post-colonialism. Although new historicism and cultural materialism have been the target of in-depth critique lately, they have played an essential role in making us all aware of the place of the literary text in its historical context. From them I have derived an interest in the ideological undercurrents within each play and in the analysis of power relations and the subversion of dominant ideologies. My debt to feminism is even more substantial, and so this book will attempt to trace the construction of gender (femininity but also masculinity) within these texts, as well as disclose facts concerning the gendered politics of authorship, production/publication, and circulation of literary texts, with the occasional argument about the male bias of academic research.

---

[35] Paul Salzman, *Reading Early Modern Women's Writing* (Oxford: Oxford University Press, 2006), pp. 2–3.

Post-colonialism queries the construction of ethnicity and race within literature, and it is particularly appropriate for the study of the representation of Europe and its Others in the early modern period. As Loomba has remarked:

> In the drama, attention to racial difference has at least two important implications. One, it becomes obvious that each hierarchical structure of domination is analogous to and linked with the others. The processes by which women and black people are constructed as the 'others' of white patriarchal society are similar and connected, and they also reflect upon other sorts of exclusion such as that based on class. Two, race further problematises feminist efforts to make analogies between or intertwine different aspects of women's subordination; the *specificity* of each emerges more clearly.[36]

The next chapter, 'Early Stuart Women Writers: Elizabeth Cary,' starts by looking into a play that has been the subject of much critical discussion. My analysis of gender (femininity/masculinity) and race politics in Cary's play attempts to unravel the complex ways in which *The Tragedy of Mariam* portrays an embattled society in which the old, conventional social order of male, white privilege is under attack by forces bent on change. Categories of race, class, and gender overlap in the play and are in constant flux, with some characters (women, particularly those of Idumean descent like Salome) trying to bring about change, while others (men like Constabarus) resist it and defend the benefits of conventional, compartmentalized society, leading to the tragic resolution that highlights the utter destruction of an old social order.

Chapter 3, 'The Interregnum: Margaret Cavendish's Dramatic Experiments,' discusses a number of plays composed by the Duchess of Newcastle while in exile in Antwerp and published in London upon her eventual return in 1662. Writing some fifty years after her predecessor Elizabeth Cary, and like many other women of her generation, Cavendish was empowered by the turmoil of the English Civil War. Cavendish did not systematically endorse dramatic conventions, and, more often than not, she simply identified a dramatic piece as 'a play.' Consequently, many pieces by this author defy conventional categories. This chapter undertakes the analysis of three plays that make use of tragic and heroic motifs.

Chapter 4, 'The Restoration Commercial Stage: Frances Boothby and Aphra Behn' examines the emergence of the professional woman playwright by putting side by side a play by a virtually unknown Frances Boothby (the first woman writer to have an original play performed in one of the new Restoration playhouses) and the early works of the most successful woman writer of the period, Aphra Behn, all of them tragicomedies. With the exception of her tragedy *Abdelazer* (1676), Aphra Behn maintained her distance from this genre in spite of her long theatrical career, and it was her comedies which brought her the most fame and recognition, even to this date. The study of Behn's tragedy and tragicomedies may allow us an insight into Behn's ideas on women's heroism throughout some twenty years of writing for the stage.

---

[36] Ania Loomba, *Gender, Race, Renaissance Drama*, pp. 1–2.

Chapter 5, 'Late Stuart Writers I: Mary Pix and Delarivier Manley,' interrogates Jacqueline Pearson's remark that ethnic otherness held particular interest for women dramatists of the Restoration because 'racial and ethnic difference provided useful tropes for gender difference'.[37] Often such tropes are developed in the context of tragedies set in one of two exotic locations entailing a geographical and/or a chronological displacement: Islamic medieval Spain or the Turkish Empire. The comparison of Mary Pix's and Delarivier Manley's plays to earlier women-authored tragedies such as *Abdelazer* will allow us to trace meaningful changes in the way Restoration women playwrights handled their materials, both at the level of aesthetics and of politics.

Chapter 6, 'Late Stuart Writers II: Catharine Trotter and the Historical Tragedy,' argues favorably about the dramatic undertakings of a woman writer who has received limited critical attention up to now. Like other female writers of the so-called 1690s generation, Catharine Trotter was rediscovered in the 1980s by several feminist critics who reprinted her work. Perhaps the most interesting question posed by Trotter's drama is her choice of tragedy over comedy as her dramatic genre. Only one of her five plays is a comedy, the rest are tragedies with a historical setting. These choices are puzzling when one considers that other women playwrights of the period (for example Aphra Behn, as discussed in chapter four) preferred comedy over tragedy, yet Trotter's choice stems from her knowledge of dramatic theory and from a protracted meditation on the moral aim of theatre.

Finally, Chapter 7, 'The Last of the Stuarts: Jane Wiseman and Anne Finch,' analyzes the transition into the Augustan period through the study of two women-authored tragedies, Jane Wiseman's *Antiochus the Great* and Anne Finch's *Aristomenes; or, the Royal Shepherd*. While Finch also penned a tragicomedy, only *Aristomenes* would find its way to publication in the folio edition of 1713, while her tragicomedy remained in manuscript form. Both authors engage with such topics as legitimate rule, tyranny, kingship, and exile, although Finch's conveys most clearly her anxieties concerning the Stuart succession, the exile of James II, as well as her own—personal and familial—Jacobite sympathies. Like Cavendish before her, Finch portrays a kingdom torn by war and threatened by foreign invasion, where aristocratic values continue to offer hope for survival and prosperity. Although Hellenistic motifs and topics never actually disappeared from the English stage, renewed interest in the classical pastoral world would seem to be particularly in tune with Augustan stylistic concerns, and thus the analysis of Finch's tragedy brings to a close our examination of the multifaceted configurations of the tragic genre as written by female playwrights throughout the Stuart period.

It would be inaccurate to assume that women playwrights found tragedy a pliable form. Male-oriented and high-class in its definition of characters and

---

[37] Jacqueline Pearson, 'Blacker than Hell Creates: Pix Rewrites Othello,' in *Broken Boundaries: Women and Feminism in Restoration Drama*, ed. Katherine M. Quinsey, Lexington: The University Press of Kentucky, 1996, pp. 15-16.

themes, it tended to resist women's efforts. Although I have used here the term 'women's tradition' to describe an emerging (and revisable) genealogy of women's writing, I do so advisedly, much aware of Margaret Ezell's reservations about the term and its flawed reliance on the continuity and commonality of all women's writing and lives.[38] Therefore, *Stuart Women Playwrights, 1613–1713* does not attempt to establish a linear progress or evolution in women's deployment of tragic forms. Rather, this book aims to map out a number of diverse, multi-nuanced appropriations and uses of tragedy and tragicomedy, all of them serving as vehicles for each playwright's social, intellectual, and/or formal concerns, among which one can identify the persistence of certain themes, plots, and stylistic approaches.

---

[38] See Margaret Ezell, *Writing Women's Literary History* (Baltimore: The Johns Hopkins University Press, 1993), particularly chapter one.

Chapter 2
Early Stuart Women Writers: Elizabeth Cary

Elizabeth Cary's *The Tragedy of Mariam, The Fair Queen of Jewry* (1613) has been the subject of much critical discussion as being a play that stages the tragic implications of women's submission in early modern society. Yet the play's manifold interest lies beyond the power of its protagonist or the striking life of its author. Published in 1613 but written approximately one decade earlier, *The Tragedy of Mariam* tackles the relationship between the Queen of the Jews, Mariam, and her husband Herod, who has risen to this position by his marriage. In its form, the play is indebted to Senecan tragedy as developed in France and circulated within the Sidney coterie, to which Cary belonged. By analyzing the gender and race politics of Cary's play, we will see how it addresses the fractures of a society in which the old social order of male, white privilege is under siege, and we will unravel some of the complexity of the play's overlapping categories of race, class, and gender. Most strikingly, the tragic resolution fails to punish the deviant forces of change, whether it is women's stepping out into the public sphere or racially displaced subjects. The play's ending highlights the utter destruction of an old social order, with the unnecessary sacrifice of those two characters who stand out conspicuously for conventional virtue and submission to the law of the land.

Tudor Precedents

For Danielle Clarke, Renaissance drama by women needs to be read politically, rather than solely from within the framework of the personal. Clarke has emphasized the way in which Elizabeth Cary's play and its close Tudor precedents by Lady Jane Lumley and Mary Sidney, Countess of Pembroke, belong in the group of politically engaged subgenres, and she has insisted that their functions should be read 'in relation to the *effects* of family alliances.'[1] Clarke follows a path opened by Diane Purkiss in her introduction to the joint edition of these three texts in 1998, castigating the 'remarkable overuse of women writers' biographies in setting the critical agenda'[2] and suggesting instead that writing was one of the ways in which these aristocratic women contributed and showed their allegiance to their families' struggle for prominence. Indeed, as Purkiss remarks, closet drama could

---

[1] Danielle Clarke, *The Politics of Early Modern Women's Writing* (Harlow: Pearson Education, 2001), p. 80.

[2] Diane Purkiss, introduction, *Three Tragedies by Renaissance Women*, p. xii. Her comment is particularly apt for Elizabeth Cary criticism, as described below.

be more politically dangerous than plays written for the public stage, since these manuscripts circulated freely within coteries without having to meet the scrutiny of the Master of the Revels.[3]

In all three cases, it is doubtful that these texts could have been produced outside the aristocratic context that birthed them, which was more obviously receptive to the influence of humanism and, more importantly, to the ideas of those humanists who, like Thomas More or Juan Luis Vives, advocated women's education. Drama figured very prominently in humanist pedagogy.[4] First because, like all literature, it offered role models for virtuous behavior or the rejection of vice. Second, humanists encouraged the learning of classical speeches and adages that encapsulated moral wisdom. Last, play-acting was regarded as conducive to the complete assimilation of the moral content of drama. Therefore, reading, translating, and learning by heart fragments of classical drama, whether taken from their original context or from one of the compilations available, must have constituted a substantial part of the education of those women who, like Jane Lumley, were privileged enough to have access to what was a luxury for a very few.

By translating Euripides' *Iphigenia in Aulis*, Jane Lumley was demonstrating to what extent she had assimilated the moral teachings of the play, while simultaneously displaying the extraordinary accomplishments that her high rank as daughter of the Earl of Arundel had placed within her reach. Written c. 1553, when Jane was already married to John Lumley, himself the translator of Erasmus's *Education of a Christian Prince*, *The Tragedy of Iphigenia* was meant to add to the prestige of her family by marriage as well as that of her birth family, and consequently, as has been suggested, ought to be regarded as a political statement on the power and wealth of both.[5] Erasmus's Latin translation of Euripides' *Iphigenia in Aulis* had turned it into one of the most popular classical plays of the period, and Lumley apparently worked with the Latin version rather than the Greek original.[6] The plot of *Iphigenia* deals with Agammenon's difficult decision to sacrifice his own daughter for the good of the military expedition against Troy, and how his decision becomes redundant when Iphigenia makes her own choice for self-immolation. The theme of women's sacrificial death, which appears to prefigure *The Tragedy of Mariam*, has invited a number of comparisons that highlight how these plays 'foreground

---

[3] Purkiss, ibid., p. xviii.

[4] I am following here the account provided by Kent Cartwright, *Theatre and Humanism* (Cambridge: Cambridge University Press, 1999), pp. 12–20.

[5] For more on Lumley's work, see Elaine V. Beilin, *Redeeming Eve: Women Writers of the English Renaissance* (Princeton: Princeton University Press, 1987), pp. 153–7, and Clarke 83–8, as well as Diane Purkiss's already mentioned introduction to her Penguin edition of the play. Gweno Williams's chapter 'Translating the Text, Performing the Self,' in Findlay et al., *Women and Dramatic Production 1550–1700*, pp. 15–41, analyzes the works of Lumley and Sidney in detail.

[6] Purkiss, 'Blood, Sacrifice, Marriage: why Iphigenia and Mariam have to die,' *Women's Writing* 6.1 (1999), pp. 27–8.

the suffering female body (as a discursive construction, not as a physical entity or presence) as a figuration or condition of a changing political order.'[7]

The suffering female body is also a feature of Mary Sidney's translation of Robert Garnier's *Marc Antoine* (1578), published in 1592 as *The Tragedy of Antonie*. However, the Countess of Pembroke was rather more prolific a writer than Lady Lumley. She is perhaps best known as the editor and publisher of her brother Philip's work after his untimely death. She also translated Mornay and Petrarch, composed several original poems, and finished a version of the *Psalms* that she had started again in collaboration with her brother and whose popularity would lead to several reprintings and much recognition. Her role as a patroness was even more prominent. As Krontiris has remarked, the Pembroke residence in Wilton became, under her direction, 'a literary centre, comparable to continental literary salons.'[8]

The Tragedy of Antonie went through several reprintings between 1592 and 1608 too. There is enough textual evidence to suggest that it would have been written for a formal household performance or staged reading.[9] It inspired a companion play by Samuel Daniel, who was one of Mary Sidney's *protégés*, and in general contributed to the popularity of the Antony and Cleopatra theme that would inspire William Shakespeare's own rendering years later. Although dramatizing the historical events surrounding the famous love affair of Marc Antony and Cleopatra, it highlights the death of the protagonists, and thus it invites meditation on the conflict between the public and the private. Moreover, Garnier's original text diverged from the popular figuring of Cleopatra as a voluptuous temptress and concentrated on the dignity of her final hours. For Mary Ellen Lamb, all of Mary Sidney's translations, *The Tragedy of Antonie* included, prove her sustained concern with the subject of the art of dying well or *ars moriendi*, and showcase her interest in the rhetoric of lamentation and mourning. This interest would derive partly from her own biography and partly from the culture of the time.[10] Yet, critical appreciation of *The Tragedy of Antonie* and, more generally, of the Countess of Pembroke's dramatic prowess, has suffered by repeated comparison to Shakespeare's *Antony and Cleopatra* (1607). This is unfair, since Sidney was following a dramatic tradition that widely differed from that of the English public theatre. Hannay contends that Sidney should be seen not as an antagonist but as a

---

[7] Clarke, *The Politics of Early Modern Women's Writing*, p. 83. Hodgson-Wright has also raised the question of a possible connection between Iphigenia and the execution of Lady Jane Grey around the period of the text's composition; see her 'Jane Lumley's *Iphigenia at Aulis*. Multum in parvo, or less is more,' in *Readings in Renaissance Women's Drama. Criticism, History and Performance 1594–1998*, ed. S. P. Cerasano and Marion Wynne-Davies (London: Routledge, 1998), pp. 129–41.

[8] Tina Krontiris, 'Mary Herbert. Englishing a purified Cleopatra,' in *Readings in Renaissance Women's Drama. Criticism, History and Performance 1594–1998*, ed. S. P. Cerasano and Marion Wynne-Davies (London: Routledge, 1998), p. 156.

[9] Gweno Williams, 'Translating the Text, Performing the Self,' pp. 34–7.

[10] Mary Ellen Lamb, *Gender and Authorship in the Sidney Circle* (Madison: University of Wisconsin Press, 1990), pp. 115–41.

forerunner of Shakespeare, insofar as she was among those first bringing the genre of historical tragedy to England:

> The formal aims of this Continental drama were essentially different from those of later English dramatists, such as Shakespeare. *Marc Antoine* is a drama of character, not of action; Garnier was not interested in events themselves, but in the refraction of events through different viewpoints, giving the perspectives of both the noble protagonists and their subjects. Such drama was eminently suitable for reading aloud on an evening at Wilton, when no professional entertainment was available.[11]

The Tragedy of Mariam and Senecan Closet Drama

While her work exhibits a number of common traits with that of her Tudor forerunners, Elizabeth Cary, Lady Falkland (c. 1585–1639), has the honor of being the earliest known woman to have an original play printed. This has placed her at an advantage in relation to Lady Lumley and the Countess of Pembroke, since translation and adaptation are regarded as relatively minor contributions by contemporary critics, even while they have to admit that this was by no means the estimation of their own age. On the contrary, Cary is entirely free of the charge of 'ventriloquizing' by virtue of the originality of her only surviving printed play.[12]

However, the popular view that Cary was a one-work writer is deceptive, most plainly because her *History of the Life, Reign and Death of Edward II* (published in 1689) has also survived. What's more, like other women whose writing circulated preferably in manuscript form, Cary's full production needs to be ascertained by recuperating other writers' allusions to it. Davies' dedicatory lines in *The Muses Sacrifice* (1612) mention two tragedies, one set in Sicily, the other in Palestine.[13] Cary's biography by one of her daughters, *The Lady Falkland, Her Life* (c. 1655) lists an assortment of translations, lyrical verse, religious polemics, and letters. Wolfe speculates:

> While only a handful of the manuscripts described ... are known to be extant, the fact that her Catholic children were aware of many of them in the decade after her death suggests that they had seen and read them when they lived with her in England, and that they perhaps took the Catholic writings with them to Cambrai.[14]

---

[11] Margaret P. Hannay, 'Patronesse of the Muses,' in *Readings in Renaissance Women's Drama. Criticism, History and Performance 1594–1998*, ed. S. P. Cerasano and Marion Wynne-Davies (London: Routledge, 1998), p. 143.

[12] Beilin used the term 'ventriloquize' to describe the process followed by Mary Sidney in learning how to articulate her piety, 'first by experimenting with the work of others,' and later by 'developing her own literary personae' (*Redeeming Eve*, p. 122).

[13] Barbara Lewalski discusses this subject at some length in *Writing Women in Jacobean England* (Cambridge: Harvard University Press, 1993), p. 183.

[14] Heather Wolfe, 'Introduction,' in *The Literary Career and Legacy of Elizabeth Cary, 1613–1680*, ed. Heather Wolfe (London: Palgrave Macmillan, 2007), p. 3.

Yet, the fact remains that very little of Cary's allegedly large output has reached us, and that of the two extant works, it has been so far *The Tragedy of Mariam* that has received the most critical attention. Catherine Belsey's *The Subject of Tragedy* first put it in the critics' sights in 1985 and led the way in feminist readings of this tragedy as one that 'explores the limits of a dutiful wife's right to resist a tyrannical husband' as well as in pursuing the representation of a conflictive subjectivity in Mariam's language.[15] Interestingly, Belsey then complained about the play's absence 'not only from the literary canon but from most histories of drama, and [about] the lack of an accessible modern edition.'[16] Twenty-odd years later, half a dozen scholarly editions are available, and the play is being included in most major anthologies of Renaissance drama. Both facts attest to the work's indubitable quality as well as to the power of feminist criticism to redraw the boundaries of the literary canon in the intervening years.

All in all, the biographical approach has predominated in literary appraisals of the play, with the spotlight on the figure of Mariam. Thus, for instance, in her essay 'The Spectre of Resistance' (1991), Margaret Ferguson read Mariam's resistance proleptically, anticipating Elizabeth Cary's own challenge to her husband, her conversion to Catholicism, and her abandonment of the family home decades later.[17] Fascinating as the striking analogies between Elizabeth Cary's life and her work may be, the biographical approach has neglected insights into the play beyond those to be gained from its protagonist. Some critics have tried to move beyond the conflation of author and character, wisely observing that this is 'part of our seemingly insatiable desire to locate a real, authentic, unmasked, untextualised female voice in Renaissance women's writing, a desire which stems from our assumption that only such untrammelled subjectivity can be truly subversive.'[18] Others, like Alison Shell, have pursued a line of analysis that, while admitting to an autobiographical connection, reads the play within the wider frame of those socio-political tensions surrounding mixed marriages between Protestants

---

[15] Catherine Belsey, *The Subject of Tragedy*, p. 171. For elaborations on Belsey's earlier reading, see, for example, Karen L. Raber, 'Gender and the Political Subject in *The Tragedy of Mariam*,' *Studies in English Literature* 35 (1995), pp. 321–43; Z. Luis Martínez, '"Human Eyes Dazed by Woman's Wit": Gendering Bodies and Minds in English Renaissance Poetry and Drama,' in *La mujer del texto al context,* ed. Laura P. Alonso, Pilar Cuder, and Zenón Luis (Huelva: Servicio de Publicaciones de la Universidad de Huelva, 1996), pp. 69–89; and A. Bennett, 'Female Performativity in *The Tragedy of Mariam*,' *Studies in English Literature* 40.2 (2000), pp. 293–309.

[16] Catherine Belsey, *The Subject of Tragedy*, p. 175.

[17] Margaret W. Ferguson, 'The Spectre of Resistance: *The Tragedy of Mariam* (1613),' in *Staging the Renaissance: Essays on Elizabethan and Jacobean Drama*, ed. David Scott Kastan and Peter Stallybrass (London: Routledge, 1991), pp. 235–50. Lynette McGrath has aptly summarized the terms of the critical debate over Cary's work and life in *Subjectivity and Women's Poetry in Early Modern England* (Aldershot: Ashgate, 2002), pp. 167–8.

[18] Purkiss, 'Blood, Sacrifice, Marriage,' p. 27.

and Catholics.[19] Shell explicates those puzzling resonances of Elizabeth Cary's subsequent life events on her *Tragedy of Mariam* as resulting from the author's auto-didactic efforts, following the tradition of using history as a source of exemplars. This view has the virtue of reconciling the analogies without resorting to an inexact conflation of life and literature.[20]

It is perhaps most helpful to regard Elizabeth Cary in relation to her Tudor predecessors, Lady Lumley and the Countess of Pembroke. Although she was not a member of the aristocracy by birth, she belonged to a well-off family on the rise. Her father Lawrence Tanfield was a successful lawyer who would be knighted not long after young Elizabeth made her advantageous marriage with Henry Cary, Viscount Falkland. Her sophisticated education was one of the accomplishments she brought into the marriage, and she must have been concerned to show her new as well as her old family under the best light. Thus, like Jane Lumley and Mary Sidney, Elizabeth Cary wrote her works as 'part of her self-fashioning ... as a member of a noble household.'[21]

Elizabeth Cary and Mary Sidney also have in common their choice of literary form. As mentioned above, Senecan closet drama was the vehicle for many political preoccupations within the Sidney circle. The core set of these concerns has been described by Straznicky:

> Varied as it was, the group was fundamentally reformist in its political sympathies and humanist in its intellectual endeavors, promoting popular sovereignty and limited monarchy, and developing a literary culture in which poetics, piety and politics were uniquely combined. As the products of this intellectual milieu, the Sidnean closet plays span literary and political fields, private coteries and public readerships.[22]

As an instrument for 'the exploration of political doctrine and dissent,'[23] closet drama was espoused by Samuel Daniel and Fulke Greville in addition to Mary Sidney herself, who in turn was closely following the example of Robert Garnier's neo-Senecan tragedies in France.

---

[19] Alison Shell, *Catholicism, Controversy, and the English Literary Imagination, 1558–1660* (Cambridge: Cambridge University Press, 1999), p. 156–8.

[20] Shell has pursued this subject further in 'Elizabeth Cary's Historical Conscience: The Tragedy of Mariam and Thomas Lodge's Josephus,' in *The Literary Career and Legacy of Elizabeth Cary, 1613–1680*, ed. Heather Wolfe (London: Palgrave Macmillan, 2007), pp. 52–67.

[21] Purkiss, introduction, *Three Tragedies by Renaissance Women*, p. xvi.

[22] Marta Straznicky, *Privacy, Playreading, and Women's Closet Drama, 1550–1700* (Cambridge: Cambridge University Press, 2004), p. 14.

[23] Andrew Hiscock, 'The Hateful Cuckoo: Elizabeth Cary's *Tragedie of Mariam*, a Renaissance Drama of Dispossession,' *Forum for Modern Language Studies* 33.2 (1997), p. 98.

The political purport of manuscripts that were not meant for the public stage places these texts in an ambivalent position, neither 'private' (as the standard charge against the importance of women's closet drama usually goes) nor 'public.' Instead, they are placed in an arena in which this dichotomy itself is explored, particularly in regard to the social construction of gender. 'Private' here, as Clarke has aptly remarked, does not necessarily mean 'domestic,' and indeed the very fact that these plays were not intended for public performance may be seen as empowering for their women authors by allowing them some more latitude in their interrogation of gender.[24] Moreover, it is perhaps useful to remember that those plays which went into print crossed over further into the public realm than those which did not.

The formal features of closet drama in general are shaped by their function as play-reading texts, which results in the inclusion of what Straznicky calls '"readerly" devices,' intended for orienting the reader, such as an introductory argument or summary of the action, long speeches, and a chorus.[25] Those very traits can be found in Cary's *Mariam*. Lewalski has identified them as 'the primacy of speech over action; long rhetorical monologues; the prominence of women as heroines and villains; and a chorus which speaks from a limited rather than an authorized vantage point.'[26]

A further important feature is the play's strict adherence to the three unities. Elizabeth Cary pressed into the time span of just one day the story of Herod and Mariam as told by the Jewish historian Josephus, which had been made available by Thomas Lodge's translation in 1602.[27] Herod was a historical character whose import had reached beyond the Bible and deeply into the rich dramatic tradition of medieval England, as attested to by those mystery cycles featuring Herod's slaughter of the innocents. But in the later sixteenth and early seventeenth centuries, interest in the story of his relationship with and assassination of his wife Mariam seems to have been sparked across Europe, as several writers reshaped the materials found in Josephus into their plays. Cary's tragedy itself departs from Thomas Lodge's translations and other renderings of the subject in a number of ways, particularly in the characterization of Mariam.[28] Connections of a different sort have been pointed out between Cary's tragedy and Jacobean plays such as Webster's *The Duchess of Malfi*, both in the creation of a powerful female

---

[24] Clarke, *The Politics of Early Modern Women's Writing*, p. 81.

[25] Straznicky, *Privacy, Playreading, and Women's Closet Drama, 1550–1700*, p. 12.

[26] Lewalski, *Writing Women in Jacobean England*, p. 191.

[27] As regards the main sources of Elizabeth Cary's play and its long-reaching connections within European drama (both English and Continental), I am following here the account given by Barry Weller and Margaret W. Ferguson, in their introduction to their edition of *The Tragedy of Mariam, the Fair Queen of Jewry, with The Lady Falkland: Her Life, by One of her Daughters* (Berkeley: University of California Press, 1994), pp. 17–24. All quotes from *The Tragedy of Mariam* have been taken from this edition.

[28] Erin E. Kelly has traced many of these departures in 'Mariam and Discourses of Martyrdom,' in *The Literary Career and Legacy of Elizabeth Cary, 1613–1680*, ed. Heather Wolfe (London: Palgrave Macmillan, 2007), pp. 35–52.

protagonist and in a domestic plot about 'women who seek to control their own sexual choices, challenging the orthodox ideal of submission.'[29]

Therefore, by virtue of its politicized genre affiliation, its complex form featuring argumentative speeches, a chorus, and a sophisticated use of rhymed iambic pentameters, as well as by reason of its engagement with a resonant episode of biblical history, Elizabeth Cary's *The Tragedy of Mariam* is well deserving of critical attention. It dramatically interrogates gender roles (both male and female) and how they relate in turn to the politics of race. My discussion of the play will tackle first the women characters in order to get a full picture of the conditions of femininity, and it will dwell on the male characters next, so as to thoroughly describe the patterns masculinity takes. Finally, the category of race needs to be introduced so as to map out the ways in which race impinges on gender and state politics. In so doing, I subscribe to Dympna Callaghan's observation that 'to change the canon is more than simply a matter of changing texts—it is to change the conditions and practices of reading all texts, and such changes, at least if they lay claim to political effectivity, must include 'race' as a category of analysis.'[30]

Displacing Men: Women's Rebellion in *The Tragedy of Mariam*

The protagonism not just of Mariam but of all women characters in Cary's play has attracted much critical commentary. Not a single male character enters the stage until Act I scene 5, and the arrival of King Herod himself is delayed until Act IV. Cary appears to be breaking new ground by providing women with the opportunity to voice their views of ongoing events for four full scenes, thus giving them the power to shape the reader's reactions at least in this initial stage. Such extraordinary female visibility may be considered one of the telltale signs of domestic tragedy, and a clear indicator of the conflation of personal and political issues in the play's plot. At its beginning, King Herod has been called away by Octavius to render him an account of his alliance with the now defeated Marc Anthony. There are rumors that Octavius has put Herod to death for his treason, and as a result the kingdom lies in disarray. Resistance to Herod's tyranny has sprung from various sources in his absence.

Most of all, such resistance appears to be coming from several women who have launched an attack on the public realm. Herod's first wife Doris, whom he repudiated for Mariam, now re-enters the city with the secret aim of defending her son's rights to the crown; Herod's mother-in-law Alexandra has taken the reins of the kingdom away from Herod's appointed governor Sohemus, and his

---

[29] Lewalski, *Writing Women in Jacobean England*, p. 200. For further connections between this play and other Jacobean tragedies, see, for example, Elizabeth Gruber, 'Insurgent Flesh: Epistemology and Violence in *Othello* and *Mariam*,' *Women's Studies* 32 (2003), pp. 393–410; Reina Green, '"Ears Prejudicate" in *Mariam* and *Duchess of Malfi*,' *Studies in English Literature* 43.2 (2003), pp. 459–74; and Jennifer Heller, 'Space, Violence, and Bodies in Middleton and Cary,' *Studies in English Literature* 45.2 (2005), pp. 425–41.

[30] Dympna Callaghan, *Woman and Gender in Renaissance Tragedy*, p. 164.

sister Salome has decided to divorce her second husband in order to marry a third, a privilege granted only to men. Each of these three women is deeply involved in a struggle to defend her lineage that empowers them to break away from conventional codes of women's behavior. Therefore, rather than being seen as part of a 'private' conflict, these women's decisions must be seen from the perspective of state politics, as their actions have dynastic import that goes well beyond their personal interests. Moreover, all of them are outspoken about their motives, their ends, and the means they are going to deploy in order to achieve them.

Mariam's mother Alexandra is a case in point. From the beginning of the play, she upbraids her daughter for her lack of purpose and her fine sentiments, insofar as they blind her as to those family interests of which Alexandra takes good care to remind her. Alexandra sees the world in black and white, those against and those in favor of her family, and she always acts accordingly. It was she who accused Herod before Caesar, and she who now takes the kingdom's rule into her own hands. She is thus renewing control over her family's inheritance, since she sees in Herod only the usurper to her family's lineage. In her raging speech to bring Mariam back to duty, Alexandra consistently defines Herod as someone completely unworthy of the crown. First of all, Herod is described as a man of low birth because he is an Idumean, one descending from Esau, who sold his birthright to his younger brother Jacob: he is a 'base Edomite, the damnèd Esau's heir,' a 'vile wretch,' 'a toad,' 'this Idumean' lifted by Alexandra's father 'from the dust,' an 'ungrateful caitiff,' and finally 'Esau's issue, heir of hell.'[31] Alexandra emphasizes the fact that several circumstances, first her own father's benevolence and later his marriage to Mariam, elevated Herod far above his expectations and merits. Second, Alexandra has contemptuous words for the use that he has made of the crown so far. Herod has a cruel nature 'which with blood is fed,' so that he 'ever thirsts for blood.'[32] This is followed by the accusation that his base nature is what 'made him me of sire and son deprive,' an accusation recurring a few lines later ('my father and my son he slew').[33] Third, Alexandra questions his faithfulness to women:

ALEXANDRA
Was love the cause, can Mariam deem it true,
That Herod gave commandment for her death?
I know by fits he show'd some signs of love,
And yet not love, but raging lunacy:
And this his hate to thee may justly prove,
That sure he hates Hircanus' family.
Who knows if he, unconstant wavering lord,
His love to Doris had renew'd again?
And that he might his bed to her afford,
Perchance he wish'd that Mariam might be slain.[34]

---

[31] *The Tragedy of Mariam*, I.II.84, 86, 89, 96, 97, and 100.
[32] *The Tragedy of Mariam*, I.II.104 and 106.
[33] *The Tragedy of Mariam*, I.II.105 and 119.
[34] *The Tragedy of Mariam*, I.II.121–30.

Alexandra's perception of the situation in Palestine is shaped by her family loyalty; love or hatred of 'Hircanus' family' is the key issue in a potent combination of state, gender, and racial politics. Those who, like her own daughter Mariam, fail to prioritize family interests get no pity from her, which may explain her 'unnatural' behavior in turning against her own daughter at Herod's return. Family survival should take precedence over any other consideration.

Another driven woman is Herod's first wife Doris, still resentful for having been forsaken for a fairer woman.[35] Nine years later, the exiled Doris returns to Jerusalem with her son Antipater (a name resounding with father-hatred), in order to ascertain the chances of having him named heir: 'With thee sweet boy I came, and came to try/ If though, before his bastards might be plac'd/ In Herod's royal seat and dignity.'[36] She thus becomes one more source of rebellion, discontent, and anarchy in the kingdom. Nevertheless, unlike Alexandra, Doris does not have the political alliances that might help her cause, and so she is reduced to plotting. Given her family loyalties, her revenge against Mariam is directed instead against her children, who in Antipater's words 'might subverted be/ By poison's drink, or else by murderous knife.'[37] Although Salome's own plot brings about Mariam's fall without Doris's help, she gloats over the fate of her long-time enemy, and curses not just her but, more particularly, her progeny: 'And plague the mother much: the children worse./ Throw flaming fire upon the baseborn heads/ That were begotten in unlawful beds.'[38] Her behavior is consistent with her characterization, which in Callaghan's words is that of a 'de-sexualized mother.'[39]

Third in this triad of rebellious women is Herod's sister Salome, who is certainly Mariam's antagonist in many ways. She is jealous of Mariam's pure blood and of her influence over her brother Herod, and she resents Mariam's pride. Like Alexandra and Doris, she is determined and active where Mariam procrastinates and fails to act. She is articulate about her will to power, and she is fearless as to the consequences of her actions. Among such powerful actions stands out her decision to draw up a separating bill from her second husband in order to marry her new lover, an unprecedented action undertaken in a society where this is a privilege that only men have:

---

[35] 'Fair' is a recurring adjective in the play, encoding the multilayered meanings of conventionally praised beauty (i.e., pale skin), conventional sanctioned behavior (virtue and modesty), and conventionally valued rank (i.e., pure lineage). As such, it is consistently and universally used for Mariam, whereas it is used only occasionally for Salome, and then only by her lover Silleus.

[36] *The Tragedy of Mariam*, II.III.255–7.

[37] *The Tragedy of Mariam*, II.III.274–5. Revenge is indeed a key concept to explicate many of the situations described in this play, so much so that Alison Findlay classifies *The Tragedy of Mariam* as a revenge tragedy in *A Feminist Perspective on Renaissance Drama* (Oxford: Blackwell, 1999), pp. 76–80.

[38] *The Tragedy of Mariam*, IV.VIII.616–18.

[39] Dympna Callaghan, 'Re-Reading Elizabeth Cary's *The Tragedy of Mariam, Faire Queene of Jewry*,' in *Women, "Race," and Writing in the Early Modern Period*, ed. Margo Hendricks and Patricia Parker (London: Routledge, 1994), p. 173.

SALOME
Why should such privilege to man be given?
Or given to them, why barr'd from women then?
Are men than we in greater grace with heaven?
Or cannot women hate as well as men?
I'll be the custom-breaker: and begin
To show my sex the way to freedom's door.[40]

This principle, however, was untenable in the context of early seventeenth-century divorce laws.[41] Consequently, as Clarke justly remarks, Salome's bid for female desire contributes to cast her as the villain, for it signals a transgressive, incontinent sexuality.[42] At the same time, Salome becomes the most active agent of disorder in the kingdom, the one who can bring about far-reaching and long-effecting changes. But it is worth pointing out that she is not only motivated by self-interest, as most critics would have it, but also by family loyalty. Salome's vindictive nature and her hatred for Mariam derive in good part from her own awareness of racial inferiority. This is evidenced in Salome's sensitivity to Mariam's insults concerning her family's Idumean descent, which virtuous Mariam throws at her during a major confrontation:

MARIAM
Though I thy brother's face had never seen,
My birth thy baser birth so far excell'd,
I had to both of you [Herod and Salome] the Princess been.
Thou parti-Jew, and parti-Edomite,
Thou mongrel: issued from rejected race,
Thy ancestors against the heavens did fight,
And thou like them wilt heavenly birth disgrace. [43]

All of these characters happen to be more articulate in claiming power and autonomy and in challenging Herod's government than Mariam herself would seem to be. Like Alexandra and Doris, Salome's self-empowerment and her entry into state politics is connected in large measure to her personal commitment to a lineage, a family, a race, although these do not exclude the women's personal interests. On the contrary, despite sporadic assertions of her high birth and some protective remarks about her children, Mariam lacks such wholehearted commitment to rank and family, and as a result she fails to implement an effective course of action. As a matter of fact, her eloquence conveys self-doubt and lack

---

[40] *The Tragedy of Mariam*, I.IV. 305–10.
[41] Jeanne Addison Roberts has related the play's concern with divorce to contemporaneous controversies surrounding the cases of Penelope Rich and of Frances Howard in 'Sex and the Female Hero,' in *The Female Tragic Hero in English Renaissance Drama*, ed. Naomi Conn Liebler (New York: Palgrave, 2002), p. 207.
[42] Clarke, *The Politics of Early Modern Women's Writing*, p. 97.
[43] *The Tragedy of Mariam*, I.III. 232–8.

of determination, and her actions might rather be called 'inactions.' When Herod returns, the man whom she detests for commanding the assassinations of her brother and grandfather, she announces that she will not continue to live with him as his wife. Although failure to perform her wifely duties should be taken as a very real challenge, passive resistance rather than direct action is her main feature. She is imaged rather for what she does not do than for what she actually does. Later, as she is wrongly accused of conspiracy against Herod, she meekly lets herself be taken to the scaffold and summarily executed. Mariam's final soliloquy is self-deprecating in tone. She contends that she was lacking in humility, and that she was wrong to consider herself safe from danger because she was beautiful, chaste, and beloved by Herod:

> MARIAM
> Had I but with humility been grac'd,
> As well as fair I might have prov'd me wise:
> But I did think because I knew me chaste,
> One virtue for a woman might suffice.
> That mind for glory of our sex might stand,
> Wherein humility and chastity
> Do march with equal paces hand in hand.
> But one, if single seen, who setteth by?
> And I had singly one, but 'tis my joy,
> That I was ever innocent, though sour,
> And therefore can they but my life destroy,
> My soul is free from adversary's power.   *Enter Doris.*
> You princes great in power, and high in birth,
> Be great and high, I envy not your hap:
> Your birth must be from dust, your power on earth;
> In heav'n shall Mariam sit in Sara's lap.[44]

Although the play highlights Mariam's conflicted subjectivity from its very first lines, displaying a self puzzled by the fact that 'one object yields both grief and joy,'[45] yet as the plot comes to its denouement, Mariam's ambivalence and self-doubt give way to the cold virtuous perfection that the Chorus prescribes for all women.[46] Mariam becomes an exemplar of those virtues enforced by patriarchal conduct books: chastity, humility, modesty. Mariam's speech typifies her stoic renunciation to earthly power and her claim of spiritual, rather than material, freedom. Her heroism emerges as a kind of saintly martyrdom, and her stance has been compared to that of 'an early Christian martyr.'[47] Mariam thus joins a line of heroic women in Renaissance culture, characterized, according to Lamb, by their sacrificial deaths:

---

[44] *The Tragedy of Mariam*, IV.VIII.559–74.

[45] *The Tragedy of Mariam*, I.I.10.

[46] For further discussion of the Chorus's contradictory politics, see Ferguson, 'The Spectre of Resistance,' 240–244.

[47] Beilin, *Redeeming Eve*, p. 170.

> Heroizing women for their willingness to die ... was a cultural cliché, set forth in a multitude of works read in the Renaissance, from Boccaccio's *De Claris Mulieribus* to Chaucer's *Legend of Good Women* to Castiglione's *Book of the Courtier*. In all these works, the willingness to die was represented primarily as a means of exonerating women from the charge of sexual guilt.[48]

Similarly, Dolan has traced numerous accounts of women's executions, particularly those recorded in John Foxe's *Acts and Monuments* (1563), and concludes that the scaffold may be 'an arena of boundary crossing, negotiation, and possibilities of agency' because women's speech may then be recorded without challenging the status quo.[49] It might be argued, however, that Mariam makes little use of such a privilege, only enlisting the Nuncio to report her death to Herod, about whom she claims she is sure that 'By three days hence, if wishes could revive,/ I know himself would make me oft alive.'[50] Nevertheless, Dolan understands that a Christian (or a Stoic) heroism of endurance construes virtuous suffering as a kind of action, their agency being created 'in and through the transcendence of bodily suffering.'[51] This kind of agency, if agency it is, establishes a marked contrast with the sort exhibited by other female characters. Mariam exhibits a Stoic's heroism, and as Braden has remarked,

> Stoicism is not finally a philosophy of political resistance. The essential Stoic strategy for dealing with a tyrant is not interference but indifference. ... Stoicism's central strength is its calculus of adaptation to unchangeable realities. Surrendering the world's goods, we find them false and learn how to want what we have instead of striving to have what we want. ... The calculus leads progressively inward, redefining individual freedom as a state of mind; the Stoic's inviolable privilege is simply his attitude toward the incontestable fate which has its way with him.[52]

Ultimately, Mariam's Stoic passivity and lack of drive serve in the play to highlight the agentive power of the other, more deviant women. She is the catalyst of female deviancy, those true 'monsters' that enforce a combined challenge of the gendered, racialized state of Palestine.

---

[48] Lamb, *Gender and Authorship in the Sidney Circle*, p. 120.

[49] Frances E. Dolan, '"Gentlemen, I Have One Thing More To Say": Women on Scaffolds in England, 1563–1680,' *Modern Philology* 92.2 (1994), p. 157.

[50] *The Tragedy of Mariam*, V.I.77–8.

[51] Dolan, '"Gentlemen, I Have One Thing More To Say,"' p. 167. It may be worth noting that Dolan is right in pointing out that Christianity and Stoicism share an ethics of renunciation and endurance. Since this play drinks from both sources, it is hard to ascertain which of them is to be accorded responsibility for Mariam's behavior at the scaffold.

[52] Gordon Braden, *Renaissance Tragedy and the Senecan Tradition: Anger's Privilege* (New Haven: Yale University Press, 1985), p. 17.

Hegemonic Masculinity under Siege in *The Tragedy of Mariam*

Compared to the women's formidable attack on the public realm, the male characters of *The Tragedy of Mariam* may appear puny and adrift, lacking willpower and direction, which might go some way towards explaining critics' fairly minor interest in them so far. Subversion in this field is also substantial, and yet, by virtue of their comparatively higher position as men, it may be considered less transgressive. Herod's brother Pheroras has taken a wife other than the one the king had appointed; his brother in law Constabarus has been hiding the sons of a known opponent to Herod's regime; and his main counselor Sohemus has refused to carry out Herod's orders that Mariam be put to death if he does not return.

The men's relative happiness and acquiescence with Herod's regime should not be wondered at. After all, they are the ones policing the borders and enjoying the privileges. They are largely part of the establishment, and they stand to gain by remaining on the side of power, so they become the target of the women's rebellion rather than agents of disorder in their own right. Perhaps the only exception is Pheroras, whose wife-taking entails a higher risk than the passive resistance of the others. He has gone beyond rejecting his brother's choice, daring to make his own. But his challenge is short-lived. When the news of Herod's return reaches him, he hastens to follow his sister Salome's instructions and promptly makes accusations against Constabarus that may deflect the king's attention from his own disloyalty, thus proving that his weak mind is an easy subject for Salome's manipulation. Salome's new lover Silleus is an Arabian foreigner who seems to be beyond the political strife of the Jewish kingdom. But his love for her makes him susceptible to her plotting, and he is similar to Pheroras in that he readily accepts all her words at face value. He is a mere pawn, unable to make his own decisions. His love is easy for the audience to perceive as an incapacitating blindness to view her and their situation as they truly are, and thus, rather than admiration, Silleus deserves the audience's pity.

Out of all the male characters, only Constabarus stands out for his virtues. Salome's husband is a character of higher stature than Herod himself, as he is consistent in his speech and his actions throughout the play. He is the first one to realize the subversive potential of Salome's doings, which threaten the gender hierarchy of the kingdom by taking away men's privileges. These are his accusations when he hears that *she* is divorcing *him*:

> CONSTABARUS
> Are Hebrew women now transformed to men?
> Why do you not as well our battles fight,
> And wear our armour? Suffer this, and then
> Let all the world be topsy-turvèd quite.[53]

---

[53] *The Tragedy of Mariam*, I.VI.421–4.

Moreover, Constabarus seems to be an objective man, one who is not bent by family or self-interest, in clear contrast to the others. He is blinded neither by love (like Silleus or even like Pheroras), nor by jealousy (like Herod). He can see through Salome's manipulations and manages to anticipate their effect on other men, with the kind of wisdom one gains from previous experiences. When Silleus tries to pick a fight, Constabarus at first declines to take him on and only does so when Silleus calls him a coward. Then while they fight, Constabarus attempts to convince Silleus that Salome is unworthy of his love, and that he is bound to be replaced when she tires of him:

> CONSTABARUS
> For her, I pity thee enough already,
> For her, I therefore will not mangle thee:
> A woman with a heart so most unsteady
> Will of herself sufficient torture be.
> I cannot envy for so light a gain;
> Her mind with such unconstancy doth run:
> As with a word thou didst her love obtain,
> So with a word she will from thee be won.
> So light as her possessions for most day
> Is her affections lost, to me 'tis known.[54]

Although Silleus proves stubbornly impervious to his warnings, Constabarus also candidly offers his help to the wounded man, to the extent that Salome's lover feels that 'Had not my heart and tongue engag'd me so,/ I would from thee no foe, but friend depart,' and Constabarus replies that he will 'take/ Thee as friend, and grieve for thy complaint.'[55] It is perhaps this virtuous concern for other people, even those whom he should count as his enemies, that makes Constabarus truly Mariam's counterpart, but like her, Constabarus is essentially passive, and his resistance to injustice or tyranny never takes a productive form. His tragic stature derives from the fact that, though not lacking in either virtue or honesty, he nevertheless falls prey to Salome's plot, very much as Mariam does. Thus, he is unable to protect himself from Herod's cruelty, and as he is led to his death he is as stoically virtuous as Mariam herself will later be, in a scene of high moral tone that prepares the audience for the scene of her sad death and the later discovery of her innocence. Like Mariam too, Constabarus embodies the fractures of conventional virtue, this time for the male gender. Even while being admirable for his honesty and plain dealing, he is a mouthpiece for the traditional values that support class privilege and gender inequality. It is an inescapable fact that, like the Chorus closing each Act, Constabarus is the one character to consistently voice the most stereotypical denunciations of women's duplicitous and inherently evil nature:

---

[54] *The Tragedy of Mariam*, II.IV.313–22.
[55] *The Tragedy of Mariam*, II.IV.391–2 and 398.

CONSTABARUS
You are to nothing constant but to ill,
You are with nought but wickedness indued:
Your loves are set on nothing but your will,
And thus my censure I of you conclude.
You are the least of goods, the worst of evils,
Your best are worse than men: your worst than devils.[56]

His is a failed attempt to restore male privilege. Under women's joint attack in the play, men have become confused and gullible, unable to see things clearly. The best case in point is Herod himself, whose arrival is put off until Act IV, when he enters Jerusalem in a haze of love, only to find a disgruntled Mariam, dressed in dark clothes, who asks him to account for the murder of her relatives. The man who has successfully evaded Caesar's justice seems hardly able to face his wife's discontent. When he discovers the clumsy attempt to poison him, he immediately trusts the butler's accusation against Mariam. He does not require proof of her deceit and infidelity, but he jumps straight away to the wrong conclusions without anyone's assistance:[57]

HEROD
Now do I know thy falsehood, painted devil,
Thou white enchantress. Oh, thou art so foul,
That hyssop cannot cleanse thee, worst of evil.
A beauteous body hides a loathsome soul.
Your love Sohemus, mov'd by his affection,
Though he have ever heretofore been true,
Did blab forsooth, that I did give direction,
If we were put to death to slaughter you.
And you in black revenge attended now
To add a murder to your breach of vow.[58]

Unlike Constabarus, Herod is changeable and insecure, easily manipulated by his sister Salome. Having had Mariam committed to prison, he is unlikely to follow this through with the order for her execution, so in Act IV scene VII, a scene that resonates with echoes of Shakespeare's *Othello*, Salome (like Iago) pushes Herod (like Othello) to take the decision he so fears to make. Herod's speech is full of dilatory moves, complaining, for example, that none of the methods of execution Salome suggests is right for his fair Mariam, to the point that his sister, tired of

---

[56] *The Tragedy of Mariam*, IV.VI.345–50.

[57] For further study of the implications of this epistemological flaw, see Elizabeth Gruber, 'Insurgent Flesh.' So close is the parallelism between Herod and Othello, that a full analysis of Herod's insecurity and vulnerability might well follow the guidelines of Ania Loomba's excellent analysis of Othello in chapter two of *Gender, Race, Renaissance Drama*, pp. 38–64.

[58] *The Tragedy of Mariam*, IV.IV.175–84.

his shenanigans, finally undertakes to give the order herself. Herod then turns against his sister, calling her his 'black tormentor,'[59] and cancels the order twice, but finally he caves in and accepts Salome's injunction that Mariam must die. The king is not completely unaware that Salome has her own agenda and that she is Mariam's enemy, but he is unable to overcome his jealousy, the mere thought of her 'wavering heart' making him rave. Here we find a portrait of the gullible husband moved by jealousy and by his own insecurities, like Othello. Eventually, when proof is found that Mariam was innocent of his charges, a careworn Herod must come to terms with his own failures and with the injustice of his decisions. At the end of the play he is a broken man, not the joyful, careless tyrant he arrived as, only one Act earlier. He now resigns himself to a lifetime of grief, and welcomes the thought of death:

HEROD
Happy day
When thou at once shalt die and find a grave;
A stone upon the vault someone shall lay,
Which monument shall an inscription have,
And these shall be the words it shall contain:
Here Herod lies, that hath his Mariam slain.[60]

Therefore, Herod is a remarkable example of what Breitenberg has termed 'anxious masculinity.' By anxiety Breitenberg is referring to the Burtonian meaning of doubt and suspicion, as well as the modern sense of feeling troubled. But for this critic, anxiety is not an exception but, rather, the normal condition of masculinity, as 'it reveals the fissures and contradictions of patriarchal systems and, at the same time, it paradoxically enables and drives patriarchy's reproduction and continuation of itself.'[61]

No restoration of the original order appears to be feasible at the end of the play. The execution of Mariam has brought about nothing worthy of note, except giving her new life as a martyred saint. Instead, the sources of subversion and change seem to have survived unchallenged. Salome's actions go unpunished, and presumably now that Constabarus is dead she can achieve unimpeded what was her end all along, her marriage to Silleus. Alexandra too, appears to escape unscathed by placing herself on the side of Herod against her own daughter, although at one point Herod threatens to tarnish her reputation for her 'unnatural' behavior. No indication of Doris and her son's fate is given, though in Mariam's execution Doris's revenge against her hatred rival has been effected too. All in all, women's 'monstrous' behavior seems to have won the day, and hegemonic masculinity lies in disarray. Those who might sustain the old structures of male privilege, like Constabarus, are dead.

---

[59] *The Tragedy of Mariam*, IV.VII.513.

[60] *The Tragedy of Mariam*, V.I. 253–8.

[61] Mark Breitenberg, *Anxious Masculinity in Early Modern England* (Cambridge: Cambridge University Press, 1996), p. 2.

The Bounds of Race: Complex Identities in *The Tragedy of Mariam*

As declared above, gender and rank are not the only categories in the play's complex staging of identity at critical junctures. One must add race, particularly since *The Tragedy of Mariam* is run through by the conflict between two Jewish lines of descent: Esau's and Jacob's. It should be noted at this point that there is a consistent connection between the kingdom and its queen. Mariam *is* Jerusalem, and other characters often utter their names in the same breath, or else variously link them, like Herod's joyous greeting to Jerusalem on his unexpected return in Act IV:

> HEROD
> Hail happy city, happy in thy store,
> Happy that thy buildings such we see:
> More happy in the temple where w'adore
> But most of all that Mariam lives in thee.[62]

Similarly, Doris commanded the city to 'bow your lofty side' on entering it surreptitiously.[63] Even though the city's foremost trait for Herod is its happiness, while for Doris it is its loftiness, both agree in signifying it as Mariam's abode and, thus, sharing in the characteristics they assign her.

In the case of Herod, his opening lines suggest rather more than one would expect from a lover's hyperbolic assertion if one considers that it is Mariam who, through marriage, legitimizes Herod's rule, he being considered a usurper by his Idumean ancestry, she, by contrast, being the bearer of a pure Jewish bloodline. The 'Argument' that introduces the play's plot literally describes this event as Herod's 'having *crept* into the Jewish monarchy' (my italics), a verb that invites thoughts of illegitimacy and duplicity. Alexandra's portrait of Herod, as seen above, emphasized such traits. Consequently, Mariam stands as the embodiment of the Jewish nation and of the city of Jerusalem, and as a powerful symbol of the embattled situation in which the Jewish nation lives. The body politic and the gendered body come together in her, just as family politics is tangled with state politics, as described above.

From the very beginning of this play, then, race and rank are intimately associated by means of the kingdom and of this marriage of Othello-like unequals, as Callaghan explains:

> Palestine provided an unusually suitable site for the depiction of male tyranny and female resistance, and for a protagonist who embodies an unstable mixture of antithetical elements—female virtue and rebellion. Both fantasized and actual, Palestine is a place where Cary can unbalance the polarized binarisms which constituted the category "woman."[64]

---

[62] *The Tragedy of Mariam*, IV.I. 1–4.
[63] *The Tragedy of Mariam*, II.III. 1.
[64] Dympna Callaghan, 'Re-Reading,' pp. 169–70.

The terms used by Elizabeth Cary to depict the struggle come from a historically available source of binary oppositions such as white/black, fair/dark, virtuous/evil. Moreover, this battery of terms has been historically gendered as well. Callaghan has remarked that '"Race" is not self-explanatory; it is currently the site of intense cultural contestation. The term merits quotation marks because, historically, racial marking functions as a denigratory process of cultural othering rather than a positive mode of self-definition.'[65] The most evident sign of such struggle is the consistent othering of Salome as the dark woman in relation to Mariam's fairness. Mariam herself calls her a 'mongrel,'[66] just like Herod's designing her his 'black' tormentor in Act IV Scene VII is clearly intended to recall both her darker hue and her bad acts. MacDonald has interpreted this persistent juxtaposition of a white heroine and a brown villain as yet another instance of an early modern text's singling out a racially marked woman for moral censure, as well as the writer's strategy in order to emphasize 'the affiliation of their speaking voices with dominant racial cultures, even as they may be disputing the sway of dominant constructions of gender and sexuality.'[67]

Yet, in foregrounding racial conflict in the play, one must not forget that it is consistently associated with strategies for empowerment. More often than not, the relationships in the play are couched in a language of elevation that reminds readers of the force of hierarchical structures as well as of some characters' efforts to break through them. Thus, Alexandra reminds Mariam that it was her father who 'did lift this Idumean [Herod] from the dust,'[68] while Salome questions the importance of birth, claiming that there is no difference between their ancestors and hers: 'Both born of Adam, both were made of earth,/ And both did come from holy Abraham's line.'[69] Yet she in turn later upbraids her husband Constabarus, whose 'low estate' she deems to have upreared.[70] Salome is demanding from her husband the kind of gratitude that Pheroras' chosen wife Graphina expresses when she admits that: 'Your hand hath lifted me from lowest state/ To highest eminency wondrous grace,/ And me your handmaid have you made your mate,/ Though all but you alone do count me base.'[71] But in choosing her, whose 'brow's as white, her cheeks as red' as Mariam's,[72] Pheroras was certainly not unaware of racial categories. Doris herself, who we may infer to be of Idumean descent like her estranged husband, is full of anger at the loss of status that came with her divorce, and in returning to Jerusalem she dreams of its inhabitants' renewed homage, so

---

[65] Callaghan, 'Re-Reading,' p. 164.
[66] *The Tragedy of Mariam*, I.III. 236.
[67] Joyce G. Macdonald, *Women and Race in Early Modern Texts* (Port Chester, NY: Cambridge University Press, 2002), p. 64.
[68] *The Tragedy of Mariam*, I.II.95–6.
[69] *The Tragedy of Mariam*, I.III.241–2.
[70] *The Tragedy of Mariam*, I.VI.397.
[71] *The Tragedy of Mariam*, II. I.57–60.
[72] *The Tragedy of Mariam*, II. I.40.

that 'You royal buildings bow your lofty sides/ And stoop to her that is by right your Queen.'[73] Whether it is marriage or other sorts of kinship, all interpersonal relations bear the imprint of both rank and an implicit color hierarchy.

These are only some examples of the complex, manifold ways in which categories of race, class, and gender overlap in the play. As we have seen, they are constantly in flux, with some characters (women, particularly those of Idumean descent like Salome) trying to bring about change, while others (men like Constabarus) resist it and defend the benefits of conventional, compartmentalized society. Most strikingly, the tragic resolution fails to punish the deviant forces of change, whether it is women's stepping out into the public sphere or the Idumeans' equalizing efforts. The play's tragic ending highlights the utter destruction of an old social order, with the unnecessary sacrifice of those two characters that stand out conspicuously for conventional virtue and submission to the law of the land: Mariam and Constabarus.

Thus, a biographical approach centered exclusively on the ambiguous figure of Mariam and on the politics of the writer's life cannot truly aspire to bring to light the complexity of Cary's take on issues of social citizenship, power, and privilege. On the contrary, by engaging in a thorough analysis of gender and race politics in *The Tragedy of Mariam*, one can see how Elizabeth Cary's play manages to break new ground in portraying early modern identity and belonging as a contested site, fraught with discrepancies and contradictions. Furthermore, *The Tragedy of Mariam* stages early modern society as the embattled ground where the categories of gender, class, and racial differences are acted out.

It is tempting for critics to find meaning and transcendence in the protagonist's suffering, to portray Mariam as a female hero engaged in a politics of resistance. Yet, the power of the play lies more in how its inconsistencies bring to light related fractures in a tyrannical social order put to the test by several contending forces. Similarly, as we will see, the Stoic resilience displayed by Elizabeth Cary's Mariam will prove attractive to later women playwrights, as it allows for a non-confrontational (though questionable) form of female hero.

---

[73] *The Tragedy of Mariam*, II.III. 1–2.

Chapter 3
The Interregnum: Margaret Cavendish's Dramatic Experiments

Margaret Cavendish and English Drama during the Interregnum

Until recently, the Interregnum has been considered a theatrical wasteland. The Puritan rule and the closing of the theatres were thought to have precluded any significant theatrical activity. However, some critics have questioned this approach because it oversimplifies the situation, ignoring the wealth of (often privately held) theatrical events that continued to take place throughout the period.[1] Undoubtedly, the underestimation of this literary period has also resulted at least partly in belittling the importance of Margaret Cavendish's own contribution, although recent critical studies are on the way to correct the imbalance.[2] Margaret Cavendish, née Lucas, was an extraordinary young woman who followed the royal family into exile in France, where she met and married in 1645 the widowed William Cavendish, later Duke of Newcastle.[3] The couple settled in Antwerp, and there during the 1650s Margaret composed several plays that would be published in London on their return in the first of two folio collections of dramatic works, *Plays Written by the*

---

[1] On the subject of Civil War and Interregnum theatre, see Susan Wiseman, *Drama and Politics in the English Civil War*.

[2] Cavendish's dramatic works have been receiving more attention in the last few years, as mentioned in chapter one. This is perhaps the result of a general increase in critical interest, as attested to by special issues of the journal *Women's Writing* (4.3, 1999) and *In-Between: Essays and Studies in Literary Criticism* (9.1 & 2, 2000) as well as two monographs (Anna Battigelli's *Margaret Cavendish and the Exiles of the Mind* and Emma L. E. Rees's *Margaret Cavendish: Gender, Genre, Exile*) and three further collections of essays, *A Princely Brave Woman*, ed. Stephen Clucas, *Authorial Conquests*, ed. Line Cottegnies and Nancy Weitz, and *Cavendish and Shakespeare*, ed. Katherine Romack and James Fitzmaurice. However, judging from the contents of these works, one could well say that her plays do not yet rate quite as highly as her prose and poetry in the critics' estimation.

[3] Although she has had several biographers, the best source of information on Margaret Cavendish's life is to be found in her own writings. For short but informative profiles of this author, see Sara Heller Mendelson, *The Mental World of Stuart Women: Three Case Studies* (Brighton: Harvester, 1987), and Moira Ferguson, 'A "wise, wittie and learned lady": Margaret Cavendish,' in *Women Writers of the 17th Century*, ed. Katharina M. Wilson and Frank J. Warnke (Athens: University of Georgia Press, 1989), pp. 305–40.

Thrice Noble, Illustrious, and Excellent Princess, the Marchioness of Newcastle (1662). This was followed in 1668 by *Plays, Never Before Printed*.

Writing some fifty years after her predecessor Elizabeth Cary, and like many other women of her generation, Cavendish was empowered by the turmoil of the English Civil War. Women of all paths of life were thrown into the most unlikely situations and had to perform roles other than those institutionally approved. Royalist women in particular were occasionally forced to defend their households and properties in the absence of their husbands.[4] Cavendish's marriage into the high aristocracy and her husband's unfailing support and encouragement—as reported in all of her writings—no doubt facilitated the publication of her work. Even so, entering the theatrical world was by no means easy for a woman. Cavendish's choice of the prestigious folio format instead of separate quartos, as was more usual, was in itself a tour de force. It placed her, despite her own marginal voice, in the company of those dramatists such as Jonson and Shakespeare whom she admiringly mentions in her 'General Prologue to all my Playes.' At the same time, her lack of status as a dramatist is evidenced in the folio itself. Examining this 1662 edition of Cavendish's plays, Jeffrey Masten remarks that:

> Unlike the Beaumont and Fletcher folio or its famous predecessors, Cavendish's collection includes no succession of male poets commending her plays. ... In significant contrast to ... the Jonson, Shakespeare, and Beaumont and Fletcher folios, the bulk of the Cavendish preliminary materials, it must be emphasized, is signed by Cavendish herself.[5]

The very range and scope of Cavendish's interests and intellectual endeavors remains exceptional for her time and deserves admiration, though it has often been conducive to a perception of the writer as disorderly and amateurish. Sylvia Bowerbank has claimed that Cavendish's exile from the intellectual community was owing to 'her sex and her untamed method.'[6] Her dramatic works challenge generic labels and experiment with form, characterization, and plot. Moreover,

---

[4] Karen L. Raber offers some particular instances of such women warriors and discusses the subject at some length in 'Warrior Women in the Plays of Cavendish and Killigrew,' *Studies in English Literature* 40.3 (2000), pp. 413–33; see also Alexandra Bennett's 'Margaret Cavendish and the Theatre of War,' *In-Between* 9:1 & 2 (2000), pp. 263–73, for a detailed analysis of the parallels between fact and fiction.

[5] Jeffrey Masten, *Textual Intercourse: Collaboration, Authorship, and Sexualities in Renaissance Drama* (Cambridge: Cambridge University Press, 1997), p. 157.

[6] Sylvia Bowerbank, 'The Spider's Delight: Margaret Cavendish and the "Female Imagination,"' *ELR* 14.3 (1984), p. 402. Dale B. J. Randall's rather patronizing approach to Cavendish also emphasizes that 'as a writer she is almost totally without discipline,' in *Winter Fruit: English Drama 1642–1660* (Lexington: The University Press of Kentucky, 1995), p. 330. On this topic, see also Hero Chalmers, 'Dismantling the Myth of "Mad Madge": the Cultural Context of Margaret Cavendish's Authorial Self-Presentation,' *Women's Writing* 4.3 (1997), pp. 323–39; Susan Wiseman, *Drama and Politics in the English Civil War*, p. 93; and Emma L. E. Rees's *Margaret Cavendish: Gender, Genre, Exile*, pp. 11–14.

the fact that they were never staged in her lifetime (and several hypotheses have been advanced as to why they were not) has worked against them in the critics' consideration, some of whom have claimed that they are 'plays of ideas' with limited stageability.[7]

Nevertheless, Cavendish was far from inexperienced in theatre matters. She had been to performances in England before the war and also during her years of exile on the continent, where she had the opportunity to see actresses on the stage. She also had recourse to her husband's wide expertise as a playwright—Cavendish mentions in the 1662 Epistle Dedicatory that it was in fact her husband's reading of his plays to her that first made her want to write them herself—and as a patron of such reputed authors as Ben Jonson and James Shirley. And though she was lacking in formal education, Cavendish's plays show the influence of major dramatists, as is now beginning to be acknowledged.[8] Indeed, recent Cavendish criticism has sought to stress continuity with the Caroline period's forms and topics rather than

---

[7] Linda R. Payne, 'Dramatic Dreamscape: Women's Dreams and Utopian Vision in the Works of Margaret Cavendish, Duchess of Newcastle,' in *Curtain Calls: British and American Women and the Theater, 1660–1820*, ed. Mary Anne Schofield and Cecilia Macheski (Athens: Ohio University Press, 1991), p. 30. Payne has further claimed that three of Cavendish's plays were likely to become successful performance texts if extensive editing was introduced: *Loves Adventures*, *Bell in Campo*, and *The Convent of Pleasure*. For the controversy over the producibility of Cavendish's plays, see Alison Findlay, Gweno Williams, and Stephanie J. Hodgson-Wright, '"The Play is ready to be Acted": Women and Dramatic Production, 1570–1670,' *Women's Writing* 6.1 (1999), pp. 129–48; and Judith Peacock, 'Writing for the Brain and Writing for the Boards: the Producibility of Margaret Cavendish's Dramatic Texts,' in *A Princely Brave Woman*, ed. Stephen Clucas, pp. 87–108. Although there is now some general consensus on the plays' stageability, some argue for preserving the play-text as it is, while Peacock contends that all plays undergo changes when staged. In his recent essay 'Shakespeare, Cavendish, and Reading Aloud in Seventeenth-Century England,' James Fitzmaurice has examined household readings as the target audience for Cavendish's plays, in keeping with the tradition of reading aloud of which closet drama partakes, as described in the previous chapter (in *Cavendish and Shakespeare, Interconnections*, ed. Katherine Romack and James Fitzmaurice, pp. 29–46).

[8] See, for instance, Hero Chalmers's 'The Politics of Feminine Retreat in Margaret Cavendish's *The Female Academy* and *The Convent of Pleasure*,' *Women's Writing* 6.1 (1999), pp. 81–94, where she argues that 'Confronting the view that her plays have no identifiable sources the author shows how they draw on plays of the 1630s which register the Caroline interest in feminine retreat,' p. 81. Julie Sanders also abounds on this topic, and pursues Jonsonian influences (via Shirley) on several plays in '"A woman write a play!": Jonsonian Strategies and the Dramatic Writings of Margaret Cavendish; or, Did the Duchess Feel the Anxiety of Influence?' in *Readings in Renaissance Women's Drama*, ed. S.P. Cerasano and Marion Wynne-Davies, pp. 293–305. More recently, the editors of *Cavendish and Shakespeare, Interconnections*, Katherine Romack and James Fitzmaurice, have set out to prove that 'Cavendish drew heavily on Shakespeare in creating dramatic situations and dialogue. Her plays commonly contain characters and language reminiscent of Shakespeare's and her plots often work to offer commentary on his,' p. 1.

her uniqueness as a playwright.[9] Wiseman and Raber have persuasively argued that what might seem Cavendish's eccentric experiments with form (for instance, long plays written in two parts) in fact have a lot in common with the output of other Royalist writers in the period, particularly Thomas Killigrew.[10]

Margaret Cavendish's interest in drama seems to stem from its didactic potential. In the fourth letter to the 'Noble Readers' of the 1662 folio edition, she argues in favor of the teaching of drama for the young aristocracy:

> [T]he noble sort, that Act not for mercenary Profit, but for Honour, and becoming, would not only strive to Act well upon the Stage, but to practise their actions when off from the Stage, besides, it would keep the youths from misimploying time with their foolish extravagancies, deboist luxuries, and base Vices, all which Idleness and vacant time produceth; and in my opinion, a publick Theatre were a shorter way of education than their tedious and expensive Travels, or their dull and solitary Studies; for Poets teach them more in one Play, both of the Nature of the World and Mankind, by which they learn not only to know other men, but their own selves, than they can learn in any School, or in any Country or Kingdome in a year; but to conclude, a Poet is the best Tutor; and a Theatre is the best School that is for youth to be educated by or in.[11]

The same idea surfaces again and again in her writings, and is occasionally voiced by the female characters of her plays, such as Lady Sanspareille in *Youths Glory and Deaths Banquet, Part I*, for whom the theatre is likewise a site of moral learning and good examples.[12] For Mendelson, this is precisely one of the two major principles underlying Cavendish's dramatic oeuvre: theatre as a medium for education and theatre as autobiographical self-fashioning. Of the two, Mendelson identifies the autobiographical impulse as seemingly stronger, as it is generally in Cavendish's writing, and thus for this critic it is its irruption that produces the generic instabilities of the work, or what she calls the 'subversion of genre'

---

[9] The attempt to bridge the Civil War gap informs Susan Wiseman's *Drama and Politics in the English Civil War*, as well as Karen L. Raber's *Dramatic Difference: Gender, Class, and Genre in the Early Modern Drama* (Newark: University of Delaware Press, 2001). Sophie Tomlinson has addressed the connections between Caroline dramatic aesthetics and the works of the Cavendish family in several essays, most extensively in her book *Women on Stage in Stuart Drama* (Cambridge: Cambridge University Press, 2005).

[10] See Susan Wiseman's *Drama and Politics in the English Civil War*, p. 92, and Karen L. Raber's *Dramatic Difference*, chapter 5 (pp. 188–236), which revises her article 'Warrior Women in the Plays of Cavendish and Killigrew,' *Studies in English Literature* 40.3 (2000), pp. 413–33.

[11] Anne Shaver, ed. *Margaret Cavendish, Duchess of Newcastle:* The Convent of Pleasure *and Other Plays* (Baltimore: The Johns Hopkins University Press, 1999), pp. 258–9.

[12] *Youths Glory and Deaths Banquet, Part I* (London, Printed by A. Warren, for John Martyn, James Allestry, and Tho. Dicas, 1662), I.iii, pp. 126–7. Further references to the play come from this edition.

when autobiographically based materials cannot be 'contained within the classical unities.'[13] Although the autobiographical import should never be underestimated in the case of this author, the didactic drive would perhaps be more explanatory concerning so-called eccentricities in the dramatic organization of the plays' themes. Cavendish is remarkably consistent, for instance, in the use of names that disclose the characters' different 'humours' or main psychological features in Jonsonian fashion—Lady Contemplation, Lady Poor Virtue, Lady Bashful, Lord Amorous, Sir Humphrey Interruption, Monsieur Sensible, to name but a few—which suggests just how much stock she placed on the moral teaching potential of her drama.[14] Her plots similarly span a variety of women—mostly upper-class—in diverse situations and paths of life, making choices that are remarkably divergent. This has puzzled critics who would like to see a consistently 'feminist' viewpoint, and therefore perceive a notable 'ambivalence' in Cavendish's opinions.[15] Similarly, the fact that Cavendish often fails to weave together the different strands of her plays, with mere juxtaposition taking the place of more specific inter-relations (cause-effect, temporality, etc.) can create a feeling of confusion or at the very least the discomfort of unfamiliarity in readers. Cavendish herself discussed this in her prefatory materials, explaining that she considered it very unlikely

> that the several persons presented should be all of an acquaintance, or that there is a necessity to have them of one Fraternity, or to have a relation to each other, or linck'd in alliance as one Family, when as Playes are to present the general Follies, Vanities, Vices, Humours, Dispositions, Passions, ... and all of these Varieties to be drawn at the latter end into one piece, as into one Company, which in my opinion shews neither Usual, Probable, nor Natural.[16]

In other words, Cavendish finds aesthetic choice subordinate to verisimilitude. She prefers plausibility over tidy endings, and moral teaching over formal neatness, as being more 'natural.' This is the basis of what Venet has termed an 'aesthetic of fragmentation' and should also be read as an epistemological position.[17] Such a choice, heavily imbued with didacticism, explains the multi-plotted structure of

---

[13] See Sara Mendelson, 'Playing Games with Gender and Genre: the Dramatic Self-Fashioning of Margaret Cavendish,' in *Authorial Conquests*, ed. Line Cottegnies and Nancy Weitz, pp. 199–204. Emma Rees has also considered the problem of genre in her book *Margaret Cavendish: Gender, Genre, and Exile*, but her analysis addresses mostly the prose writings.

[14] Restoration comedy would later make use of the same device in its satirical critiques of court and country.

[15] Payne's comment is that 'within the plays Cavendish's contrasting visions of female power are juxtaposed jarringly against each other' ('Dramatic Dreamscape,' p. 30).

[16] See her third letter to the 'Noble Readers' in Anne Shaver, ed. *Margaret Cavendish, Duchess of Newcastle:* The Convent of Pleasure *and Other Plays*, pp. 255–6.

[17] See Gisèle Venet, 'Margaret Cavendish's Drama: An Aesthetic of Fragmentation,' in *Authorial Conquests*, ed. Line Cottegnies and Nancy Weitz, pp. 213–28.

Cavendish's plays, where she puts together many 'examples' of women's stories and lives. Cavendish works through techniques of contrast and juxtaposition, both of which are more familiar to modern-day readers and viewers of novels and films, although never altogether absent from drama. Although the didactic deployment of 'exempla' has its roots in medieval scholastic practices, Cavendish puts them to renewed use by refusing to tie up loose ends or to voice a neat, round moral. Instead, Cavendish's plays open up spaces for reflection and response in performing 'jarring' disjunctions, whereby we are called upon to make our own judgment and to work out the moral, if any, to be learned from the events performed.

As mentioned above, Cavendish's plays often also challenge generic labels. Occasionally she even coined her own term, like 'come-tragedy.' The tragic mode pervades her drama, though more clearly the 1662 folio, when her experiences of war and exile remained fresh. It emerges in the midst of a full-fledged comedy such as *The Lady Contemplation*, with stories such as that of Cinderella-like Lady Poor Virtue, whose father gave his life for king and country and whose estate was confiscated, even though it ends in fairy-tale happiness. Although only one bears the name, two of the pieces in *Playes* are tragedies in tone and dramatic structure: *Youths Glory and Deaths Banquet, Parts I and II*, and *The Unnatural Tragedie*. In these texts, however, Cavendish drops the conventional blank verse and writes prose throughout. Often, in their mixing 'humours' and tones, the plays veer towards tragicomedy, though generally, like in the above-mentioned *The Lady Contemplation*, the author opts for a comic resolution. In this chapter, I examine Cavendish's own version of the tragic and the tragicomic in three plays: *The Unnatural Tragedie, Youths Glory and Deaths Banquet, Parts I and II*, and *Bell in Campo*. The focus is on her dramatic experiments, ranging from the juxtaposition of (sometimes unrelated) plots and the hybrid generic modulation, to her use of the Chorus.

Domesticity Examined: *The Unnatural Tragedie* and *Youths Glory and Deaths Banquet*

Margaret Cavendish's approach to tragedy differs widely from Elizabeth Cary's practice. While the earlier dramatist drew from biblical sources, made sophisticated use of dramatic verse, and focused on the domestic politics of a royal family in power, Cavendish's plays lack direct sources, are written in prose, and follow the tragic lives of women of the aristocracy without a close connection to the kingdom's court. Needless to say, this does not make them any less interesting. They problematize domesticity and showcase women's choices, or lack of them, outside the home.

In *The Unnatural Tragedie*, as its title suggests, Cavendish was working within the dramatic conventions of tragedy. In its main plot, Monsieur Frere is recalled home from his travels in Italy by his father in order to marry a rich heiress, but on arrival he encounters his newly married sister, Madame la Soeur, whom he has not seen since they were children, and he falls in love with her at first sight.

He then postpones his own engagement on a variety of pretexts, becomes visibly melancholy, and finally starts following his sister around the house, sighing and groaning. Although Madame la Soeur at first has no inkling of her brother's feelings, soon the signals become too clear to be misunderstood. The tension continues to build up on her as her brother declares his passion and threatens to kill himself if she does not lie with him. She resists him and upbraids his behavior, even threatens to disclose the situation to their father and her husband, and for a time Monsieur Frere tries to curb his feelings. He nevertheless fails, and so he decides to use guile to achieve his end. First he contrives to calm his family's concerns by proclaiming that he has decided to get married after all; next, he devises a pretext to keep them away while he goes into Madame la Soeur's chamber and, on finding her still unyielding, he rapes her. As the import of his actions dawns on him, he kills her first and then himself.

Incest has been, from classical times, one of tragedy's most recurrent themes. Its importance in English Renaissance and Restoration drama itself cannot be understated and has been the subject of many studies.[18] Moreover, the similarity of the plot of *The Unnatural Tragedie* to the conventions of Jacobean and Caroline domestic tragedies is irrefutable, in particular as regards the construction of a claustrophobic domestic scenario and a spectacularly violent outcome. Cavendish may have been familiar with at least some of those plays during her early theatre-going years, though the fact that her play is not about parent-child but sibling incest has suggested a connection with John Ford's 1632 *'Tis Pity She's a Whore*.[19] There are, however, abundant differences between the violent passion and rape portrayed by Cavendish and a mutually consented relationship between brother and sister like the one in Ford's play. Other works, perhaps James Shirley's *Coronation* (1634), may have been familiar to our dramatist too. Indeed, there is no lack of examples, for the topic would be a recurring theme for authors well into the Restoration period, like Aphra Behn in *Love Letters between a Nobleman and His Sister* and John Dryden in *Don Sebastian*.[20]

---

[18] See, among others, Marc Shell, *The End of Kinship* (Stanford: Stanford University Press, 1988); Bruce Thomas Boehrer, *Monarchy and Incest in Renaissance England* (Philadelphia: University of Pennsylvania Press, 1992); Richard A. McCabe, *Incest, Drama and Nature's Law 1550–1700* (Cambridge: Cambridge University Press, 1993); and Zenón Luis-Martínez, *In Words and Deeds: The Spectacle of Incest in English Renaissance Drama* (Amsterdam: Rodopi, 2002).

[19] On the similarities and differences between both tragedies, see Marguérite Corporaal, 'An Empowering Wit and an "Unnatural" Tragedy: Margaret Cavendish's Representation of the Tragic Female Voice,' *Early Modern Literary Studies* Special Issue 14 (2004), pp. 12.1–26. Karen Raber has pursued the connections between Cavendish's tragedy and Shakespeare's *Measure for Measure* in '*The Unnatural Tragedy* and Familial Absolutisms,' in *Cavendish and Shakespeare, Interconnections*, ed. Katherine Romack and James Fitzmaurice, pp. 179–91.

[20] See T. G. A. Nelson, 'The Ambivalence of Nature's Law: Representations of Incest in Dryden and His English Contemporaries,' in *Incest and the Literary Imagination*, ed. Elizabeth Barnes (Gainesville: University Press of Florida, 2002), pp. 117–37.

Moreover, incest is a suitable field of enquiry for someone with Cavendish's lifelong interests in philosophy and science and with her outspoken defense of Nature and all things natural. One of the theories about incest is precisely that attraction within the family unit is 'natural,' due to the similarity of family members who are bound together by blood. The title of Cavendish's only tragedy is, therefore, far from a mere coincidence. Rather, it hints at the play's manifold interrogation of what is (un)natural. The term and the concept it stands for are recurrently taken up and examined by different speakers throughout the tragedy, but most of all by Monsieur Frere, the character suffering from this 'unnatural' passion.

In Act II Scene xii, Monsieur Frere responds to his sister's request for information about women in foreign lands with a description of Italian women as falling into two categories: honest women, who are kept under close surveillance by their male relatives and never seen outside, and courtesans, who are crafty, artificial, and dishonest. When Mme. La Soeur complains at the jealousy of Italian fathers and husbands that so enslaves their women relatives, Frere replies that 'they are wise, and know Nature made all in common, and to a general use: for particular Laws were made by Men, not by Nature.'[21] Frere is thus subscribing to a Hobbesian view of nature as the state before government and, therefore, before private property. Frere also uses the term '(un)natural' with an altogether different meaning, to recall his sister to the duty of sibling affection: 'Sisters should not be so unnatural, as to be weary of a Brothers company, or angry at their grief; but rather strive to ease the sorrow of their hearts, than load on more with their unkindness.'[22] Both meanings come together in the scene in which he declares his love and makes an appeal for her to follow the rules of Nature: 'Sister, follow not those foolish binding Laws which frozen men have made, but follow Natures Laws, whose Freedome gives a Liberty to all.'[23] Here he is trying to break the rule of private property by enjoying the commodity that is a woman's body, socially prescribed as being a husband's possession, and at the same time he is emphasizing the meaning of 'natural' as innate, as in the link that ties brother and sister. All in all, this male character is portrayed as someone who is willing to use rhetoric to obtain his ends without consideration of moral values.

Another male character to whom the term '(un)natural' is linked is Monsieur Malateste, the tyrant husband in the secondary plot of the tragedy. He treats his exemplary wife Madame Bonit with neglect—preferring to bed her maid Nan—and with unreasonable demands, complaining about her modest dress and domestic employment, and selling away her jointure. This worthy lady accepts such behavior meekly, saying simply that 'men that love variety, are not to be

---

[21] *The Unnatural Tragedie* (London, Printed by A. Warren, for John Martyn, James Allestry, and Tho. Dicas, 1662), II.xii, p. 334. Further references to the play come from this edition.

[22] *The Unnatural Tragedie* IV.xxiv, p. 348.

[23] *The Unnatural Tragedie* IV.xxv, p. 349.

alter'd, neither with compliance or crosness.'[24] Here too the notion of 'natural' as that which is 'inherent in the very constitution of a person' becomes the key to understand this character. When Madame Bonit dies, he takes a second wife, a young woman who takes his fancy because, as he says, 'my Nature loves a free spirit.'[25] Yet Madame Malateste now subjects her husband to the same treatment he used on Mme. Bonit, in an interesting reversal of the 'taming of the shrew.'[26] Her demands are just as unreasonable as the ones he used to make. For instance, she wants a completely new house built, for she finds the old residence dreary and, as she hates to live in the country, she goes away to the city to live on her own on her husband's income. She finally manages to drive Malateste to an early grave that, ironically, he now wants to share with the very woman he himself hounded to death, Mme. Bonit.

By neglecting and mistreating her husband, Mme. Malateste is being as 'unnatural' or as monstrous as he once was. This is no mere coincidence, for she happens to be one of a group of 'sociable virgins' who in alternating scenes meet to discuss a variety of themes under the guardianship of two grave matrons. The connection between this set of scenes and the Malateste plot is thus rather loose, and this is perhaps because the meetings of these young women were never meant to stand as a separate plot altogether. Rather, I would contend that Cavendish's experiment is to make them function as a kind of tragic chorus, by amplifying many of the motifs and themes in the two other plots. It is to be noted, for example, that in their first meeting, in the last scene of Act I, the young virgins want to 'rail against men,' and one of them declares against marriage, until finally they settle to discuss Nature, thus introducing what are going to be the most pervasive concepts of the play. Moreover, in Act II Scene x they discuss women's capacity for public employment, a topic that is brought to an end by the matrons because it is not suitable for young virgins, thus stressing the claustrophobic quality of this tragedy, in which women have nowhere to go outside the home, the very site where they are the object of abuse, violence, or neglect. Eventually, in the crucial scene of III.xxiii they discuss Mme. Bonit's untimely death and Malateste's maltreatment, once more returning to the issues of marriage and husbands' tyranny over wives. It is now that one of the virgins declares that she will marry Malateste, and on this gentleman coming to visit the virgins, he finds her well suited and offers her his hand. With the transformation of one of the sociable virgins into Mme. Malateste, a new but still related cycle begins, and the Sociable Virgins disappear from the play, but not without introducing one of them into the Malateste plot with a new but interesting variation, for rather than becoming another victim like Mme. Bonit,

---

[24] *The Unnatural Tragedie* II.xiv, p. 339.

[25] *The Unnatural Tragedie* III.xxiii, p. 347.

[26] The scenes in which a strong-willed Mme. Malateste confronts her husband and finally gets her way are, in their reversal of the previous situation, masterfully ironical, and would be very funny if they were not placed in such a tragic play. See *The Unnatural Tragedie* III, scenes xxvii, xxx, and IV, scenes xxxii and xxxix in particular.

this young virgin acts as an agent of poetic justice who is going to metaphorically take revenge for all maltreated women.

The tragedy thus thematizes the 'unnatural' behavior of two men who managed to bring death and destruction to those who love them. Frere kills Mme. La Soeur, but also indirectly, brings about a number of deaths (their father's, his intended bride's). Frere dies unrepentant, rejoicing that 'Now she is dead, my Mind is at rest, since I know none can enjoy her after me; but I will follow thee: I come, my Mistris, Wife, and Sister all in one.'[27] Malateste repents, too late, of the ill-treatment he gave his first wife: 'Devil as I was, to use her as I did, making her a slave unto my whore and frowns, conjecturing all her Virtues to a contrary sense: for I mistook her patience for simplicity, her kindness for wantonness, her thrift for covetousness, her obedience for flattery, her retir'd life for dull stupidity.'[28] All in all, in this tragedy the word 'unnatural' is gendered male.

Cavendish's other tragedy, *Youths Glory and Deaths Banquet, Parts I and II*, also employs juxtaposed plots in order to contrast the fates of two young women, Lady Sanspareille and Lady Innocence. While the former lives in a protective family environment, with Father and Mother Love entirely devoted to their only child, Lady Innocence is young and helpless, and after the death of her father she is left to the care of her fiancé Lord de L'Amour, a complete stranger who is living in adultery with his married lover, Lady Incontinent. In alternating scenes, we witness the stark difference in their lives. Lady Sanspareille thrives under her parent's loving care and is permitted to opt for an unconventional lifestyle despite her mother's more conservative opinion, giving up on marriage prospects and striving to obtain fame as a scholar. Lady Innocence's education is supervised by Lady Incontinent, who maliciously stunts her ward's improvements in those accomplishments which, in her view, might charm Lord de L'Amour away from her arms; she takes pleasure in reporting to her lover that Lady Innocence is a crafty, dishonest creature. In parallel progress, we witness Lady Sanspareille's circle of acquaintances and admirers growing as she makes her way into the public sphere, lecturing to an increasing audience, while Lady Innocence's domestic space more and more closes in on her, without family, friends, or supporters. Cavendish sets up a marked contrast between both plots at the beginning of Part II, when Lord de L'Amour upbraids Lady Innocence due to the ill reports he hears of her behavior, while Lady Sanspareille's fame has grown to such an extent that she receives the Queen's visit.

Accordingly, the plots seem to be leading to diverging ends, tragic the one, happy the other. But that is not the case. Cavendish plays with our expectations in this play by ending both stories tragically. Lady Sanspareille suffers a sudden, terminal illness when she is at the cusp of her fame as a scholar. Lady Innocence is falsely accused of robbery and, left without hope that anyone would trust and defend her innocence, she commits suicide. The similar ending to such differing

---

[27] *The Unnatural Tragedie* V.xliv, p. 361.
[28] *The Unnatural Tragedie* V.xlv, p. 362.

plots is puzzling, and it should lead us to a reassessment of the significance of these two women's stories, or more accurately, why a character like Lady Sanspareille, whose very name announces that she is extraordinary or 'peerless,' and who has achieved everything she set out to do, should meet a tragic end. Payne considers this a 'disturbing manifestation of Cavendish's ambivalence': 'Was it just too inconceivable,' she asks, 'that this remarkable woman could continue to bloom in a public role, particularly when further estranged from her sex by her vow of celibacy?'[29] Mendelson explains her death as the result of the age's conventional belief that scholars of genius died young, and cites the case of John Evelyn's son, although the health risks for women, whose bodies were considered more vulnerable, must have been thought even higher.[30] For D'Monté, however, Lady Sanspareille's fate is inscribed as success rather than tragedy:

> Cavendish represents the figure of the virgin as someone who is not meek and passive, but, rather, assertive and active. In addition, by withdrawing their bodies from society, Cavendish seems to suggest that women can add value to what has not been possessed. ... Through rejecting the corporeal in favour of the spiritual, Lady Sanspareille thus ensures that her virtuousness and the lessons that she has preached will always be remembered. Moreover, she permanently safeguards her chastity whilst ensuring that this will be forever associated with her wisdom, and in doing so, receives validation from both heaven and earth.[31]

D'Monté further stresses how Lady Sanspareille is consistently shown to be in control of her own life and, even more important, of her own voice and image, by insisting on holding only public rather than private, one-to-one meetings. On those occasions, she stands on a raised stage and talks on a topic that is suitable to the interests of her listeners—Nature to a group of natural philosophers, feelings and passions to moral philosophers, learning to young scholars, justice and government to the Queen, and finally, romantic love and marriage to a group of suitors. For this critic, Cavendish's character purports to manipulate her audience with a careful staging that redirects the male gaze.[32]

Yet, Lady Sanspareille is not actually in total control of her own representation; she only appears to be. This is one more illusion in the theatrical game of mirrors that this play sets up. The real "master of ceremonies" is her father, a kind of go-between who sets up the meetings, welcomes the visitors, and otherwise controls the staging of this *rara avis*, a woman scholar. As a result, one can infer that a woman cannot be in control of her own body. After all, the raised stage that she commands is placed within the walls of her father's home, and thus Lady Sanspareille remains always safely within the bounds of patriarchal authority. She

---

[29] Payne, 'Dramatic Dreamscape,' p. 29.
[30] Sara Mendelson, 'Playing Games with Gender and Genre,' pp. 206–7.
[31] Rebecca D'Monté, '"Making a Spectacle": Margaret Cavendish and the Staging of the Self,' in *A Princely Brave Woman*, ed. Stephen Clucas, pp. 118–9.
[32] D'Monté, '"Making a Spectacle,"' pp. 111–2.

performs for a predominantly male audience—with the exception of the Queen—for whom she is, most of all, an object of desire and wonder. She does not appear to be an inspiration for other women, however. She has chosen to live a man's life and has renounced the company of other women, including her mother. Her life is tragic insofar as it is lived under glass. She receives the cold rewards of a beautiful tomb and statues in the colleges, after what is seemingly a dry intellectual existence without any warmth or intimacy. As Pearson has remarked:

> [B]y accepting a masculine education and the access to language that it allows, Sanspareille risks losing her female identity, as well as the possibilities of marriage and motherhood and a close relationship with her mother. ... A woman who is educated breaks her link with other women, and cannot function as a woman within society.[33]

Conversely, neither is a women's society a guarantee of a happy life. Rather the contrary, judging from Lady Innocence's plight, who finds herself slandered by her rival Lady Incontinent and two women servants acting under her instructions. In this plot too, men hold the power, while women are rivals for their love and respect and contrive to obtain them, whatever the moral cost. Importantly, too, the play illustrates the role of rumor and hearsay in creating or destroying a woman's reputation. Gentlemen's conversations in interspersed scenes transmit the wisdom of Lady Sanspareille, building up her fame and encouraging our admiration within and without the world of the play. Conversely, Lady Incontinent's ill-intentioned reports to Lord de L'Amour create the picture of a dishonest woman and condemn Lady Innocence beforehand, so that her spirited defense of her innocence is misconstrued as a stubborn resolution not to confess.[34] Yet, though women may also make use of the power of language in public and private (lectures, gossip, rumor), it is ultimately men's opinion that carries the most authority and weight. For Alexandra Bennett, in this play Cavendish revises Shakespeare's *The Winter's Tale*, most particularly its motif of women's fragile reputations, and she concludes: 'For Shakespeare, the point is that both men and nations become weakened when women's veracity is denied; for Cavendish, the simple fact is that women are destroyed when their reputations are.'[35]

---

[33] Jacqueline Pearson, '"Women may discourse ... as well as men": Speaking and Silent Women in the Plays of Margaret Cavendish, Duchess of Newcastle,' *Tulsa Studies in Women's Literature* 4.1 (1985), p. 40.

[34] *Youths Glory and Deaths Banquet, Part II*, III.xiii, p. 168.

[35] Alexandra G. Bennett, 'Testifying in the Court of Public Opinion: Margaret Cavendish Reworks *The Winter's Tale*,' in *Cavendish and Shakespeare, Interconnections*, ed. Katherine Romack and James Fitzmaurice, p. 102.

Heroic Tragicomedy: *Bell in Campo*

Gender anxieties in Margaret Cavendish's work surface in a different way in two further plays, the tragicomedy *Bell in Campo* and the comedy *Loves Adventures*, both of them written in two parts.[36] There she turns to the theme of the warrior and the heroic mood in order to interrogate the related construction of femininity and masculinity. Both, despite belonging in different generic categories, feature cross-dressing women who become, so to speak, 'better men' than the men themselves. Here it would be necessary to remember that the war troubled long-standing views not just about women's roles but also, crucially, the dominant understanding of masculinity:

> War creates a number of anxieties about gender and masculinity. Drill, training, and above all the corporate imperative to stand firm, not to give way or retreat because the greatest slaughter happens in a rout, genders the correctly military and male body as closed, hard, tight, and, paradoxically, at one with the similarly disposed bodies of other men. Yet war also arouses the desire to escape the self, to avoid literal death by the figurative death of flight. The tension between these two powerful impulses shakes assumptions that the masculine self is natural and inevitable, unseating notions of the naturalness of the hard male body.[37]

My examination will address mainly *Bell in Campo*, although *Loves Adventures* will be useful for the sake of comparison. Technically speaking, *Bell in Campo* is not a tragedy, nor is it identified as one in its original folio printing. Like other pieces in the collection, this one defies conventional categories. The play has been variously labeled 'heroic romance,' a 'dramatic utopia,' a 'comedy,' and a 'tragicomedy'—the latter being, in my view, the best definition—although some critics wholly bypass the question of genre, implicitly attesting to the playwright's reputed eccentricity.[38]

The cross-dressing female warrior was not Cavendish's own invention. There was already in place an iconography that the author could and did draw from. It started in France in the 1640s around the figure of Anne of Austria, Queen Regent from 1643 to 1652, and of women like her niece Anne Marie d'Orléans, the ´Grand

---

[36] In my discussion of these plays I am quoting from Ann Shaver's 1999 edition, *Margaret Cavendish, Duchess of Newcastle:* The Convent of Pleasure *and Other Plays*, pp. 21–106 for *Loves Adventures* and pp. 107–69 for *Bell in Campo*.

[37] Diane Purkiss, *Literature, Gender and Politics during the English Civil War* (Cambridge: Cambridge University Press, 2005), p. 35.

[38] It is a heroic romance for its editor Anne Shaver, p. 7, but a dramatic utopia for Erin Bonin in 'Margaret Cavendish's Dramatic Utopias,' *SEL* 40.2 (2000), pp. 339–54; Gweno Williams calls it a comedy in 'No Silent Woman: the Plays of Margaret Cavendish, Duchess of Newcastle,' in *Women and Dramatic Production, 1550–1700*, ed. Alison Findlay and Stephanie Hodgson-Wright with Gweno Williams, p. 107; it is a tragicomedy according to Raber's 'Warrior Women;' finally, Alexandra Bennett bypasses the question of dramatic genre altogether in her 2002 edition of the play for Broadview Press.

Mademoiselle,' who participated in the French civil wars known as 'la Fronde.'[39] Their counterpart in England was Queen Henrietta Maria:

> Decorous figures of female valour began to appear in Caroline masques and drama from the mid-1630s and with the onset of civil war Henrietta Maria embraced the chance to act out her role as a 'martial lady.' In her letters to Charles she draws amused attention to this role, dubbing herself 'her she-majesty, generalissima.'[40]

Drawing once more from the biographical component, Alexandra Bennett further reminds us that 'Cavendish's own stepdaughters Jane and Elizabeth also attempted (albeit unsuccessfully) to hold the family properties of Bolsover Castle and Welbeck Abbey against the Roundheads, and she further remarks that 'the actions of real female warriors amid the male armies during the English Civil War could provide plentiful raw material for a dramatist's pen.'[41] In addition to the actual events of the Civil Wars in France and England, the most obvious inspiration for Cavendish's warrior women is the classical myth of the Amazons, which had been kept alive in other literary works of the period and would survive in the Restoration work of poets such as Anne Killigrew. Cavendish must have felt the appeal of an all-woman army as a separate society in which women would be allowed to pursue their skills and talents truly uninhibited, a subject that recurs in other dramatic works with a more comic approach, like *The Female Academy* and *The Convent of Pleasure*, just as it would occupy the thoughts of later thinkers such as Mary Astell. Similarly, the heroic theme is briefly glimpsed in *The Lady Contemplation*, where this lady's wide-ranging daydreaming once lights on a war scenario in which a worthy general is taken prisoner by his enemies, causing his troops to lose faith, thinking him dead. When the general's wife rallies them on, they manage to win the day and rescue their leader, thus providing his wife with the perfect opportunity to prove her worth at those tasks customarily reserved for men.[42] It seems plausible that what is a relatively unimportant component of this play became the seed of the main plot of *Bell in Campo*.

---

[39] Amy Scott-Douglass has traced the impact of the *frondeuses* on Margaret Cavendish's plays in 'Enlarging Margaret: Cavendish, Shakespeare, and French Women Warriors and Writers,' in *Cavendish and Shakespeare, Interconnections*, ed. Katherine Romack and James Fitzmaurice, pp. 147–78.

[40] Sophie Tomlinson, '"My brain the stage": Margaret Cavendish and the Fantasy of Female Performance,' in *Women, Texts and Histories 1575–1760*, ed. Clare Brant and Diane Purkiss (London: Routledge, 1992), p. 148. See also Hero Chalmers, *Royalist Women Writers, 1650–89* (Oxford: Clarendon, 2004), pp. 40–55, for a critique of Tomlinson's views.

[41] Bennett, 'Margaret Cavendish and the Theatre of War,' 267–8.

[42] *The Lady Contemplation, Part II* (London, Printed by A. Warren, for John Martyn, James Allestry, and Tho. Dicas, 1662), II.x, pp. 220–223. Further references to the play come from this edition.

In *Bell in Campo*, the Kingdom of Faction and the Kingdom of Reformation are at war. Lady Victoria convinces her husband, the Lord General of the Kingdom of Reformation, to allow her to accompany him to the front, and many other wives follow her example. But once there the women are sent to live in a garrison town and thus kept out of the way and far from danger, a situation which they come to resent. Under Lady Victoria's leadership, several thousand women agree to take over the garrison town and arm themselves in order to help the male war efforts against the Kingdom of Faction, which are not going as well as could be expected. As they are training, the news arrives of a battle with grave casualties on their side, and the army of 'heroickesses,' as Margaret Cavendish/Lady Victoria terms them, advances towards the enemy and wins the day. Even though the men are grateful for this providential help, they refuse to let the Female Army into their plans, and so they continue to fight on their own, successfully completing the siege of a town that proves to be the key to the final victory for the Kingdom of Reformation. The king acknowledges the women's prominent participation by granting special favors to all women in general, Lady Victoria most of all.

Tomlinson finds this happy ending wanting insofar as the privileges and rights granted by the king fail to perform a complete revision of the prevailing gender system and consist only of minor changes in the domestic rather than the public domain; but I agree with Chalmers that the play achieves its purposes in valorizing female heroism—and, I would add, not only for an isolated individual but for women as a group.[43] Lady Victoria's initial impulse to raise an army springs from men's patronizing behavior, as she argues in her address to the women:

> LADY VICTORIA
> Then thus, we have a body of about five or six thousand women, which came along with some thirty thousand men, but since we came, we are not only thought unusefull, but troublesome, which is the reason we were sent away, for the Masculine Sex is of an opinion that we are only fit to breed and bring forth Children, but otherwise a trouble in a Commonwealth, for though we encrease the Common-wealth by our breed, we encumber it by our weakness, as they think, as by our incapacities, as having no ingenuity for Inventions, nor subtill wit for Politicians; nor prudence for direction, nor industry for execution; nor patience for opportunity, nor judgment for Counsellers, nor secrecy for trust; nor method to keep peace, nor courage to make War, nor strength to defend our selves or Country, or to assault an Enemy; also that we have not the wisdome to govern a Commonwealth, and that we are too partial to sit in the Seat of Justice, and too pittifull to execute rigorous Authority when it is needful.[44]

Therefore, Lady Victoria's agenda is no other than to prove men wrong, and to show them that women are indeed multifaceted beings deserving of full citizenship. At the end of the play, the king's proclamation, together with the

---

[43] Chalmers, *Royalist Women Writers*, p. 45.
[44] *Bell in Campo Part I*, II.9, p. 119.

men's admiring comments, highlights this extraordinary achievement, no matter the relative terms in which it is couched.

In order to bring this project to a successful end, Lady Victoria displays all the talents of a true born hero. She shows courage and initiative, she is resourceful and determined, and she fights against the odds. Moreover, the Female Army's success in the battlefield is not presented as sheer luck or a one-off, but as the commonsensical result of a careful, well-contrived plan, both in training the troops and in designing the war strategy. One whole scene of the play is dedicated to a rather tedious explication of the rules given by Lady Victoria for the organization and training of the Female Army, in order to bring home the message of the lady's accomplishments and thus to prepare the readers for the later news of her victories.[45]

Wiseman, who has paid attention to the dynamics of gender and class in Margaret Cavendish, has faulted this kind of female heroism. She contends that it is based on a discourse of class privilege that contradicts the text's claims to gender equality: 'The right to power, for women in Cavendish's writing, is a privilege attendant upon birth and status; her plays dramatize the differences between noble women warfarers and other women, especially citizen women.'[46] This is partly true. Although one should acknowledge the many fractures in the discourses of gender and class in Cavendish's works as a whole, this play is remarkably consistent in the construction of a hero that works towards the common good of all women, regardless of their social rank. Obviously Cavendish's Royalist partisanship prevents her from envisioning a woman who can be a leader *and* a commoner, and it is her understanding that true merit is much more likely to be found among the high-born. But such nobility of mind and character is precisely what allows Lady Victoria to look beyond her own self-interest. This fact becomes more evident if one considers the play's subplots, in which Cavendish, as is her usual practice, provides contrasting exempla. In them, two other women characters live through similar circumstances while making choices markedly different from Lady Victoria's. Both Madam Passionate and Madam Jantil accept their respective husbands' departure for the front, and both are devastated when their husbands are killed in battle. However, old Madam Passionate's grief does not last long, and she is soon married again, this time to a young, handsome, but penniless gentleman, who swiftly takes control of her assets and her household, leaving her quite literally out in the cold:

MADAM PASSIONATE
[F]or this idle young fellow which I have married first seized on all my goods ... and now he ... sells all my Lands of Inheritance, which I foolishly and fondly delivered by deed of gift, the first day I married, devesting myself of all power,

---

[45] *Bell in Campo Part I*, III.11, p. 121–6.

[46] Susan Wiseman, 'Gender and Status in Dramatic Discourse: Margaret Cavendish, Duchess of Newcastle,' in *Women, Writing, History 1640–1740*, ed. Isobel Grundy and Susan Wiseman (Athens: The University of Georgia Press, 1992), p. 175.

which power had I kept in my own hands I might have been used better, whereas now when he comes home drunk, he swears and storms, and kiks me out of my warm Bed, and makes me sit shivering and shaking in the Cold, whilst my Maid takes my place; but I find I cannot live long, for age and disorders bring weakness and sickness, and weakness and sickness bring Death, wherefore my marriage Bed is like to prove my grave, whilst my Husband's Curses are my passing Bell, hay ho.[47]

Madam Passionate's behavior stands as a cautionary tale for women of all social rank, rich or otherwise. Again, Cavendish emphasizes this point by showing how Madam Passionate's maid, Doll Pacify, follows her mistress' lead and, like her mistress, is duped by her young Master, who robs her of all. Madam Passionate rejected the chance to enter the public domain and preferred to stay home. But 'home' in this play—or indeed, in other plays by Cavendish, as seen above—is not necessarily a safe haven for women, and this subplot stresses the need for women's wise management and power-taking in order to survive. Indeed, as Pearson has claimed, for Cavendish, 'female heroism is not confined to the battlefield: it is just as necessary within the confines of ordinary domestic life.'[48]

Madam Jantil's story differs completely. She is unable to overcome her grief over her husband's passing away, and so determines to devote the rest of her life to his memory. She uses her wealth to build a monumental shrine, where she retires from the outside world and leads an austere life of prayer and philosophical contemplation. On her untimely death she wills most of her money to ensure the survival of her husband's memory, while her own is most likely to be erased from public record. Thus, Lady Jantil significantly reverses the fate of Lady Sanspareille in *Youths Glory and Deaths Banquet*, for whom statues were built in the colleges. Only her maid Nell Careless will fondly remember her mistress, for she has received a pension on condition that she remain single:

NELL CARELESS
Truly I have seen so much sorrow in my Lady, and so much folly in your Lady [Madam Passionate] concerning Husbands, that had not my Lady injoyned me to live a single life, I would never have married; wherefore my Ladies generosity did not only provide for my bodily life, and for my plentiful living, but provided for the tranquillity of my mind, for which I am trebly obliged to reverence her memory.[49]

Even though Madam Jantil's plight is full of pathos, and evidently very far from the bathetic story of Madam Passionate, her example is ultimately every bit as unprofitable and barren for women as a group. In Nell's speech, they stand for sorrow and folly. Beyond their differences, these women are similar in that they

---

[47] *Bell in Campo Part II*, IV.17, p. 162.
[48] Jacqueline Pearson, 'Women may discourse,' p. 34.
[49] *Bell in Campo Part II*, V.21, p. 169.

are victims, passive creatures instead of agents, and in retreating from the public sphere their path seems to lead only to death. The last scene of the play further contrasts their deaths with Lady Victoria's happiness and triumph, both in the public and in the domestic fronts, with the Lord General's pride in his wife's heroism.

In taking up arms, Lady Victoria would seem to have become a virago, an unnatural woman, an honorary man. However, Cavendish did not aim at reversing the spheres, i.e., she never actually suggests that men should stay at home and women abroad. Instead, she appears to be proposing a theory of mutuality, or collaboration between the sexes beyond strict gender roles, that can be profitable for the nation as a whole. Lady Victoria does not encourage gender antagonism in any of her military addresses to the Female Army. Her actions are rather reactions to the unfolding events. She lets the Male Army go into battle first while she observes from a distance, ordering her own Army in only when the defeat of their side becomes evident. She offers the Male Army the opportunity to work together in the design of the military strategy to follow, but is rejected. Only when the men's continued gender prejudice endangers the royalist enterprise does she act on her own, and only in order to prove that women can play their part in the protection of their world.

Nevertheless, the fact remains that Lady Victoria affords only a provisional role model for women's heroism, one that may work out in times of war, but not in times of peace. At the end of the day, Cavendish must return women home, which is what causes the disappointment of many feminist critics. But, as Alexandra Bennett has the commonsense to ask: 'does Cavendish have a choice but to return to extant discourses in showing Lady Victoria's social recognition and triumph?'[50] A similar scenario is played out in *Loves Adventures*, but this time clearly within the conventions of romantic comedy. Here too, we find a cross-dressing heroine who is not afraid to undertake masculine exploits. But unlike Lady Victoria, who saved the whole kingdom, Lady Orphant's objective is simply to win over the man who was her destined husband according to both their fathers' wishes, but who rejects her on the grounds that all women are false and likely to cuckold their husbands. Here too, the hero is a warrior, a successful general who has left his country to fight for the Venetian rulers against the Turks, and Lady Orphant's only way to reach him is to travel across Europe wearing a man's habit for safety, and taking up the job of page to Lord Singularity under the false name Affectionata, appropriately meaning 'woman in love.'

Thus, Cavendish sets out on what is a hopelessly conflicting pursuit, at once conservative and subversive. Proving the worthiness of women to Lord Singularity means implicitly acquiescing with patriarchal definitions of women's virtue— modesty, virginity, faithfulness. But at the same time, Cavendish's method to achieve this end radically subverts those definitions by having a heroine who dons men's clothes and is actually involved in battle managing to save Lord Singularity's

---

[50] 'Margaret Cavendish and the Theatre of War,' p. 273.

life (a scene playing out once more Lady Contemplation's daydream in the play of the same title). Means and ends are at odds in this comedy, which resonates with Shakespearean echoes. Lady Orphant's respect for her dead father's wishes echoes Portia's in *The Merchant of Venice*, as does the courtroom scene in which she must appear to save her faithful servants, accused of murdering her. The war scenario between Venetians and Turks resembles the situation in *Othello*, while the cross-dressing heroine serving the man she loves under a fake, male persona, has been identified with Viola's in *Twelfth Night*.[51] In fact, the Shakespearean subtexts are so many that Mihoko Suzuki considers *Loves Adventures* a pastiche, by means of which 'Cavendish stakes out a claim to be a worthy heir, a metaphorical "adopted son" of Shakespeare.'[52] Lady Orphant/Affectionata is, in Hiscock's terms, a 'dynamic heroine bent on self-realisation,' who manages to impress Lord Singularity and his army, the Venetian duke, and even the pope, with her wisdom, courage, and gift for leadership; yet at the end of the day she settles for marriage and domesticity.[53] *Loves Adventures* thus stops short of changing society even in the minor way *Bell in Campo* did, with its comic form denying the import and transcendence of its heroic theme.

---

[51] Susan Wiseman, *Drama and Politics in the English Civil War*, p. 101.

[52] Mihoko Suzuki, 'Gender, the Political Subject, and Dramatic Authorship: Margaret Cavendish's *Loves Adventures* and the Shakespearean Example,' in *Cavendish and Shakespeare, Interconnections*, ed. Katherine Romack and James Fitzmaurice, p. 105.

[53] Andrew Hiscock, "'Here's no design, no plot, nor any ground': the Drama of Margaret Cavendish and the Disorderly Woman," *Women's Writing* 4.3 (1997), p. 412.

Chapter 4
The Restoration Commercial Stage: Frances Boothby and Aphra Behn

The Restoration Commercial Stage and Frances Boothby

By the time Margaret Cavendish had her plays published, the commercial stage in England had experienced some radical changes. Two rival patent companies—the King's Company run by Sir Thomas Killigrew and the Duke's Company under the management of Sir William Davenant—had been set up in London, and women actors had been allowed to perform in them by a royal warrant issued in 1662.[1] Playhouses had also changed, with the new Dorset Garden theatre establishing the model since 1671. Movable scenery and candle lighting had become major advantages in creating an illusion of reality for the audience. King and court had an impact on the sort of plays produced, with a strong preference for the heroic tragicomedy in the early years of the Restoration. As pointed out by Nancy Klein Maguire in her classic *Regicide and Restoration*, 'the very nature of tragicomedy (that is, in simple terms, drama which turns tragedy into comedy) made the genre suitable for marketing a restored king with a decapitated father.'[2]

Since early on in the Restoration period, women's involvement in this renewed and challenging commercial stage was multifaceted. They worked not only as actresses but also as patrons, managers, fruit sellers, singers and dancers, and, a few years later, also as playwrights. Although Katherine Philips's translation of Pierre Corneille's *Pompey* was successfully performed in 1663 and set an interesting first, the turning point came with the theatrical seasons 1668–71.[3] In 1669 Frances Boothby, a young woman whose identity remains controversial, had a tragicomedy performed by the King's Company. *Marcelia, or the Treacherous Friend*, though not a huge success, was the first original play in English written by a woman to be produced in the commercial theatre and was printed in 1670.[4] An unknown

---

[1] See Elizabeth Howe, *The First English Actresses* (Cambridge: Cambridge University Press, 1992), for a thorough account of the role of early professional actresses in Restoration drama.

[2] Nancy Klein Maguire, *Regicide and Restoration: English Tragicomedy, 1660–1671* (Cambridge: Cambridge University Press, 1992), p. 13.

[3] Jane Milling, '"In the Female Coasts of Fame": Women's Dramatic Writing on the Public Stage, 1669–71,' *Women's Writing* 7.2 (2000), p. 267. For more on Philips's *Pompey*, see Salzman, *Reading*, pp. 187–90.

[4] Derek Hughes discusses at some length the difficulties of identifying this writer in the entry on 'Frances Boothby' of the *Oxford Dictionary of National Biography*, Oxford University Press 2004–09, online edition. For the stage history of her play, see William

Elizabeth Polwhele (d. 1691) had a tragedy performed (*The Faithful Virgins*, 1671) and also wrote an unacted comedy around the same period (*The Frolicks*), although neither went on to be printed. Last but not least, Aphra Behn would see her first play staged by the Duke's Company in 1670. *The Forc'd Marriage*, also a tragicomedy, was a great success, perhaps due as well to the remarkable talent of the leading actor, Thomas Betterton, and would put its author firmly on the path to a successful professional career. Behn's handling of tragic and tragicomic materials deserves specific attention, and so it will be discussed below.

The novelty of women-authored plays must have attracted large audiences to the playhouse and, at least in the beginning, they were not received with open antagonism; neither, it would appear, did they see themselves as part of a tradition of women's writing. Their prologues usually stress the uniqueness of their endeavor and their courage in facing the house's witty criticisms.[5] Things presumably changed later when Behn attempted to make a living from the theatre rather than remain an amateur, judging from her famous preface to the printed edition of *The Luckey Chance* (1686):

> All I ask, is the Privilege for my Masculine Part the Poet in me, (if any such you will allow me) to tread in those successful Paths my Predecessors have so long thriv'd in, to take those Measures that both the Ancient and Modern Writers have set me, and by which they have pleas'd the World so well. If I must not, because of my Sex, have this Freedom, but that you will usurp all to yourselves; I lay down my Quill, and you shall hear no more of me, no not so much as to make Comparisons, because I will be kinder to my Brothers of the Pen than they have been to a defenceless Woman; for I am not content to write for a Third day only. I value Fame as much as if I had been born a *Hero*; and if you rob me of that, I can retire from the ungrateful World, and scorn its fickle Favours.[6]

Yet, the sudden presence of four different women writers on the English public stage in these years remains so extraordinary that Milling hypothesizes that, with the exception of Aphra Behn, the writers owed their productions to the powerful patronage of several theatre-going coteries. Although particularly clear in the case of Katherine Philips's *Pompey*, this may well be the case for Frances Boothby too, whose connections with the Astons and Somersets can be identified in the prologue to the play, in the dedication to the printed version, and in a manuscript poem.[7]

---

van Lennep, ed., *The London Stage 1660–1800. Part I: 1660–1700* (Carbondale: Southern Illinois University Press, 1965), p. 163. Van Lennep suggests a premiere in August 1669, hence out of the regular acting season, which ordinarily concluded in July. There are no records of its being revived.

[5] Milling, "'In the Female Coasts of Fame,'" p. 270 and 286.

[6] Aphra Behn, preface to *The Luckey Chance*, in *The Works of Aphra Behn, vol. 7*, ed. Janet Todd (London: Pickering, 1996), pp. 119–29.

[7] Milling, "'In the Female Coasts of Fame,'" p. 277–81.

Boothby's tragicomedy usually deserves little more than a brief acknowledgment in histories of drama. Boothby chose a happy ending for the tragic plot and included a comic subplot, with the text shuttling swiftly between prose for the lighter contents and rhymed couplets—the standard form in heroic drama of the 1660s—for the serious conflict. Set in Paris, both of the play's plots are connected to the court of the young fictive King Sigismund by means of a group of noblemen led by one Lucidore, a gallant who only worships money but eventually reforms when he falls in love with a virtuous (and wealthy) widow. In the tragic plot, the king's sudden desire for Marcelia triggers her kinsman Melynet's conspiracy to separate her from her fiancé Lotharicus.

For Hughes, it is 'a conservative work, showing the defeat of upstarts and the triumph of aristocratic values. In portraying the fall of an ambitious favorite, it perhaps alludes to the recent fall of Clarendon, and in depicting a king who is (temporarily) false in love, it contributes to the widespread, but as yet tactful, theatrical criticism of the king's morals.'[8] Budding criticism of the king's philandering ways is expressed by several characters, who variously remind the audience of the duty for kings to be 'Suns on which the Subjects gaze.'[9] Like many Tory plays of the period, however, such criticism is diluted in the larger number of references to the king's merits. Peregrine, newly returned to the kingdom after long travels, wonders at Sigismund's having become king when there were so many other claimants to the crown, in an open allusion to the extraordinary sequence of events that brought about the Stuart Restoration, but his friend Almeric replies that 'he merits what he wears,' a statement in which the rhetoric of divine right and the idea of meritocracy overlap.[10] Moreover, Sigismund is shown to be blissfully unaware of Melynet's plotting against (and his attempted murder of) Lotharicus. As a result, he can only be faulted for inconstancy in love and perhaps an undue trust in a favorite, both of which are lessons he proves to have learned in the final scene of the play. There Sigismund muses after banishing Melynet from his kingdom: 'Oh! How seriously ought Princes first to weigh the lives and souls of men, before they draw them to their bosoms! For Favourites that are vitious, are the Cankers of Kings Courts, and eat in their Soveraigns bosoms.'[11] Likewise, Sigismund generously returns Marcelia to her fiancé Lotharicus, while he humbly begs for his formerly rejected fiancée Calinda's mercy:

> Madam, you have all Reason to express,
> As much as you can say in scorns excess:
> But Heav'n the greatest faults that are forgive,

---

[8] Derek Hughes, 'Frances Boothby,' *Oxford Dictionary of National Biography*.

[9] Frances Boothby, *Marcelia, or the Treacherous Friend*, in *The Early Modern Englishwoman: A Facsimile Library of Essential Works, series II. Printed Writings, 1641–1700: Part 1, vol.7: Miscellaneous Plays*, gen. eds. Betty S. Travitsky and Patrick Cullen (Aldershot: Ashgate, 2000), IV.IX, K1r. All further references to the play are from this edition.

[10] Boothby, *Marcelia*, I.III, B3v.

[11] Boothby, *Marcelia*, V.VIII, M2r.

>'Tis noble, when we may kill, to let live. (...)
> And if I e'er again that gift abuse,
> May Heav'n all prayers that I make refuse:
> I much admir'd thy Excellence heretofore;
> But now Idolater shall turn, and thee adore.
> I did not think this would have bin the close:
> "Man may design, but Heav'n will still dispose."[12]

No obstacle in this play is so serious that it cannot be eventually overcome. Therefore, Boothby's play appears to veer away from the tragic mode and to lean a little further towards the comic. Nevertheless, this tragicomedy is of further interest because it lays open the generic tensions between the author's handling of women characters in the tragic versus the comic plot. Staves has simply summarized *Marcelia* as 'a double-plotted tragicomedy. In the upper plot, the heroine escapes from a lecherous king to marry her true love; in the comic plot, a canny widow outwits a fop.'[13] Staves's concise description is remarkable in her choice of words for the actions assigned to the two female characters: while one escapes, the other outwits; one is passive, the other active. Already in this early Restoration woman-authored play, we can find a contrastive pair of characters that, to a certain extent, reproduces the Mariam/Salome, passive/active conundrum that we first encountered in Elizabeth Cary's tragedy at the onset of the seventeenth century. However, the contrast now takes on new meaning as deriving from the differing demands of tragedy (female passivity) and comedy (female agency), a dilemma that Aphra Behn too will need to face in her own prolific production.

The women characters in the serious plot are both virtuous and powerless. Calinda is the king's fiancée, but, on being cast aside, her only recourse is to bitter complaining at the inconstancy of men. Overwhelmed by her grief, she listens to her wise friend Ericina's advice and listlessly asks for her to sing melancholy songs. Calinda only reappears briefly to accept the king's apologies in the closing scene and be reinstated in his favor. Comparatively less powerless but similarly passive is Marcelia herself. Happily engaged to a similarly virtuous man, Lotharicus, at the beginning of the play, her secure life goes suddenly adrift when her beauty attracts the king's sights and her kinsman Melynet sees there an opportunity for advancement. She is easily misled into believing his insidious lies regarding Lotharicus's alleged betrayal. She is not hard to convince that she should not confront him about it but should make him suffer her neglect and disdain, an unexplainable change of heart that sends Lotharicus into a spiral of bitterness and later into exile, thus playing into Melynet's designs. As a result, Marcelia is effectively silenced and deprived of agency. Guided by a sense of duty, she meekly accepts Melynet's advice to listen to the king's wooing though she continues to love Lotharicus, and she lets her true feelings transpire in public

---

[12] Boothby, *Marcelia*, V.VIII, M3v.

[13] Susan Staves, *A Literary History of Women's Writing in Britain, 1660–1789* (Cambridge: Cambridge University Press, 2006), p. 55.

only in displaying a generally downcast demeanor. Like Calinda, her grief knows no bounds when she believes her lover dead, and in learning that he is alive and has wounded Melynet, she offers to share his sufferings. Marcelia's one chance at agency comes at the end of the play, when the king asks that she freely choose between the two rivals, but even then she is so torn between love and duty that she modestly declines to make a choice:

> Heav'n leaves me not to an Election free.
> Both so deserve, Sir, that if I should chuse,
> I'd be unjust to him I did refuse.
> Oh Gods! What punishments do you design
> Marcelia, that neither must be mine!
> Love will not let me my Lotharicus leave,
> Nor Honor won't permit I him receive.[14]

Marcelia is so paralyzed by the codes of virtue ruling her life that she is unable to decide her life's direction one way or the other and must leave it to fate, which is in the hands of the various men surrounding her.

In contrast, in the comic plot, women generally exhibit more freedom and agency. Here we encounter another pair, the wealthy widow Perilla and her single friend Arcasia, who also function as bridges between both plots. Arcasia is used by Melynet against Lotharicus as his alleged new love, while Perilla is wooed by one of the court lords, Lucidore. Perilla's status as a widow allows her more latitude in her lifestyle. Unlike Marcelia, who feels compelled to lend an ear to her kinsman Melynet's advice and to answer to her brother Euryalus when he returns from his travels, Perilla does not appear to have any male kinsman breathing down her neck. She is pestered by a number of suitors who look for an easy way to fill their pockets, including Moriphanus, a fool who attempts to pass for a newly made lord, much to everyone's merriment, but she is self-confident in her dealings with them and deflects all attempts to push her into an unwanted marriage, finally settling for Lucidore, who appears to be the least controlling of all her suitors.[15] Perilla's friend Arcasia is even less inhibited. Arcasia knows exactly what she wants, and how to obtain it. When Lotharicus approaches her on Melynet's behalf, she makes clear that, though uninterested in that particular offer, she might be less loath to consider the messenger himself as a lover, an idea that, despite his initial puzzlement, she pursues:

> I perceive, my Lord, you little thought to have found a Courtship where you came to make one; but persons of Merit are often subject to such accidents. I have heard some swear they have had a hundred of them in their days; nay some,

---

[14] Boothby, *Marcelia*, V.I, M2v–M3r.

[15] Jacqueline Pearson has argued that Moriphanus and Lucidore are contrasted through their use of metaphors of service and subjugation. See *The Prostituted Muse: Images of Women and Women Dramatists, 1642–1737* (New York: St. Martin's Press, 1988), pp. 134–5

more than Arithmetic could number: I hope your Conquest is not yet arriv'd to such a large accompt: You see, my Lord, how different our intentions are, I strive to gain you for myself, and you to win me for another.[16]

As the quote above makes clear, she is witty and determined. Her talent for repartee is displayed in Act IV, Scene iii, when she and Perilla come across the fool Moriphanus as they take a walk in the gardens, and she decides that engaging in conversation such a ridiculous person will be most entertaining:

> Well, I am most strangely taken with the *Mounsieur*, as I live; I'd give a hundred Pistols he were in love with me: My Doctor tells me I am going into a Consumption; but I dare swear his company but one two moneths would cure me. O most incomparable *Don Quixot*! What faces and postures he has![17]

Interestingly, Frances Boothby chose to adopt the name Arcasia for herself in her surviving manuscript poem.[18] This surely hints that it is with this kind of character that the author more closely identified, rather than with the more conventional female characters of the tragic plot. One may only wonder what Boothby might have next written for the stage.

Aphra Behn: Early Tragicomedies

As mentioned above, Aphra Behn's critics and editors have been stunned by the fact that in a theatrical career spanning two decades, she should write only one tragedy, *Abdelazer* (1676), the rest of her plays being all comedies and tragicomedies. Behn's first produced play was a tragicomedy, *The Forc'd Marriage* (1670). She must have also written *The Young King* around the same period, although its staging was delayed until 1679, and it was published only in 1683.[19] According to Janet Todd and Derek Hughes, the reason for this preference for tragicomedy was that 'this was the prevailing mode in the 1660s, when she must for the first time have watched plays on the public English stage.'[20] One may also contend, as Kroll has done, that the form of tragicomedy was particularly suitable to the analysis of pressing political issues of the time:

---

[16] Boothby, *Marcelia*, II.III, D4r.
[17] Boothby, *Marcelia*, IV.III, H2r.
[18] Milling, '"In the Female Coasts of Fame,"' p. 278.
[19] *The Amorous Prince* (1671), though a comedy written and performed in the same period, has been likewise described by Salzman as being 'in the same tragicomic mode' (*Reading*, p. 201), and it has been analyzed as such by Janet Todd and Derek Hughes in 'Tragedy and Tragicomedy,' in *The Cambridge Companion to Aphra Behn*, ed. Janet Todd and Derek Hughes (Cambridge: Cambridge University Press, 2004), p. 97, allegedly because of thematic continuities with *The Forc'd Marriage* and *The Young King*. However, *The Amorous Prince* entirely lacks the background of warfare and state conflict that figures prominently in those two.
[20] Janet Todd and Derek Hughes, 'Tragedy and Tragicomedy,' p. 83.

These plays—often spoken of as "tragicomedies" became, for Dryden and others, heuristic devices by which their age could deliberate on issues which were for it the profoundest sources of anxiety. Because tragicomedy by definition was generically indeterminate, often pitting incommensurable ways of seeing the world against each other, it permitted various kinds of thought experiment, as it were, in the single and most obviously contested arena in the seventeenth century, namely political theory. It enabled dramatists and their audiences to ask a number of related questions: what were the sources of power in the state; what was the extent of the king's prerogative; how far was the king obliged to traditional sources of counsel in the political nation of parliament; and what was the relation between the common law and the dispensing power?[21]

Kroll is not alone in making a case for a political reading of Restoration drama, perhaps the best example being Susan J. Owen's groundbreaking book *Restoration Theatre and Crisis* (1996), which set out to disclose the theatre's engagement with partisan politics by means of a case study of drama during the Exclusion crisis.[22] Aphra Behn's own Tory partisanship is so well established as to be pretty much beyond debate, but other, more circumstantial, reasons may have weighed on these early choices. For Hughes, comedy was not at its best during the early 1670s; with Wycherley's *Love in a Wood* the only remarkable première in the years 1669–71, Hughes concludes that 'it is hardly surprising that she did not immediately see comedy as her natural medium, and chose tragicomedy.'[23]

Like Boothby's one year earlier, the prologue in *The Forc'd Marriage, or the Jealous Bridegroom* makes much of its being a woman's play, describing how women are no longer satisfied just with beauty and will 'joyn the Force of Wit to Beauty now.'[24] It was spoken by a male actor, who encouraged the audience to 'discourage but this first attempt, and then,/ They'le hardly dare to sally out again.'[25] He was then rebuked by an actress who took over the prologue in order to

---

[21] Richard Kroll, *Restoration Drama and the 'Circle of Commerce': Tragicomedy, Politics, and Trade in the Seventeenth Century* (Cambridge: Cambridge University Press, 2007), p. 3.

[22] Susan J. Owen, *Restoration Theatre and Crisis* (Oxford: Clarendon Press, 1996).

[23] Derek Hughes, *The Theatre of Aphra Behn* (London: Palgrave, 2001), p. 16. Yet, as Janet Todd reports, the play was well received, opening the season of the Duke's Company on 20 September 1670 and lasting for six days. Interestingly, the play is connected to the careers of two people who would contribute much to tragedy. Thomas Otway was to act in it in the part of the old king, but his case of stage fright was so severe that he turned to playwriting instead. Also making her debut, although more successfully than Otway, was Mrs. Lee, who would become a major tragic actress in later years (Introduction to *The Forc'd Marriage*, in *The Works of Aphra Behn, vol. 5*, ed. Janet Todd (London: Pickering, 1996), p. 3.)

[24] Aphra Behn, prologue to *The Forc'd Marriage*, in *The Works of Aphra Behn, vol. 5*, p. 15.

[25] Prologue to *The Forc'd Marriage*, pp. 25–6.

conventionally appeal for the ladies' favor, but also for the men's, since 'Who is't that to their Beauty wou'd submit,/ And yet refuse the Fetters of their Wit.'[26]

In common with *Marcelia*, Behn's tragicomedy shifts its focus partly towards private politics by setting up several unfortunate love affairs at court while keeping well in sight the ruler's moral behavior, particularly in relation to his subjects and favorites. *The Forc'd Marriage* starts with the king's desire to reward one such individual's notable effort at the ongoing war. Alcippus has proved so courageous that, in the king and the young prince's estimation, he deserves to be made general, but by speaking up to ask for Erminia's hand he sets in motion a series in catastrophic events. Obviously Alcippus could not know that Erminia and Prince Phillander were in love. And yet, while the king's impulse to reward his subject is perceived as entirely appropriate, Alcippus' speaking out of turn is not. The subject's unbridled desire is not legitimized in Behn's play. On the contrary, it is condemned as a sin of pride, and Alcippus will have to learn, to his cost, to want only that which he is given by his betters. Similarly, Erminia's father Orgulius is shown to be in the wrong when, on finding out her secret relationship with Phillander, he decides to hasten the wedding:

ORGULIUS
Though by his fondness led he [Prince Phillander] were content
To marry thee, the King would ne'er consent.
Cease then this fruitless passion and incline
Your will and reason to agree with mine.
Alcippus I dispos'd you to before,
And now I am inclin'd to it much more.
Some days I had design'd t've given thee
To have prepar'd for this solemnity;
But now my second thoughts believe it fit,
You should this night to my desires submit.[27]

Orgulius' language ('incline/ your will and reason to agree with mine,' 'you should this night to my desires submit') is forceful in making a tyrant's demands on his daughter, and it resonates with echoes of Desdemona's father Brabantio who, when enraged at her marriage to Othello, denounced him before the Duke of Venice. It is precisely the idea of the oppressive authority of the father on her daughter that Behn emphasized both in the play's title and in its performance. Act II opens with a dumb show representing the rushed wedding of Alcippus to an unwilling Erminia, to the consternation of many witnesses, whose body language conveys their feelings more expressively perhaps than words could. Prince Phillander has his sword half-drawn but is being held by his sister Galatea, who in her fixed gaze on the bridegroom makes clear her love for Alcippus. Erminia herself is looking at Phillander, and Galatea remains unaware of Pisaro's passionate stare.

---

[26] Prologue to *The Forc'd Marriage*, pp. 45–6.
[27] Aphra Behn, *The Forc'd Marriage*, in *The Works of Aphra Behn, vol. 5*, I.III.53–62.

In this succinct scene the main conflict of the play is masterfully laid out before the audience's eyes, anticipating most of its unfolding tensions. For Hughes, the wedding ceremony in *The Forc'd Marriage* is a good example of Behn's theatrical skills:

> From the outset of her career, Behn thought in terms of the tangible, visible and spatial aspects of theatre as well as the purely textual. Her ability to shape plays visually as well as textually is illustrated by this opening ceremony of masculinity, which lays bare the basis and distribution of power, and which acts as a repeated visual point of reference at later stages of the play.[...] The scene is pure dumbshow, separated from the surrounding action (unusually) by the rising and falling of the curtain. The characters are reduced to voiceless, paralysed prisoners in a spatially choreographed system of power.[28]

Furthermore, Behn brings her characters to the very edge of a tragic denouement when Phillander's plot to elope with Erminia while Alcippus is away from court backfires with the unexpected return of Alcippus. Enraged by what seems to be evidence of Erminia's adultery, Alcippus strangles her and flees. Erminia's father demands his daughter's murder be revenged, but he is upbraided by Galatea, who caustically remarks:

> —But might it not your present griefs augment,
> I'd say that you deserve this punishment,
> By forcing her to marry with the General,
> By which you have destroy'd Phillander too,
> And now you would Alcippus life undoe.[29]

Galatea relocates the source of the conflict and, by extension, of all gendered violence in the arranged marriage of unsuited partners. Interestingly, Galatea and Erminia together become the agents of their ensuing revenge. In true revenge tragedy fashion, the ghost of the victimized Erminia starts to be seen on several locations, covered by a thin veil, frightening those who watch her pass, while Alcippus himself is distraught, tormented by his guilt.[30] When Erminia discloses to Phillander, Galatea, and others that she is not truly dead, Galatea engineers a plan to recuperate Alcippus and to reunite Phillander and Erminia. Once more, Behn creates two theatrically effective scenes that come to undo the multifaceted conflict as staged in the dumb show at the opening of Act II. In Act V scene II, Alcippus awakens to a dream-like masque during which Erminia, dressed like an angel with wings, and to a soft background music, informs him that she is truly happy in her new incorporeal state and that he is vainly mourning 'what the

---

[28] Hughes, *Theatre of Aphra Behn*, pp. 32–3.

[29] *The Forc'd Marriage*, IV.VII.73–7.

[30] The theme of the unjustly accused woman who is taken for dead and then resurrected has powerful Shakespearean resonances, particularly from *Much Ado About Nothing* and *The Winter's Tale*.

Gods must ever keep.'[31] Furthermore, she discloses that the gods' pardon will be manifest soon, that Alcippus is to be a great conqueror, and that his fate is linked to that of Galatea:

> 'Tis she must make your happiness;
> 'Tis she must lead you on to find
> Those blessings Heaven has design'd,
> 'Tis she'le conduct you where you'll prove
> The perfect joys of grateful love.[32]

Insistently, Alcippus' mind is forced to turn away from Erminia (who, as the angel states, could never have been his wife because she belonged solely to the prince) and towards Galatea. The message is reinforced by the appearance onstage of several characters in allegorical costumes. Glory, Honor, Mars and Pallas, Fortune and Cupid, all take a turn on the stage and dance with Love in the center, bearing him offerings which he rejects and which the characters then lay at Alcippus' feet. Finally, they all retire, with Erminia again urging that this is the Gods' will and that 'You must obey what they command.'[33]

Despite this intensive brainwashing session, Alcippus remains doubtful. He continues to be angry at Phillander, considering him guilty of adultery, to the point that, on their next encounter in Act V scene V, both men draw on their swords. It falls to the king himself to remind Alcippus now that he owes unquestioning obedience to his prince:

> —Is this an object for your rage to work on[?]
> Behold him well, Alcippus, 'tis your Prince.
> —Who dares gaze on him with irreverend eye?
> The good he does you ought t'adore him for,
> But all his evils 'tis the Gods must punish,
> Who made no Laws for Princes.[34]

Behn's Tory message of uncritical loyalty to the Crown comes through loud and clear in this final scene, which recuperates the rebellious subject by curbing and redirecting his desire. Facing the resurrected Erminia, he admits that 'Madam, you were wife unto my Prince,/ And that was all my sin.'[35] Orgulius, too, has earlier confessed to his error in setting up the unfortunate arranged marriage. Yet, the clash between Behn's partisan politics and her gender politics surfaces when it comes to forgiving Alcippus for his violent treatment of Erminia. Alcippus requests forgiveness on his knees, but he states that his behavior 'was a fault the

---

[31] *The Forc'd Marriage*, V.II.80.
[32] *The Forc'd Marriage*, V.II.98–103.
[33] *The Forc'd Marriage*, V.II.134.
[34] *The Forc'd Marriage*, V.V.83–8.
[35] *The Forc'd Marriage*, V.V.183–4.

most excusable,/ That ever wretched Lover did commit.'[36] His repentance is not of the act itself, which he claims would have been 'just and brave revenge.'[37] Rather, it is solely based on the acknowledgment that Prince Phillander, much superior to him in rank, had a previous claim on her. Gendered violence remains legitimate and largely unquestioned; at best, it is accounted for as an inadequate response to the circumstances.

In *The Young King, or the Mistake* (performed between March and August 1679, although of earlier composition), Aphra Behn continued to pursue the implications of the conjunction of gender and partisan politics. The playwright wove together two stories from markedly different sources. The love plot she took from La Calprenède's *Cléopâtre* (whose twelve volumes had been translated into English in several portions, the last books being published in 1663); the king's plot was inspired by the Spanish playwright Calderón de la Barca's very successful *La vida es sueño* (*Life is a Dream*), published in Spain in 1636, which may have reached her either in its French translation or by way of its Dutch performances. While following some aspects of Calderón's text, Behn introduced substantial changes, particularly in enhancing the role of women and in toning down the Spanish play's theological underpinnings.[38] The love plot focuses on the Amazon Princess Cleomena, heir to the throne of Dacia. Her brother Orsames, disqualified for the crown due to their mother the queen's firm belief in the prophecy that foretells he will be a tyrant king, is the focus of the second, interrelated plot. Orsames, who corresponds to the Segismundo of Calderón's *La vida es sueño*, grows up in total isolation from the world, under the care and close supervision of a wise tutor, Geron. The same prophecy that has caused the prince's ostracism has predicted Cleomena's future as the queen of Scythia, so both kingdoms are at war.

Once more against a background of war, Behn tackles issues concerning gender roles as well as the duties and rights of a king. As Todd has remarked, Behn's revisions of her earlier draft for production in 1679, that is, at the very peak of the Exclusion Crisis, were made 'to express Behn's support for legitimacy in the person of the heir to the throne, James Duke of York, and hatred of improper ambition, embodied in the illegitimate eldest son of Charles II, James Duke of Monmouth.'[39] In contrast to the intricate love plot, which abounds in false identities and disguises, the Orsames plot stresses the 'natural' impulses of the untutored male and the equally 'natural' endowments of a king. Taken out of his prison for a test of his attitude in Act III scene I, Orsames wakes up sitting on a throne, dressed with royal robes, and surrounded by courtiers. He is informed by Geron that he is a king, and when he demands further information, Geron replies:

---

[36] *The Forc'd Marriage*, V.V.174–5.

[37] *The Forc'd Marriage*, V.V.181.

[38] For a detailed analysis of Behn's debt to Calderón's play, see Dolors Altaba-Artal, *Aphra Behn's English Feminism: Wit and Satire* (London: Associated University Presses, 1999), pp. 26–45.

[39] Janet Todd, introductory notes to *The Young King: or, the Mistake*, in *The Works of Aphra Behn*, vol. 7, p. 81.

> Your Frowns destroy, and when you smile you bless;
> At every nod, the whole Creation bows,
> And lay their grateful Tributes at your feet;
> Their Lives are yours, and when you daign to take 'em,
> There's not a mortal dares defend himself:
> But that you may the more resemble Heaven,
> You should be merciful and bountiful.[40]

Geron's description highlights the king's power and its quasi-divine attributes, in line with theories of the divine right of kings that had been consistently held by the Stuart monarchs, most prominently by James I in his *Basilikon Doron* (1599). Only the last two lines suggest that there may be duties involved as well as rights to hold. Consequently, Orsames understands this as a call to make real all his dreams without constraint. High among those wishes is a sexual attraction towards the other sex that he has freshly discovered when Urania came into the prison in search of her fiancée Amintas. This 'natural' impulse does not discriminate among women, as evidenced when Orsames most shockingly addresses his advances to the Queen Mother. On being informed of the impropriety of his actions, he gets angry at being contradicted and orders Geron's execution.[41] Most of all, it is this inability to rein in his 'natural' appetites during that scene that renders Orsames unfit to be king for the time being, and this suggests a strong critique of Charles II's notorious sensual drive. However, it is not enough of a fault to entirely dismiss him, and the playwright contrives to engineer the restoration of the rightful king, who by then has learned from his 'dream' to display more sensible behavior.

While the prison affords a retired space where Orsames muses on his life and identity, his sister Cleomena inhabits a world shaken by strife and rivalry, in which alliances can easily shift and identities are unstable. The connection between the torn country of Dacia and the divided, conflicted self of its princess is made through the Queen of Dacia's offering Cleomena's hand to whoever can obtain the kingdom of Scythia for her. Raised as a warrior princess, Cleomena undertakes a variety of disguises, variously fighting under a male name (that of Clemanthis, when he is believed dead) and later posing as a harmless shepherdess (in order to infiltrate the Scythian camp and murder Prince Thersander, whom she believes has had Clemanthis killed). Thus, as someone who has been bred 'more like a General than a Woman,'[42] Cleomena is one of Behn's drama's most agentive female characters, engaging in matters of state usually reserved to men, like setting up the restoration of her brother Orsames. Yet, in the disjointed times in which she lives, Cleomena feels that she must shoulder unduly heavy tasks, including her forced marriage to a man she hates, Prince Thersander (whom

---

[40] *The Young King: or, the Mistake*, in *The Works of Aphra Behn*, vol. 7, III.i.7–13.

[41] Interestingly, Behn's examination of the concept of what is 'natural' echoes Margaret Cavendish's in *The Unnatural Tragedy* (see previous chapter). In both cases, 'nature' leads men to incest and, ultimately, to violence that is often directed against women.

[42] *The Young King*, I.i.73.

she fails to recognize as her beloved Clemanthis). Another female character, the Scythian lady Urania, is likewise forced to adopt disguises. Like Affectionata in Margaret Cavendish's *Loves Adventures*, Urania follows her fiancée Amintas to the battlefield without his knowledge. Dressed as a boy, she remains close to him, rendering him small services, until he is captured and taken to Orsames's prison in Dacia. Even then, with the help of a shepherdess and resuming woman's dress, Urania continues her endless search for Amintas. The already familiar contrast between a more agentive female character and a more passive one is less striking than in *The Forc'd Marriage*. Although Urania's femininity is more conventional than Cleomena's, she is spirited and resourceful. Consequently, in *The Young King* Behn scrutinizes the notion of female heroism more obviously than in any other of her early plays. This is a theme she will return to in fairly similar terms in her later tragicomedy set once more in a war-torn environment, *The Widdow Ranter*, as discussed below.

Nevertheless, even while forced to undertake tasks beyond those traditionally reserved to their sex, these women characters feel the pull of the pastoral world that gives the lie, again and again, to the ravaged battlefields of the play. At its opening, Cleomena muses on the charms of the grove of trees she has unexpectedly walked into in the course of a hunt:

> How much more charming are the works of Nature
> Than the productions of laborious art!
> Securely here the wearied Shepherd sleeps,
> Guiltless of any fear, but the disdain
> His cruel Fair procures him;
> How many Tales the Ecchoes of these Woods
> Cou'd tell of Lovers if they wou'd betray,
> That steal delightful hours beneath their Shades![43]

Similarly, on leaving this pastoral world to join once more the turmoil of the war between Dacia and Scythia, and still in the temporary dress of a shepherdess, Urania wishes:

> Oh, my Amintas, wou'd I were what I seem,
> And thou some humble Villager hard by,
> That knew no other pleasure than to love,
> To feed thy little Herd, to tune a Pipe,
> To which the Nymphs should listen all the day;
> We'd taste the waters of these Chrystal Springs,
> Which more delight than all delicious Wines;
> And being weary, on a bed of Moss,
> Having no other Canopie but Trees,
> We'd lay us down and tell a thousand stories.[44]

---

[43] *The Young King*, I.ii.13–20.
[44] *The Young King*, IV.ii.18–27.

No matter how strong the pull of the Golden Age is, however, it is ultimately suppressed. Urania is, after all, a Scythian wife and a soldier's wife, and her duty is none other than to obey her husband and learn to bear his bow and arrows, as Amintas unkindly reminds her.[45] And yet, the dreamlike appeal of the pastoral that so often surfaces in tragicomedy is so strong that it is invoked once more at the closing of the play, with a dance of shepherds and shepherdesses, and in the last few lines of the epilogue:

> Greatness, be gone, we banish you from hence,
> The noblest state is lowly Innocence.
> Here honest Wit and Mirth in triumph reigns,
> Musick and Love shall ever bless our Swains,
> And keep the Golden Age within our Woods and Plains.[46]

Aphra Behn's *Abdelazer*: Revenge Tragedy, Partisan Politics, and Women's Agency

Like *The Young King*, Behn's only tragedy manifests a Spanish influence. Behn was no exception to the great fascination exerted by Spain over Restoration writers, who used materials, topics, and settings connected to the Iberian Peninsula fairly regularly. Indeed, John Loftis remarked that 'in the whole range of English history, there is no other period when dramatists turned more frequently to Spain for sources and formal models.'[47] Behn's tragedy *Abdelazer* (first staged in 1676)[48] is set in the late Middle Ages, when Spain was acquiring its permanent territorial shape by displacing the Moorish and Portuguese presences on the peninsula. As Bridget Orr has argued, 'the extended depiction of Peninsular empire on the stage under the later Stuarts is clearly playing out that dialectic of identification and difference by which free, Protestant England defined herself against absolutist, Catholic Spain.'[49] *Abdelazer* tells the tale of the revenge of the Moorish prince on the Spanish royal family that, in defeating his father, took away his inheritance and rightful place in the world. To bring about this revenge, the Moor deploys the passion he has awakened in the Queen Mother, Isabella, who is willing to

---

[45] *The Young King*, IV.ii.50–52.

[46] *The Young King*, Epilogue 38–42.

[47] John Loftis, *The Spanish Plays of Neoclassical England* (New Haven: Yale University Press, 1973), pp. x–xi.

[48] The Duke's Company staged it with a strong cast including Thomas Betterton, Henry Harris, and William Smith in the lead male roles and Mary Lee, Mrs. Barry, and Mary Betterton as Isabella, Leonora, and Florella respectively. There are no records of its revival until 1695, when it was acted by Rich's Company (Lennep, *The London Stage*, pp. 443–4).

[49] Bridget Orr, *Empire on the English Stage, 1660–1714* (Cambridge: Cambridge University Press, 2001), p. 137.

do away with all obstacles on the path to the fulfillment of her desires. Playing the several parties at court against each other, Abdelazer manages to wreck the kingdom before dying a villain's death.

The general picture drawn by Behn is vaguely recognizable as that of the late Middle Ages, with the Christian kingdoms of Castile and Aragon allied against several small Moorish kingdoms and against Portugal, all of them vying for further expansion and ultimate control of the peninsula. Behn chose to depict a period during which Spain was a contact zone. Given its multicultural and multiethnic situation, conflicts broke up rather easily. This was not uncharted territory in Restoration drama, since a few years earlier John Dryden had tackled the topic in his very successful heroic tragedy *The Conquest of Granada* (published in 1672). The story of Abdelazer as the son of a defeated Moroccan king living at the Christian court was in itself fairly plausible, since the borders of the kingdoms as well as the power dynamics among them tended to fluctuate at the time, with the smaller kingdoms paying tribute to the larger and more powerful ones, and with a relatively stable exchange of goods and people going on in both directions. However, Abdelazer is also living proof of the imperialistic, expansionist drive of the Castilian king, and his resentment is the seed for his revenge:

> My Father, Great Abdela, with his Life
> Lost too his Crown: both most unjustly ravisht
> By Tyrant Philip; your old King, I mean.
> How many wounds his valiant breast receiv'd,
> Methinks I see him cover'd o're with bloud,
> Fainting amidst those numbers he had conquer'd;
> I was but young, yet old enough to grieve,
> Though not revenge, or to defie my Fetters,
> For then began my Slavery: and e're since
> Have seen that Diadem by this Tyrant worn,
> And shou'd adorn mine now;—shou'd! nay and must;—[50]

Owen has identified the topic of court corruption associated with rebel noblemen as one that features prominently in the dramatic language of Tory politics around the time of the Exclusion Crisis, especially in connection to the rebels' ingratitude, and such is the case here: 'Rebels are also guilty of the unnatural crime of ingratitude, since the patriarchal model suggests that subjects should be as grateful for the benefits of kingly government as children are to parents. The faction and ingratitude of villains is often associated with the wrongful banishment or exclusion of loyal heroes.'[51]

Once again, the topic of the rightful use of the king's power is at the center of Behn's drama. Here it takes the form of two opposing concepts of the Monarchy emerging at court at the death of the old king, each of them represented by one

---

[50] *Abdelazer, or the Moor's Revenge*, in *The Works of Aphra Behn, vol. 5*, I.i.167–79.
[51] Owen, *Restoration Theatre and Crisis*, p. 131.

of the young princes. Ferdinand, the older son, privileges private joys over the public good and would rather devote all his energies to lovemaking. On being acclaimed as the new king of Castile, he declares: 'Had Hev'n continu'd Royal Philips life,/ And giv'n me bright Fiorella for a wife,/ To Crown and Scepters I had made no claim,/ But ow'd my blessings only to my flame.'[52] Such a sentimental assertion, foregoing any claim on state power, can be considered 'feminine,' and it bodes no good to Ferdinand in a play that, as Hughes has remarked, is full of aggressive males; and indeed, he soon falls a victim to his desires.[53] Ironically, it is the younger brother, later to be falsely named a bastard, who is his father's true heir. Philip appropriately bears the old king's name, for he boasts the same kind of soldierly feats of conquest that brought the older man his laurels. On arriving from the wars, he finds out that his father has died, and refusing to believe the news, he complains that his welcome 'from the toyls of War' is much too cold.[54] Next, and much like Hamlet, he paints a picture that highlights his mother's wantonness and his father's warrior virtue:

> My Father whilst he liv'd, tir'd his strong Arm
> With numerous Battels 'gainst the Enemy,
> Wasting his brains in Warlike stratagems,
> To bring confusion on the faithless Moors,
> Whilst you, lull'd in soft peace at home,—betray'd
> His name to everlasting Infamy;
> Suffer'd his Bed to be defil'd with Lust,
> Give up your Self, your honour, and your vows,
> To wanton in yon Sooty Leacher's arms.[55]

While the older generation thus defined its fortunes in relation to the Moors, the younger generation that Philip stands for has set its sights on Portugal. Thus, not much later in the play we learn that Portugal is in fact the place where Philip has been waging war. There he will return, he claims, if things get rough for him: 'If all fail, Portugal shall be my Refuge,/ Those whom so late I conquer'd, shall Protect me.'[56] Portugal is mentioned elsewhere in the play, once as one of the three crowns that Ferdinand would like his beloved Fiorella to wear, the other as an added argument to support Abdelazer's claims to power, for the Spaniards rightly fear the threat of civil war at home and rebellions abroad.[57]

Above all, Philip is his father's son insofar as he embodies the virtues of leadership and courage that must adorn a true king. Behn thickly lays the colors of these virtues by bringing to the fore the comparison with Roman heroic role models, such as Caesar, when she portrays Philip in the battlefield. Similarly, in the

---

[52] *Abdelazer*, I.ii.26–9.
[53] Hughes, *Theatre of Aphra Behn*, p. 68.
[54] *Abdelazer*, I.ii.50.
[55] *Abdelazer*, I.ii.83–91.
[56] *Abdelazer*, II.ii.140–141.
[57] *Abdelazer*, III.iii.65 and V.i.26–30.

following conversation with one of Philip's soldiers, Behn contrasts the soldier's ignorance and common-sense ideas of self-preservation with Philip's high-minded vision and his inspired (and inspiring) rhetoric:

SEBASTIAN
We are as bad as one already, Sir, for all our Fellows are craul'd home, some with ne're a Leg, others with ne're an Arm, some with their Brains beat out, and glad they escap'd so.

PHILIP
But my dear Countrymen, you'l stick to me.

1 SOULDIER
Aye, wou'd I were well off.

PHILIP
Speak stout Sceva, wilt thou not?

1 SOULDIER
Sceva Sir, who's that?

PHILIP
A gallant Roman, that fought by the Caesar's side,
Till all his Body cover'd o're with Arrows,
Shew'd like a monstrous Porcupine.

1 SOULDIER
And did he dye, Sir?

PHILIP
He wou'd not but have dy'd for Caesar's Empire.

1 SOULDIER
Hah—why Sir I'm none of Sceva, but honest Diego, yet would as willingly dye as he, but that I have a Wife and Children; and if I dye, they beg.

PHILIP
For every drop of bloud which thou shalt lose,
I'le give thee Wife—a Diadem.

1 SOULDIER
Stark mad, as I'm valiant.[58]

Audiences are thus encouraged to discern Philip's true royal quality despite his reduced circumstances, the idea of 'discernible superiority' being, as Owen remarks, 'a commonplace of the heroic plays of the 1660s and 1670s.'[59]

---

[58] *Abdelazer*, IV.390–407.
[59] Owen, *Restoration Theatre and Crisis*, p. 127.

Therefore, Behn's play establishes a clear antagonism not only between villain and hero, Abdelazer and Philip, as critics have pointed out, but also, and even more importantly from my point of view, between a monarch who is weakened by a pursuit of private pleasures that renders him blind to the conspiracies raging at court and another monarch who has the powers of clairvoyance and leadership and, as such, is better equipped to restore the kingdom to its pristine situation of justice at home and conquest abroad. Such antagonism between Ferdinand and Philip goes a long way to clarify the connections between Behn's play and the Exclusion Crisis. In *Abdelazer*, Behn is making a case for the succession of Charles II's younger brother James, although some uncertainty is understandable if one considers Behn's calculated ambiguity. Thus, the closing scene does not wholeheartedly celebrate the triumph of good versus evil, but undermines it by intimating, in Philip's closing speech, that this has been only one battle in a protracted war:

> So after Storms, the joyful Mariner
> Beholds the distant wish'd-for shore afar,
> And longs to bring the rich-fraight Vessel in,
> Fearing to trust the faithless Seas again.[60]

Much critical discussion of Behn's tragedy has addressed the character of the Queen Mother, Isabella, who is the agent of several murders: first her husband, then Abdelazer's wife. In order to promote her lover's ploys, she even falsely confesses to an adulterous affair that, as mentioned earlier, temporarily deprives her second son Philip of his rights to the Spanish crown by proclaiming him illegitimate. According to Thomas, in adapting her source play, *Lust's Dominion*, Behn much emphasized the queen's agency: '[The queen] is Abdelazer's equal in villainy and a far more powerful and domineering presence than her counterpart in *Lust's Dominion*; she has more to say and more to do.'[61] For Thomas, this alteration is related to another, downplaying Abdelazer's blackness. She contends that by emphasizing the queen's villainy, Behn is proportionally diminishing the Moor's blame in the destruction of the kingdom, and Thomas persuasively argues that associations of blackness with evil and whiteness with virtue are few and so scattered that, unlike the source, they fail to convey blackness as inherently evil.[62] Thomas's project is to rid Behn of accusations of racism and vindicate her work as one which resists the stereotypical representation of women and black people. To her, the author of *Oroonoko* could not possibly have written 'an overtly racist play.'[63]

---

[60] *Abdelazer*, 5.821–4.

[61] Susie Thomas, 'This Thing of Darkness I Acknowledge Mine: Aphra Behn's *Abdelazer, or, The Moor's Revenge*," *Restoration* 22 (1998), p. 21.

[62] For a discussion of racial issues in Behn's source play, see Jesús López-Peláez Casellas, 'The Enemy Within: Otherness in Thomas Dekker's *Lust's Dominion*,' *Sederi* 9 (1998), pp. 203–7.

[63] Thomas, 'This Thing of Darkness,' p. 25.

Thomas's thesis, however, is weaker as concerns the representation of women. Although Behn may have altered the racist script in *Lust's Dominion*, she did not materially resist the characterization of women as either passive virgins or forward whores that we have often encountered to different degrees in earlier plays of the period. As Hughes remarks, '[w]omen have more public freedom of movement than in the earlier plays, but they die in the bedroom, sexually threatened or sexually expectant; and they die by Abdelazer's dagger, which they have themselves briefly held in unsustainable moments of power.'[64] Thomas may find that the queen's having more to say and more to do may be a positive trait *per se*, but her agency and loquacity continue to be signs of deviance, just like those associated to Salome in Elizabeth Cary's *Tragedy of Mariam* earlier in the century, and should be read as indications of the female monstrous as long as passivity remains the paradigm of female normality. Like the source, Behn's play sees in Isabella the threat of unleashed lust, a female succubus, as suggested by Abdelazer himself:

> And thou shalt see the balls of both those Eyes
> Burning with fire of Lust.—
> That bloud that dances in thy Cheeks so hot,
> That have not I to cool it
> Made an extraction ev'n of my Soul,
> Decay'd my Youth, only to feed thy Lust!
> And wou'dst thou still pursue me to my Grave?[65]

This portrayal of Abdelazer de-emphasizes his lust to present him as the queen's prey, or 'the Minion of the Spanish Queen,'[66] where the term minion suggests 'Abdelazer's sexual servitude, and characterizes the state as an unnatural and unjust feminization (…). More strikingly, the term may also implicitly masculinize the queen.'[67] As quoted above, Philip makes similar accusations of deformity and treason against his mother in Hamlet-like fashion. Insistence on Isabella's deviance is maintained throughout the play, whereby she is made a scapegoat that must eventually be punished with death for her lust and ambition. With true poetic justice, she falls victim to the designs of her lover. This adds an ironic touch that reinforces the moral of normative femininity: not only must an adulteress perish but she may also be sacrificed by the very hand that led her to sin.

Other female characters in the play, though conforming to more standard feminine roles, can hardly be said to fare any better. The Infanta Leonora only speaks to state her grief for her father's death at the beginning of the play, she is conventionally silent when her brother the new king grants her hand to Alonzo, and she briefly reappears in Act V to weep again over the death of her mother and to cry

---

[64] Hughes, *Theatre of Aphra Behn*, p. 57.
[65] *Abdelazer*, I.i.53–9.
[66] *Abdelazer*, I.i.65.
[67] Joyce Green MacDonald, *Women and Race in Early Modern Texts* (Cambridge: Cambridge University Press, 2002), p. 155.

for help in a near-rape scene ('Oh, take my Life, and spare my dearer Honour!'[68]). The interest of this character rests solely in the effect it has on Abdelazer. First, because in her spotless virtue and beauty and in her noble origins she induces dreams of perfect happiness and power in Abdelazer. Second, because Leonora-as-virtue is later rejected by him as a weakening, feminizing influence, just as in the case of Isabella-as-lust, though if the latter fed upon his body and strength, the former now preys upon his Soul and affections:

> How tame Love renders every feeble sense!
> —Gods! I shall turn Woman, and my Eyes inform me
> The Transformation's near:—death! I'le not endure it,
> I'le fly before sh'as quite undone my soul.—[*Offers to go*]
> But 'tis not in my power—she holds it fast,—
> And I can now command no single part—[69]

Florella too bears a similar effect on the Moor, her husband ('She has the art of dallying with my soul,/ Teaching it lazie softness from her looks'[70]), even though in this case too he is ready to sacrifice her to his ambition. Like Leonora, Florella's speeches are few and perfectly conventional. She expresses her total faithfulness to her husband, she pleads his cause before the king, and she is willing to take on any further duty demanded her by her lord and husband. Only once is she shown to harbor individual thoughts and to resist Abdelazer's will in some measure. When commanded to kill the king, she bravely refuses:

> Murder my King!—The man that loves me too!—
> What Fiend, what Fury such an act wou'd do?
> My trembling hand, wou'd not the weapon bear,
> And I shou'd sooner strike it here,—than there. [*Pointing to her breast*]
> No! though of all I am, this hand alone
> Is what thou canst command, as being thy own;
> Yet this has plighted no such cruel vow:
> No Duty binds me to obey thee now.
> To save my King's, my Life I will expose,
> No Martyr dies in a more Glorious Cause.[71]

Interestingly, here the public imposes its rules over the private, and royalist sentiments take precedence over all other duties and ties. The same hierarchy of values would seem to apply for the whole play, as indeed for Behn's whole dramatic output. In this, her only tragedy, Behn did not introduce major modifications in the representation of women. The basic types remain in place, as Canfield points out: 'The passivity of Florella and Leonora, relative to the queen, constitutes the

---

[68] *Abdelazer*, V.566.
[69] *Abdelazer*, V. 538–43.
[70] *Abdelazer*, I.ii. 261–2.
[71] *Abdelazer*, III.i. 222–31.

typical patriarchal dichotomy between assertive and recessive women, the former being improperly uppity, centrifugal, and the latter properly meek, centripetal.'[72] In fact, women characters are of consequence only in so far as they oppose the royalist cause (Isabella) or advance it (Leonora and Florella). If the former, they are villains that must perish; if the latter, they may either survive (Leonora) or die as martyrs (Florella).

Behn's notions of women's agency thus came to clash with her royalist allegiance. In this tragedy, the monarchy is threatened by the combined forces of marginal subjects (female lust and black ambition), a lethal combination that plays havoc in the country.[73] Derek Hughes considers this play 'evidence of the gathering political crisis,'[74] as it warns of the dangers of cutting off rightful heirs from their place in the line of succession. Thomas too acknowledges that

> Behn's adaptation of *Lust's Dominion* ... is tailored to suit the preoccupations of her audience. Abdelazer is portrayed as a defeated usurper and bogus "Protector" in a play which begins with regicide, then deals with civil war and an exiled king, before ending with the restoration of the rightful monarch. At the same time, the play challenges the prejudices of her audience through its sympathetic representation of black Moors.[75]

For Vaughan, it is Queen Isabella's 'perversion of maternity' that suggests 'concerns about legitimacy and succession.[76] As discussed above, further evidence of the political import of the play is to be found in the contrasting pair of brothers, princes Ferdinand and Philip. Obviously, and this is an implication that Thomas prefers not to pursue, Behn was attracted to the old play for its adequacy to her royalist political agenda, and racial and/or feminist preoccupations were secondary, if they had any bearing at all. If Behn managed to suppress some of the racist abuse of the source play (as both Thomas and Hughes have asserted), she only did so at the cost of enhancing its misogynist content. Women's villainy, and their final silencing, is the price Behn has to pay here in order to strike the royalist moral home. Race itself is less significant than the play's title would seem to indicate. Abdelazer is more 'a kind of visual shorthand for other issues of sexual and gender ill-ease'[77] than a true exploration of the dynamics of race in the multicultural environment of medieval Spain.

---

[72] Canfield, *Heroes and States*, p. 37.

[73] Interestingly, the marginality of these forces is visually reinforced through onstage movement: Hughes has remarked on how Abdelazer is always isolated, always the observer or the intruder on other groups, especially in scenes of full regalia (Hughes, *Theatre of Aphra Behn*, pp. 58–9).

[74] Derek Hughes, *English Drama, 1660–1700* (Oxford: Clarendon, 1996), p. 112.

[75] Thomas, 'This Thing of Darkness,' p. 32.

[76] Virginia Mason Vaughan, *Performing Blackness on English Stages, 1500–1800* (Cambridge: Cambridge University Press, 2005), p. 142.

[77] Macdonald, *Women and Race*, p. 162.

Return to Tragicomedy: Aphra Behn's *The Widdow Ranter*

After *Abdelazer*, Aphra Behn's dramatic output turned consistently towards the comic and the farcical. Rachel Carnell has convincingly argued that the key to her abandonment of tragedy lies in the conflict between Behn's royalist and feminist politics.[78] Restoration tragedy as practiced, for example, by John Dryden, conflated both discourses, so that a loyalist message of male obedience to the crown would entail female domestic submissiveness. Carnell further contends that Behn continued to pursue the tragic mode in a new genre, the novel, which provided more latitude to the woman writer than dramatic tragedy. However, Behn turned once more to tragicomedy in her last play, *The Widdow Ranter*, perhaps because such a mixed genre gave a more mature author more scope. In this double-plotted tragicomedy, she experimented with striking a balance between tragic and comic messages.

The Widdow Ranter, or the History of Bacon in Virginia (1689) was performed posthumously, but must have been composed roughly around the same time Behn was penning her most famous novel, *Oroonoko* (1688), closely related to her youth experiences in Surinam.[79] Both works are related in both the setting—the English colonies in the New World—and in subject matter, for both feature male tragic heroes, Bacon and Oroonoko. The historical source of the tragic plot in *The Widdow Ranter* is the 1676 rebellion of Nathaniel Bacon in Virginia, which offered Behn the raw materials to stage the topic of the good man who fights for the right reasons but ultimately does wrong. Bacon had armed himself in order to protect his possessions from the attacks of the natives, but in doing so he usurped royal authority and brought on more chaos and disorder.[80] Bacon abducted the wives of the Virginian aristocrats in his struggle against the Governor, and he was so successful that he even took possession of Jamestown, but on his sudden death the rebellion ended. The confusing situation in Virginia, with three parties at war, Bacon's rebels, the Virginia loyalists, and the Indians, was conducive to Behn's

---

[78] Rachel K. Carnell, 'Subverting Tragic Conventions: Aphra Behn's Turn to the Novel,' *Studies in the Novel* 31.2 (1999), pp. 133–51.

[79] The play was premiered in November 1689, with a cast in which only Bracegirdle (in the role of Semernia) had some preeminence. There is no known revival, and the author of the Dedication claimed that it 'had not that Success which it deserve'd,' due, partly, to a mismatched cast (Lennep, *The London Stage*, p. 378).

[80] Several critics have addressed Behn's use of historical sources: Wilbur Henry Ward, 'Mrs. Behn's *The Widow Ranter*: Historical Sources,' *South Atlantic Bulletin* 41.4 (1976), pp. 94–8; Jorge Figueroa Dorrego, 'Cultural Confrontations in Aphra Behn's *Oroonoko* and *The Widow Ranter*,' in *Culture and Power IV: Cultural Confrontations*, ed. Chantal Cornut-Gentille D'Arcy (Zaragoza: Universidad de Zaragoza, 1999), pp. 193–201; Bridget Orr, *Empire on the English Stage*, pp. 232–8; Heidi Hutner, *Colonial Women: Race and Culture in Stuart Drama* (Oxford: Oxford University Press, 2001); Aspasia Velissariou, '"Tis pity that when laws are faulty they should not be mended or abolisht": Authority, Legitimation, and Honor in Aphra Behn's *The Widdow Ranter*,' *Papers on Language and Literature* 38.2 (2002), pp. 137–66; and Jenny Hale Pulsipher, '*The Widow Ranter* and Royalist Culture in Colonial Virginia,' *Early American Literature* 39.1 (2004), pp. 41–66. The focus of these essays is Bacon's rebellion, with the exception of Hutner's book, which discusses the representation of the women characters.

usual interrogation of royalist and sexual politics. She did so by constructing a play with two plots, one tragic and the other comic, whose female protagonists establish an interesting contrast that has to do as much with genre as with gender.

In the tragic plot, the Indian Queen Semernia suffers in silence her love for her enemy Nathaniel Bacon, whom she first saw at the tender age of twelve, before being forced to marry the Indian King Cavernio, in what is perhaps an echo of the Pocahontas myth.[81] The play is sympathetic to the Indians' side of the colonial venture, letting the Indian king voice his complaints over the English occupation of their land, arguing that 'we were Monarchs once of all this spacious World; Till you an unknown People landing here, Distress'd and ruin'd by destructive storms, Abusing all our Charitable Hospitality, Usurp'd our Right, and made your friends your slaves.'[82] What's more, through an English colonist, Friendly, the responsibility of the English in mismanaging the situation is acknowledged.[83] However, the colonists also defend their ancestral right to the land, as Bacon replies to the Indian king: 'I will not justify the Ingratitude of my fore-fathers, but finding here my Inheritance, I am resolv'd still to maintain it so.'[84] The elements of tragedy are here served, in the irreconcilable conflict between both men over the land, but also over the Indian queen's body and heart, for she symbolically stands for the colony. Their jealous rivalry is played out in open combat during the battle, with Bacon killing the king and capturing the queen, who had stayed behind, praying in the Temple and full of strange foreboding. Some Indians manage to infiltrate Bacon's camp and rescue the queen, whom they dress in men's clothes and take away. Bacon pursues them and falls on them in a murderous rage, accidentally dealing the blow that kills the (to him unrecognizable) queen. While Bacon grieves over the body of the dying queen, the royalists attack and, fearing he has been defeated and is most likely to suffer a traitor's death, Bacon prefers to commit suicide.

In the figure of the Indian queen, then, we find the staple elements of the tragic heroine, who welcomes death because it rescues her from the conflicting emotion of love towards her enemy and because it safeguards her honor. Her female body stands as a trophy to be fought over by men of both races, like the land. The racial script that stipulates that the English must take over the land is superimposed on the gender script. Interestingly, however, class supersedes race in the same way as race supersedes gender when all these categories come into play. As Rubik has observed, 'the Indian royal couple have completely internalized the European code of civility.'[85] Like Dryden's, Behn's representation of the higher classes remains constant regardless of the race of the subject.

---

[81] Hutner, *Colonial Women*, p. 99.

[82] Aphra Behn, *The Widdow Ranter or, the History of Bacon in Virginia*, in *The Works of Aphra Behn, vol. 7*, II.i.11–14.

[83] Behn, *The Widdow Ranter*, I.i.95–6.

[84] Behn, *The Widdow Ranter*, II.i.15–16.

[85] Margarete Rubik, 'Estranging the Familiar, Familiarizing the Strange: Self and Other in *Oroonoko* and *The Widdow Ranter*,' in *Aphra Behn (1640–1689). Identity, Alterity, Ambiguity*, ed. Mary Anne O'Donnell, Bernhard Dhuicq, and Guy Leduc (Paris: L'Harmattan, 2000), p. 36.

In the passive configuration of the tragic heroine, cross-dressing as a male is for Semernia just one more ill-starred accident, which, instead of providing her with agency and autonomy, hastens the way to her tragic death. The casting of Anne Bracegirdle for this role surely must have been meant to underline the virginal, submissive attitude of the queen. The 'moral paralysis' of this character has received a different reading from Ross:

> Semernia's moral paralysis when forced to choose between "the King" and "The General" is, on the one hand, an obvious nod at the choice England faced when Cromwell usurped the power of Charles I. At the same time, she embodies the post-revolutionary subject, the being caught between the two camps of the old "fictions of authority" but is herself a "foreigner" within the old system. On the outskirts of the *status quo*, she is both a part of it and excluded from it, essentially incapable of acting within it.[86]

Whether or not one wants to follow this close parallelism with the affairs of the Interregnum, what matters for our purposes here is that Behn balances this exemplar of female passivity with an alternative role model in the comic plot. The title of the play refers to Ranter, who came to the colonies as a servant, married her older master, and after his death wants to marry again a man of her own choice. He happens to be one of Bacon's brave commanders, Dareing, but unfortunately for Ranter he is passionately in love with a more conventional heroine, a young maid. Ranter is indeed rather unconventional, for like the male colonials she loves to smoke and also drinks and swears, an indication of her lower social extraction. For other characters, Ranter may appear 'primitive,' a description that according to Ross establishes a connection between her and Semernia.[87] Such vulgar, 'masculine' behavior is quite unsuitable for a rich young widow, but she takes it one step further when, in the middle of the confusion, she dons man's clothes and joins the campaign. In that sense, as Ross perceptively comments, '[w]hile Semernia remains trapped within the standard love versus honor debate of Restoration tragedy, Ranter settles issues of love with action.'[88] Dareing is convinced by the widow's actions to give up the young maid and to accept this partner, someone who will 'fit his humour' better and who comes with a sizeable fortune too.

DAREING
Give me thy hand Widow, I am thine—and so intirely, I will never—be drunk out of thy Company:—[Parson] Dunce is in my Tent,—prithee let's in and bind the bargain.

RANTER
Nay, faith, let's see the Wars at an end first.

---

[86] Shannon Ross, '*The Widdow Ranter*: Old World, New World—Exploring an Era's Authority Paradigms,' in *Aphra Behn (1640–1689). Identity, Alterity, Ambiguity*, ed. Mary Anne O'Donnell, Bernhard Dhuicq, and Guy Leduc (Paris: L'Harmattan, 2000), p. 85.
[87] Ross, '*The Widdow Ranter*,' p. 86.
[88] Ross, '*The Widdow Ranter*,' p. 86.

DAREING
Nay, prithee, take me in the humour, while thy Breeches are on—for I never lik'd thee half so well in Petticoats.

RANTER
Lead on, General, you give me good incouragement to wear them.[89]

Soon, however, the enemy's attack separates the lovers, and Ranter is taken prisoner. When she is eventually reunited with Dareing, she complains:

RANTER
Faith, General, you left me but scurvily in Battel.

DAREING
That was to see how well you cou'd shift for your self; now I find you can bear the brunt of a Campaign you are a fit Wife for a Soldier.[90] (1996: 350)

This sequence of events echoes the situation of Urania and Amintas in *The Young King*, while improving on it, for the relationship of the later couple is much more egalitarian. In the comic plot, as seen here, Ranter is endowed with masculine qualities that may not be apparent at first sight. In breaking away from the ideal of modesty (by swearing, drinking, smoking), Ranter would seem to be too masculine, and therefore unmarriageable. What's more, she dares enter the public sphere in donning men's clothes and joining the campaign. Beyond the erotic appeal that cross-dressing had on the Restoration stage, here it also suggests that Ranter has qualities beyond those considered 'natural' or desirable for her gender. She is resourceful and determined, and she does not respect pre-established borders. She is as daring as the man she loves, and the turmoil of war empowers her. Thus Behn hints, more powerfully than she did in *The Young King*, that certain features cannot be statically assigned to one gender, that they can and should be renegotiated in each particular instance. According to Bridges, this is a significant departure:

> Her identity, far from being fixed and written as Bacon's is, is dynamic and growing … [S]he refuses to be constrained by what others believe her, or women in general, to be. Ranter takes as her model neither Restoration London nor an ancient past. Rather she prefers to write herself into the moment and the future.[91]

By showing a brave woman who is not afraid to decide her own destiny, Behn states that such a course of action is not only possible but also desirable. Behn's

---

[89] Behn, *The Widdow Ranter*, IV. 277–84.
[90] Behn, *The Widdow Ranter*, V. 359–62.
[91] Liz Bridges, '"We were somebody in England": Identity, Gender, and Status in *The Widdow Ranter*,' in *Aphra Behn (1640–1689). Identity, Alterity, Ambiguity*, ed. Mary Anne O'Donnell, Bernhard Dhuicq, and Guy Leduc (Paris: L'Harmattan, 2000), pp. 79.

deployment of the New World as a setting is probably relevant as well, since she envisions a place where white women of the middle class can experience gender empowerment as well as upward social mobility.[92] Yet, the comic tone of this plot undermines the feminist message. Although her transgressive actions are acceptable, Ranter is a one-off, an eccentric, the exception to the rule, as Hutner has perceptively remarked:

> With Ranter, Behn brings together servant women ... religious dissenters, and upper-class women. In effect, through the linking of disparate socioeconomic, political, racial, and gendered identities in Ranter's body, Behn attempts to resolve, or at least unify, the intense social and political oppositions at war in the late seventeenth century in England and Virginia. It is not surprising, however, that Ranter can only be figured as a joke, or a mockery.... Ranter's hybridity, her blurring of distinctions, calls attention to the crisis of categories—for she is a blatant dramatic invention in an historically 'real' context.[93]

In 1989, Dympna Callaghan's crucial essay *Woman and Gender in Renaissance Tragedy* warned feminist critics that there was no need to search for female heroes in the genre. She encouraged us to look instead for the idea of transgression, which often decenters the male hero of tragedy. Callaghan's work valorized the role of the often absent, mute, or dead women characters.[94] In this later tragicomedy, Behn for the first time envisioned a low-class would-be female hero, the bourgeois woman of the next century, although her attempt did not completely succeed. There is indeed, as Callaghan pointed out, no female hero, perhaps because the genre, as Behn seems to have intuited, was impervious to women's heroism. The clash of ideological positions remained unbridgeable and unnegotiated. Behn did at least succeed in suggesting ways in which the official paradigm of femininity fell into incoherence, and in destabilizing essentialized notions of the masculine heroic. Tragedy would remain contested ground for women writers of the late Stuart period, as we will see next.

---

[92] The very name Ranter is an allusion to the radical group of dissenters, and therefore suggests the challenge to established beliefs and categories. However, the kind of gender empowerment that Bridges describes for middle-class Englishwomen is simply not available for Native ones, as Semenia's death blatantly illustrates.

[93] Hutner, *Colonial Women*, p. 105. A striking precedent of the Widow can be found in the anonymous comedy *The Woman Turned Bully*, in the figure of another spirited widow, Madam Goodfield, who also indulges in heavy smoking and drinking. See María José Mora et al., eds., *The Woman Turned Bully* (Barcelona: Edicions Universitat de Barcelona, 2007), pp. 34–6.

[94] Callaghan, *Woman and Gender*.

Chapter 5
Late Stuart Writers I: Mary Pix and Delarivier Manley

The Second Generation of Professional Women Playwrights

For several years after Aphra Behn's death, London theatres lacked the regular input of a female playwright. The 1680s and early 1690s were difficult for the theatre in general, since the political atmosphere immediately before and after the Glorious Revolution of 1688 was not conducive to seeking or providing entertainment. By the mid-1690s, an increasing stability coincided with changes in theatre management to facilitate the staging of women's plays. Milhous has noted how the competition between the King's Company and the Duke's Company during Charles II's reign had influenced the amount and the kind of drama then produced. When the two companies merged in 1682, such competition had ceased. A conservative period followed during which few new plays were produced. When Thomas Betterton broke away from the United Company in 1695, establishing a rival company in a new playhouse, Lincoln's Inn Fields, the immediate result, as Milhous records, was 'a flood of new plays (again more than twenty each year).'[1] The early 1690s were also characterized, in Backscheider's words,

> by nearly unprecedented debate and discussion about the nature and place of women. Not only were they written about but they were writing, and evidence suggests that middle- and higher-class women were beginning to display what Ernesto Laclau calls 'mobilization,' the 'process whereby formerly passive groups acquire deliberative behaviour.' Interest in women had never been greater, and they had become an increasingly significant group of 'culture consumers.' Their contemporaries saw them as an important part of the theater audience and believed that they had begun to have considerable influence.[2]

In the season of 1695–96, four female playwrights had their plays produced by either company: a young lady writing under the pen name 'Ariadne' (*She Ventures and He Wins*), Catharine Trotter (*Agnes de Castro*), Mary Pix (*Ibrahim, or the Thirteenth Emperor of the Turks*), and Delarivier Manley (*The Lost Lover* and *The Royal Mischief*). Nothing is known of the identity of 'Ariadne,' and, like Frances Boothby in the previous generation, no further plays written by her

---

[1] Judith Milhous, *Thomas Betterton and the Management of Lincoln's Inn Fields, 1698–2001* (Carbondale: Southern Illinois University Press, 1979), p. ix.

[2] Paula Backscheider, *Spectacular Politics: Theatrical Power and Mass Culture in Early Modern England* (Baltimore, The Johns Hopkins University Press, 1993), p. 72.

appear to have been produced. Unlike those women first entering the stage in 1670–71, the three remaining writers of this later generation seem to have been already well aware of belonging to a tradition of women's writing, within which two authors, Katherine Philips (known as 'Orinda') and Aphra Behn ('Astrea') stood out. Despite substantial differences in their class and upbringing, they also outspokenly supported each other in what they perceived to be very much a man's world.[3] In Catherine Trotter's prefatory poem to Manley's *The Royal Mischief*, for instance, the latter is celebrated for being women's champion and having vanquished men, her talent being so great that it is only unclear 'in which you'll greater Conquest gain,/ The Comick, or the loftier Tragick strain.'[4] Similarly, a laudatory poem by Manley was included alongside other prefatory materials in Trotter's *Agnes de Castro*, and on the death of John Dryden they all contributed poems to the collection *The Nine Muses*. Their arrival on the public stage was not well received. One of the theatrical hits of the following season was *The Female Wits; or, the Triumvirate of Poets at Rehearsal*, a satire written in the tradition of Buckingham's *The Rehearsal* by an anonymous Mr. W.M. The play scorned the three women on several accounts, but it was particularly virulent against Manley. In the long run, the term 'female wits' has become consistently linked to this generation of women writers, and it has contributed to the perception of these playwrights as a group, rather than as three individuals.

It is remarkable that in their first works three of the four young women writers would turn towards tragedy. Marsden has attributed the resurgence of serious drama in these years to two causes. First, the popularity of she-tragedies by Otway and Banks in the 1680s, which had 'shifted its emphasis from the hero to the heroine, usually a virtuous woman beleaguered and overwhelmed by sorrows.'[5] Second, interest in tragedies would have been spurred by the box-office success in the previous season of Thomas Southerne's *The Fatal Marriage, or, the Innocent Adultery*, based on Aphra Behn's novel *The Nun, or the Fair Vow-Breaker*.[6] The shift from male-centered heroic plays to women-centered pathos was easily accommodated by theatre companies, whose casting strategies included pairing off actresses with diverse strengths. Elizabeth Barry and Anne Bracegirdle at Lincoln's Inn Fields and Frances Knight and Jane Rogers at Drury Lane were two such

---

[3] For biographical information on Pix, Trotter, and Manley, see Nancy Cotton, *Women Playwrights in England, c. 1363–1750* (Lewisburg: Bucknell University Press, 1980), pp. 81–121.

[4] 'To Mrs. Manley. By the Author of Agnes de Castro,' in *Eighteenth-Century Women Playwrights, vol. 1: Delarivier Manley and Eliza Haywood*, ed. Margarete Rubik and Eva Mueller-Zettelmann (London: Pickering & Chatto, 2001), p. 51.

[5] Jean I. Marsden, 'Tragedy and Varieties of Serious Drama,' in *A Companion to Restoration Drama*, ed. Susan J. Owen (Oxford: Blackwell, 2001), p. 236. See also Laura Brown, 'The Defenseless Woman and the Development of English Tragedy,' *Studies in English Literature, 1500–1900*, 22.3 (1982), pp. 429–43, for a fine description of the she-tragedy's main characteristics and development throughout three decades.

[6] Marsden, 'Tragedy and Varieties of Serious Drama,' p. 238.

celebrated pairs, with one skillfully acting out passion while the other embodied virtuous demureness.[7] More and more often, passion was to be condemned in a cultural climate that, unlike the libertinism of the early Restoration period, emphasized morality and virtue. During the reigns of the later Stuarts, societies for the reformation of manners proliferated, and the theatre came under attack by moralists who regarded it as nursing libertinism and irreligion.[8]

Mary Pix's and Delarivier Manley's Orientalist Tragedies

Despite all these changes, some overall continuity can be established in the topics and concerns of this later generation of women writers. In devising their first tragedies, both Mary Pix and Delarivier Manley made renewed use of the Eastern script that earlier Restoration playwrights had successfully deployed. The exoticism of Mediterranean cultures had made a strong impression on Restoration London theatre-goers from the spectacular staging of Sir William Davenant's *The Siege of Rhodes* (1663), and was rekindled in the 1670s by plays such as John Dryden's *The Conquest of Granada* (1671) and Elkanah Settle's *The Empress of Morocco* (1673). However, this can hardly be considered a new development, since Restoration writers were in turn tapping into a spatter of Elizabethan and Jacobean plays on the Mediterranean Muslim kingdoms. Trade with the Mediterranean had prospered in the late sixteenth century, so that the English had increasingly more contact with Muslim trade partners, particularly the Kingdom of Morocco and the Ottoman Empire. These locations, though dangerous, offered beguiling prospects to enterprising subjects. Not surprisingly, Moors and Turks soon began to feature in the plays of the time with similarly ambivalent connotations, awakening fear and admiration. Orr has estimated that at least forty plays set in Asia or the Levant were produced in London between 1660 and 1714.[9] When it came to figuring out sexual politics in particular, westerners were left to their own fantasizing. No male traveler was allowed into the women's quarters, and so 'the blank space of the harem ... only magnified the temptation.'[10] However, these plays should be understood not as ethnographic portrayals but, rather, as reflections on difference,

---

[7] Howe, *The First English Actresses*, pp. 152–61. Elizabeth Barry and Anne Bracegirdle were also sharers in Betterton's company.

[8] Staves, *A Literary History*, p. 107. For further analysis of the changes in the cultural climate of Revolutionary London and the role played by the societies for the reformation of manners, see Manuel J. Gómez-Lara, 'The Politics of Modesty: The Collier Controversy and the Societies for the Reformation of Manners,' in *The Female Wits: Women and Gender in Restoration Literature and Culture*, ed. Pilar Cuder-Domínguez, Zenón Luis-Martínez, and Juan A. Prieto-Pablos (Huelva: Servicio de Publicaciones de la Universidad de Huelva, 2006), pp. 117–34.

[9] Orr, *Empire on the English Stage*, p. 61.

[10] Ruth Bernard Yeazell, *Harems of the Mind: Passages of Western Art and Literature* (New Haven: Yale University Press, 2000), p. 1. In this book, Yeazell traces the history of the orientalist accounts of the harem in French and English literature between 1683 and 1923.

change, and possibility,[11] more often than not masking underlying domestic preoccupations.[12] Although the writers' politics differed, both Pix's *Ibrahim* and Manley's *Royal Mischief* feature strong women whose desires interpellate the social order of a kingdom and, though supposedly far away from England, betray anxieties much closer to home. In fact, as Orr has argued:

> Where the male playwrights of the Restoration exploited the exoticism of the seraglio, celebrated the contrasting purity of Christian womanhood and praised European sexual relations as marked by freedom and ease, Pix and Manley seem fascinated by the overt sensuality of the harem, the license to exploit one's female sexuality and the political authority attached to such covert erotic power.[13]

Despite its title, Mary Pix's *Ibrahim, the Thirteenth Emperor of the Turks* is less about Ibrahim than about his mistress Sheker Para, who involves him in her revenge against virtuous Amurat for daring to reject her advances.[14] Although this is also a revenge tragedy like Behn's *Abdelazer*, here Sheker Para is the agent of the action and not a mere collaborator. She is a strong woman who uses whatever means necessary to obtain her desires and who gloats on her power and influence over the emperor:

> I have charm'd the wandring God
> More variable than the Heathens Jove,
> He darts but like a falling Star upon
> The yielding fair, dissolves, and then
> To her is seen no more; yet his Soul
> Is rivetted to mine, hangs on the Musick
> Of my tongue, nay late at my request
> For the first blossoms of the early year, he gave
> The obliging donor, the rich Kingdom of Natolia:
> I look down on the Sultana Queens, despise
> Their Pregnancy, and want of power.[15]

---

[11] Daniel Vitkus, *Turning Turk: English Theater and the Multicultural Mediterranean, 1570–1630* (London: Palgrave Macmillan, 2003), pp. 29–31. On this subject, see also Nabil Matar, *Turks, Moors, and Englishmen in the Age of Discovery* (New York: Columbia University Press, 1999), Matthew Birchwood, *Staging Islam in England, Drama and Culture, 1640–1685* (Cambridge: D.S. Brewer, 2007), and a shorter but interesting account given by Jesús López-Peláez Casellas in '"Race" and the Construction of English National Identity: Spaniards and North Africans in English Seventeenth-Century Drama,' *Studies in Philology* 106 (2009), pp. 32–51.

[12] Orr, *Empire on the English Stage*, p. 11.

[13] Orr, *Empire on the English Stage*, p. 87.

[14] *Ibrahim*, acted by Rich's company, cast Mrs. Knight as Sheker Para and Mrs. Rogers as Morena. Amurat was acted by Mr. Powell.

[15] Mary Pix, *Ibrahim the Thirteenth Emperor*, in *The Plays of Mary Pix and Catharine Trotter*, vol. 1, ed. Edna L. Steeves (New York: Garland, 1982), pp. 10–11.

Using her skills, Sheker Para has managed to defeat a gender economy that turns women's bodies into disposable objects for the emperor's consumption, but, in order to do so, she must join that very economy and cater to Ibrahim's appetites. Orr finds Sheker Para fascinating because 'her role reflects the eclipse of the traditional source of female authority, maternity (as embodied in the Queen Mother), and reveals the fissures in masculine identity through her manipulation of Ibrahim.'[16] Yet Sheker Para may also repel, particularly because she is ready to victimize other women in order to advance her own agenda. She punishes Amorat's rejection by bringing the existence of his beautiful fiancée Morena to the attention of Ibrahim, knowing full well that the emperor's lust accepts no boundaries. Morena's violated female body acquires emblematic value and comes to stand for everything that is wrong in the political order. Although a rebellion puts an end to Ibrahim's tyranny, it is ultimately unable to rescue Morena from dejection and self-loathing. Mary Pix's play betrays her Whig sympathies because, like other post-1688 works, it justifies active resistance against tyranny.[17] However, Pix's gender politics reveal ambivalence and contradiction. Lowenthal has underlined Morena's courage against the tyrant, for in the scene immediately preceding her rape Morena marshals rhetoric, violence, and even the threat of rebellion in her defense.[18] Consequently, Lowenthal contends that Morena represents a new kind of female hero that fights against the tyrant for her self-preservation, even if she finally and conventionally swoons, overwhelmed by her plight.[19] Yet one must concur with Marsden that Morena's status as a new kind of hero is somewhat compromised by the fact that her violence is ultimately directed against herself, and not the tyrant.[20]

Pix seems to be caught in the same kind of double bind as Cary and Behn were. Patriarchally defined virtue leaves women exposed to male violence, while their agency can only be figured as deviancy. *Ibrahim* resounds with unresolved gender anxieties, most of them linked to the character of Sheker Para, whose ambition is conveyed in terms of excessive masculinity. When she propositions Amurat, she

---

[16] Orr, *Empire on the English Stage*, p. 89.

[17] Orr, *Empire on the English Stage*, p. 86 and 88; Jean I. Marsden, *Fatal Desire. Women, Sexuality, and the English Stage, 1660–1720* (Ithaca: Cornell University Press, 2006), p. 108.

[18] Rape was by no means a novelty on the English stage. One need only think of plays such as William Shakespeare's *Measure for Measure* or *Titus Andronicus* to realize that it had a long theatrical lineage. Deborah G. Burks provides an interesting historical account of the topic in *Horrid Spectacle: Violation in the Theater of Early Modern England* (Pittsburgh: Duquesne University Press, 2003). Howe goes so far as to state that 'Anne Bracegirdle actually specialised in having her virgin innocence brutally taken from her,' *The First English Actresses*, p. 43.

[19] Cynthia Lowenthal, *Performing Identities on the Restoration Stage* (Carbondale: Southern Illinois University Press, 2003), pp. 169–72.

[20] Marsden, *Fatal Desire*, p. 109.

describes herself as wishing she were 'a Man, your Companion/ in the War,'[21] and in Act V, as the rebellion rages, she wishes once more to be a man in order to fight for her lord. Sheker Para has no trouble in adopting the heroic language of war just as she has proved apt in the power politics of the kingdom. In contrast, dignitaries such as the Mufti and Mustapha complain in Act I about the feminization of the realm, ruled by a 'degenerate' man because 'softness and ease,/ Flatterers and Women, fill alone our Monarch's Heart.'[22] Morena's violated body is paraded as a sign of the kingdom's corruption in the last two acts of the play. It is exposed again and again, first to her father and her fiancé's father, then her fiancé and his friend. The continued male gaze onstage also stands figuratively for the spectators.'[23] The effectiveness of this spectacular display as a theatrical device is beyond doubt, but by objectifying women's bodies and exposing them to lustful looks, Pix comes close to acting out Sheker Para's own role when, at the beginning of the play, she gives orders for twenty young virgins to parade before the emperor. Eroticism and pathos are closely imbricated in this play, and it could be argued that they result in the victimization of women.[24]

Manley's *The Royal Mischief* was staged by Betterton's company (with Mrs. Barry in the role of Homais and Mrs. Bracegirdle as Bassima) in the same season as *Ibrahim*.[25] It echoes with similar anxieties but resolves them in a different way. Here too a *femme forte* engineers the plot, this time set in contemporary Persia.[26] Homais, married to the old Prince of Libardian, nurses a passion for the younger Prince Levan Dadian after hearing of his heroic feats in the war against the Abcans and viewing his portrait. Unlike Sheker Para, Homais is under strict surveillance by her husband, who distrusts her to the extent that when he goes to war he leaves her under heavy guard in their castle. Both are women who dare to be the subject of desire rather than its object, and therefore their main motivation is sexual, but in Homais's case it is mingled with resentment over her confinement rather than with ambition.

---

[21] Mary Pix, *Ibrahim the Thirteenth Emperor*, in *The Plays of Mary Pix and Catharine Trotter*, vol. 1p. 12.

[22] *Ibrahim*, p. 1.

[23] Howe pointed out that the moving shutters played an important role in providing titillation by hiding and disclosing the eroticized body at the playwright's will: 'Such use of the moving scene enhances the sense of the actress's body being offered to the audience as a piece of erotic entertainment—a kind of pornographic painting brought to life,' *The First English Actresses*, p. 46.

[24] See Jean I. Marsden, 'Rape, Voyeurism, and the Restoration Stage,' in *Broken Boundaries: Women and Feminism in Restoration Drama*, ed. Katherine M. Quinsey (Lexington: The University Press of Kentucky, 1996), pp. 185–200, for a full discussion of these issues.

[25] The play was first meant for Rich's Company but was given to Betterton's after Manley had an argument with George Powell. See Milhous, *Thomas Betterton and the Management of Lincoln's Inn Fields*, p. 162.

[26] On Manley's possible sources and choice of setting, see Orr, *Empire on the English Stage*, p. 128, and Ruth Herman, *The Business of a Woman. The Political Writings of Delarivier Manley* (Newark: University of Delaware Press, 2003), p. 188.

These overall similarities in plot and characterization indicate that Manley is working here with the contrasting pair of forward vs. demure women that we have encountered elsewhere. Like Behn and Pix, Manley too seems to be caught in the bind of condemning women's sexual agency and endorsing women's passivity. It is noteworthy that her play changes the source story in order to punish 'Homais's ambition, reinforcing a royalist Tory ideology.'[27] Yet, feminist readings of the play have emphasized Homais's rebellious nature and her refusal to comply with conventions and repent even at her tragic end. Carnell praises the heroic stature of this 'magnificently unrepentant' character, and Andrea points out that Homais is 'beautifully terrifying and terrifyingly beautiful.'[28] Further, Homais's rebellion against her confinement and maltreatment by her husband may also be read, as Andrea has, as a counter-discourse against 'the patriarchal orientalist projection of the impassioned harem slave and her obverse, the overseeing phallic mother.'[29]

Interestingly, Manley has tempered many of the conventional contrasts between virtue and vice. Rather than white and black, in this play, Manley paints all shades of grey. All her characters (women *and* men) are somehow flawed, and all fail to embody extremes of virtue or evil, suggesting that this is 'an age when there are apparently no real heroes left to rule the country.'[30] Unlike Pix, who set up a stark contrast between Sheker Para and Morena, the virtuous female characters in *The Royal Mischief* fail to provide successful role models. Princess Bassima follows the rules more out of habit than with true conviction, whereas Selima, deeply embittered by her husband's indifference and neglect, acts out of jealousy rather than principle.

Manley's portrayal of the male characters is similarly ambivalent. Levan Dadian, unlike Amurat in Pix's play, gives in to temptation and commits adultery with Homais as well as incest, for she is his aunt by marriage. But perhaps the best example of the many fractures in the ideological script of Manley's tragedy is the Prince of Libardian, the jealous husband who keeps his wife strictly confined and forbids all visits. This feature works to undermine his status as a figure of virtue and righteousness in the spectators' minds, as he conforms to the stereotype of Oriental jealousy and tyranny. But Manley's Tory politics influence the play's ending, in which she manages to bring about a final restoration of order, rather than leave the kingdom in utter disarray as Pix does in *Ibrahim*. Herman has contended that Manley's plays became the arena in which she debated her own political positions and worked out her own doubts and that, in *The Royal Mischief*, the Prince of

---

[27] Rachel Carnell, *A Political Biography of Delarivier Manley* (London: Pickering and Chatto, 2008), p. 103.

[28] Carnell, *A Political Biography*, p. 103; Bernadette Andrea, *Women and Islam in Early Modern English Literature* (Cambridge: Cambridge University Press, 2007), p. 99.

[29] Andrea, *Women and Islam*, p. 98.

[30] Carnell, *A Political Biography*, p. 104.

Libardian came to stand for the exiled James II.[31] Although the play's prince may not be perfect, he performs a sacred mission in restoring harmony and dispensing punishment to the forces of evil, including the execution of his adulterous wife, Homais. As a result, although Manley may have seen some truth in popular claims about James II's irregularities and overbearing behavior, her play was implicitly counter-arguing that this was not enough cause to remove the kingdom's ruler.

While the Persian kingdom provided Manley with a sounding board for her gender and party politics preoccupations, one decade later she would once more turn to an Eastern location in order to sound out these issues. *Almyna, or the Arabian Vow* (performed in December 1706 by the Queen's Company and published the following year) was loosely based on the framing story in the *Arabian Nights*, which had recently reached England in French translation.[32] The Spanish-sounding sultan Almanzor, enraged by his wife's adultery, has taken a vow to marry a woman each night and to have her executed the following morning. The vizier's eldest daughter, Almyna, a woman who has received a privileged education, decides to marry Almanzor and convince him to go back on his vow, thus saving many women's lives. Rather than acting impulsively out of personal ambition like Sheker Para in *Ibrahim,* or of sexual desire like Homais in *The Royal Mischief*, Almyna's motivation is reasoned out and completely selfless. This has led some critics to consider the play of little interest, as being 'more lecture than drama,' and even to argue that Almyna is a Christ-like figure.[33] It is certainly true that Manley's later tragedy is less sensually titillating than her first, and passion only features as a vice to be avoided by women, for 'passions ... but seldom mend a wrong.'[34] Such a radical shift from passion to reason is remarkable for Manley, and the play itself is more interesting than current critical neglect might lead one to suppose.

Most strikingly, Manley lets go of the contrasting pair of women and settles for two equally virtuous sisters. Although the cast is still built on the acting strengths of Mrs. Barry and Mrs. Bracegirdle, Almyna and her younger sister Zoradia do not convey the habitual contrast between forwardness and demureness. The already familiar pattern of female rivalry over a man is here cancelled out by their strong alliance. In this, as Andrea suggests, Manley echoes the strong relationship between Scheherezade and her sister Dunyazade in the source text.[35] Act II focuses on their tender friendship, in an intimate garden scene in which Zoradia reveals to

---

[31] Ruth Herman, *The Business of a Woman,* pp. 189–90. Yeazell believes that the influence of Jean Racine's orientalist tragedy *Bajazet* (1672) must have been strong as well, since Manley was fluent in French (*Harems of the Mind*, p. 187).

[32] Herman, *The Business of a Woman*, p. 193.

[33] Marsden, *Fatal Desire*, pp. 128–9. In meeting her sacrificial death with dignity (although eventually pardoned), one can find similarities with Mariam in Cary's tragedy.

[34] Delarivier Manley, *Almyna: or, the Arabian Vow* (London: Printed for William Turner, 1707), p. 26.

[35] Andrea, *Women and Islam*, p. 102. Yet, as Yeazell contends, Manley's rendering is still far from the source text's marrying off the original pair to the sultan and his brother, so as the two sisters will never be separated (*Harems of the Mind*, p. 192).

her caring older sister that she is in love with Abdalla, Almanzor's younger brother and heir, and that they have been secretly engaged. She further informs her that, though he has now shifted his attentions to Almyna, she cannot possibly hate her beloved sister as she should hate a rival. Thus, Zoradia masochistically turns her hatred towards herself like other virtuous heroines, and her body becomes a living emblem of her suffering.[36]

Although Zoradia fits within the stereotype of the passive victim, and thus will suffer the general fate of death, in Almyna, Manley has managed to create a female character that is agentive and outspoken without becoming monstrous. At the beginning of Act Four, she exhibits courage and determination, daring to upbraid both the sultan and his brother for their behavior and to demand justice and changes. Her main objective consists of dispelling the sultan's strong conviction that women do not have a soul and so her case is carefully constructed on former examples of female heroicness:

> If yet thou doubt whether our Sex have Souls,
> What Presidents, my Lord, cou'd I not bring thee?
> (...)
> What was not fam'd Semiramis the Queen of Nations,
> Whom mighty Alexander, emulated?
> Thence after her, resolv's his Indian Wars,
> At which the stoutest of his Warriors trembled.
> He trod that World, a Woman first explor'd,
> By her example, gain'd his noblest Conquest.
> What was not our fair Neighbouring Judith,
> When th'Assyrian Monarch had resolv'd,
> To sweep whole Nations, like the Durst before him?
> Had she not a Soul? And an exalted one?
> That Durst one alone attempt, what all Dispair'd off.
> Her Honour at the stake she rusht thro' all,
> And by one stroke, redeem'd the East from ruin.
> Or cou'd the Roman Ladies, their Virginia,
> Lucretia, Portia, Clelia, thousands more,
> Without a Soul, have gain'd such endless Fames?
> Or Cleopatra, that Heroick Queen,
> In Death, she nobly follow'd Anthony.
> But I shoul'd much intrude, shou'd I but tell
> The Half of what our Sex have dar'd for Glory.[37]

Powerless to cancel the sultan's vow, she must walk the narrow path towards martyrdom, meekly accepting death for the sake of all her peers. But Manley contrives to bring about a happy ending; we find the sultan is only testing her virtue to the breaking point when he declares himself 'Quite vanquished, by thy

---

[36] Here my reading departs substantially from Andrea's, who sees Zoradia engaged in 'a male-identified contest with Almyna over Abdalla,' *Women and Islam*, p. 102.

[37] *Almyna*, p. 45.

heroic Deeds/ We gain in losing of so false a Cause./ Henceforth be it not once imagin'd/ That Women have not Souls, divine as we./ Who doubts, let 'em look here, for Confutation,/ And reverence with us Almyna's Vertue.'[38] Here as in no other play, Manley has managed to reconcile her gender and party politics. Almyna, a woman who speaks up for a just cause, a champion of women's sisterhood, is rewarded with the highest position in the kingdom, while the more passive woman who accepts maltreatment dies an accidental death. Almyna's empowerment can be identified with the female playwright's, both as evoked by her name (a near anagram of 'Manley') and in her verbal prowess, as the character rehearses the arguments of the defense of women in the speech above in terms familiar to a late seventeenth-century audience.[39] Furthermore, Manley here revises the figure of Scheherezade: 'Instead of the hapless heroine keeping herself alive through the endless provision of stories, she actively takes up the challenge of dissuading the Sultan from his barbarous views through logical and historical argument, not narrative prowess.'[40]

Almanzor is able to rectify his mistakes and to restore order and satisfaction in the kingdom, while his less deserving heir dies, which allows Manley to keep the Tory script in place. This tragedy, composed so close to the death of the last Stuart and to the Hanover settlement, powerfully resonates with Jacobite echoes, particularly in the scene in which Almanzor appoints his younger brother Abdalla his successor and courtiers take an oath accepting his succession. As Herman has suggested, this was a powerful reminder of the dilemma 'in which good Tory subjects found themselves, wishing they could support the "rightful" heir to the throne but finding it impossible.'[41] Perhaps that explains the lack of popularity of a play that must have made many people at court uncomfortable, although in her preface to the publication Manley excused the fact that the play was discontinued on Mrs. Bracegirdle's retirement. Moreover, in providing a triumphant ending for her hero and heroine and allowing only for the death of secondary characters, the author failed to meet the demand of a truly tragic ending, probably because she was 'more intent on eliminating the expendable rivals in her love triangles than on fulfilling generic expectations.'[42]

In the previous season to Manley's *Almyna*, and approximately thirty years after Behn's *Abdelazer*, Mary Pix made use of similar materials for a completely different end in *The Conquest of Spain* (performed in May 1705 by the Queen's Company and published the next year), a tragedy featuring once again a country torn between the Islamic and the Christian parties. This earlier play must have had some impact on Pix, since she may have seen the revival of *Abdelazer* at Drury

---

[38] *Almyna*, p. 64.
[39] Ros Ballaster, *Fabulous Orients: Fictions of the East in England, 1662–1785* (Oxford: Oxford University Press, 2005), pp. 84–9.
[40] Orr, *Empire on the English Stage*, p. 132.
[41] Herman, *The Business of a Woman*, p. 197.
[42] Yeazell, *Harems of the Mind*, p. 192.

Lane in 1695, the same year she launched her career as a playwright. Pix's play is vaguely set in the early eighth century, when the Christian Goths' rule over the Iberian Peninsula is about to end, as they are meeting successive invading armies from across the Strait of Gibraltar. Pix's choice of topic and plot may not be incidental, for England was at this point in the middle of the War of the Spanish Succession and, as Orr points out, 'the play was produced after the capture of Gibraltar and the victory at Blenheim.'[43] Although probably inspired by such current affairs and influenced by Behn, Pix's direct source is William Rowley's *All's Lost by Lust*, which in turn romanticizes details of a story told in Spanish medieval romances such as the *Romance de la Cava*.[44]

In *The Conquest of Spain,* the virtuous Jacincta is raped by the lustful King Rhoderique while the kingdom is being invaded by Moorish forces led by Mullymullen. Like Morena in Pix's earlier tragedy *Ibrahim*, Jacincta's violated body has the power of bringing into sharp relief what is wrong in the kingdom. But, while in *Ibrahim* the action takes place within the seraglio, that is, the private section of the palace, here Pix plays with the contrast between Rhoderique's castle and the battlefield outside, the private and the public. Jacincta approaches her father disguised as a Moorish woman, which suggests the defilement and alienation she has undergone while also projecting a symbolic image of the future of Christian Spain. In Act III Scene I, under cover of her Moorish veil, she movingly denounces the wrong she has suffered while offering a titillating picture of sexualized femininity:

> See here the injur'd, ravish'd, lost Jacincta, [*Throwing up her Veil.*]
> The blotted Relict of a ruin'd Maid;
> Pity my Shame, and spare my faultring Tongue
> The hated repetition of my Wrongs.[45]

Although Pix skillfully exploits the tensions between both parties in the play's action, in terms of their ideological import, Christians and Moors are fairly interchangeable. One can hardly tell the difference between Theomantius and Mullymumen, for instance. Both adhere, in words and deeds, to a chivalric code of behavior; both want to possess Jacincta and are willing to wreak havoc in the process. What is at stake in the main plot is, after all, a mere trafficking of women. Male rivalry over women and the country thus seals the trope of woman as nation that Pix successfully deploys in *The Conquest of Spain*, whereas in *Ibrahim* the political implications of the plot were perhaps less obvious. In both plays the

---

[43] Orr, *Empire on the English Stage*, p. 179.

[44] For more information on this theme and for an analysis of Pix's handling of such diverse materials, see my article 'The Islamization of Spain in William Rowley and Mary Pix: The Politics of Gender and Nation,' *Comparative Drama* 36.3–4 (2002–03), pp. 321–36.

[45] Mary Pix, *The Conquest of Spain*, in *The Plays of Mary Pix and Catharine Trotter*, vol. 1, p. 36.

king has failed to protect the kingdom; immersed in hedonistic pleasures like Emperor Ibrahim in the earlier play, Rhoderique has been careless in his duties to the extent that he has left the kingdom open to a foreign invasion. The familiar symbols of kingship and warrior heroism, so deeply entwined with the dramatic genre of tragedy, are here deflated. Ultimately, Spain ceases to exist as a Christian nation, just as Jacincta's defiled body is not recuperable either, so in Act V she dies an accidental death (rather than self-inflicted like Morena's) in the confusion of the battle.

Although Jacincta is a passive character, the emblem of victimized femininity, and thus very far from the agentive assertion of Sheker Para in *Ibrahim*, the parallelism between the ravished female body and the invaded nation allows Pix to question both monarchy and patriarchy by showing them as equally abusive and oppressive. It is remarkable that in *The Conquest of Spain*, like Manley's *Almyna*, there is no instance of female deviancy. The only other major female character, Margaretta, mirrors Jacincta's virtue, producing a doubling effect in the play rather than the slight contrast achieved by Manley. Margaretta too must oppose the unwanted advances of a man who uses deceit to get into her bed, and she too remains perfectly loyal to the man she loves. However, she is luckier than Jacincta and is saved from 'pollution' in the nick of time. Such lack of female deviance in Pix's world suggests that women's agency is not at fault for the collapse of the social structure. Instead, women's virtue is subjected to arbitrary fate and mere chance.

Pix's new use of pathos disrupts the surface message that the violated woman transmitted in her earlier play. It is true that the male gaze is present here as well, and that the ravished woman on stage may become a visual source of erotic pleasure. But in this later play, Pix endows her with several new meanings. Rape in this play is the means by which to throw into sharp relief the inconsistencies of a patriarchal structure that fails to protect those who live within its fold. As Callaghan has remarked in the case of Renaissance tragedy, '[female tragic characters] are frequently constructed as catalysts of tragic action, throwing moral order into confusion rather than merely ratifying its boundaries; they serve not just to define limits but also to uncover the limiting structures of society.'[46]

Lowenthal contends that the rape narrative was used by women playwrights to explore the possibility of 'a new, female, heroic, different from the manly sort with its emphasis on the clash between love and honor.'[47] In Pix's and Manley's early work (as in Behn's), the tragic pattern seems to have functioned as a kind of straightjacket against which the authors chaffed, as they were compelled to write within the limits of a contrasting characterization of virgin vs. whore. Yet, one can see commonalities insofar as the exploration pointed out by Lowenthal was made by means of exotic settings and characters. As Jacqueline Pearson has remarked, ethnic otherness held particular interest for women dramatists of the

---

[46] Callaghan, *Woman and Gender*, p. 63.
[47] Lowenthal, *Performing Identities*, p. 169.

Restoration because 'racial and ethnic difference provided useful tropes for gender difference.'[48] Nevertheless, the racial script often hid more immediate concerns and imbrications with the political agenda of their day and time, as well as a permanent engagement with the performance of women's lives. Manley's works in particular seem to have veered away from the orientalist portrayal of Eastern societies pervading travelogues and other writings of the period, particularly in refraining from 'establishing an orientalized other against which the "freeborn" English woman can secure her imperialist self-definition.'[49] However, as we will see next, the East was not Manley's or Pix's exclusive engagement.

Mary Pix, Delarivier Manley, and the Politics of History

At some point in their playwriting lives, both Mary Pix and Delarivier Manley turned away from exotic faraway kingdoms and towards English history for their source materials. Pix did so fairly early on, when her tragedy *Queen Catharine: or, the Ruines of Love* was produced in 1698. In contrast, Manley delved into the subject at the very peak of her writing career, and *Lucius, the First Christian King of Britain* (1717) would be her last play.[50]

It is uncertain whether Pix's *Queen Catharine* met with box-office success, as no records of its run have been found.[51] Like many other plays of the period, it was never revived, so it seems safe to assume that it was received with some indifference. However, it must have had at least some influence, judging from the fact that soon afterwards Colley Cibber had staged *The Tragicall History of Richard III*, a play that drew upon some of the historical characters and events in *Queen Catharine*.[52] Luis-Martínez has placed these two plays in the context of the Restoration's adaptations and alterations of Shakespearean works,[53] and Pix herself acknowledged her debt in the prologue, announcing 'A heavy English Tale to day, we show/ As e'er was told by Hollingshead or Stow,/ Shakespear did oft his Countries worthies chuse,/ Nor did they by his Pen their Lostre lose.'[54] While Pix was certainly following the lead of Shakespeare in choosing to plot situations from the English chronicles, like many of her contemporaries she

---

[48] Pearson, 'Blacker than Hell Creates,' pp. 15–6.

[49] Andrea, *Women and Islam*, pp. 103–4.

[50] Strictly speaking, *Lucius* falls outside the chronological span of this study by a few years, but in its main features it belongs with the rest of Manley's dramatic output.

[51] Lennep, *The London Stage*, pp. 496–7.

[52] On Cibber's tragedy, see Derek Hughes, *English Drama*, p. 432.

[53] Zenón Luis-Martínez, 'Mary Pix's *Queen Catharine* and the Interruption of History,' in *Re-shaping the Genres: Restoration Women Writers*, ed. Zenón Luis-Martínez and Jorge Figueroa-Dorrego (Bern: Peter Lang, 2003), pp. 178–9.

[54] Mary Pix, Prologue to *Queen Catharine*, in *Eighteenth-Century Women Playwrights, vol. 2: Mary Pix and Catharine Trotter*, ed. Anne Kelley (London: Pickering and Chatto, 2001), p. 73, lines 8–11.

was not so bound by tradition and authority that she was afraid to suit the extant materials to her own ends.

Queen Catharine tackles a momentous episode in the War of the Roses before the decisive Battle of Towton in 1461, staging the capture and execution of Owen Tudor in the final weeks leading to the victory of the House of York under Edward IV. The historical Owen Tudor was among the strongest Lancastrian supporters, as then-king Henry VI was his son-in-law by his marriage to Catharine, Henry V's widow. However, the historical Katherine de Valois had long been dead by this time. Pix's daring move to turn her into the protagonist of her tragedy shakes the very foundations of the history play as practiced by Shakespeare and is part and parcel of her project to introduce women characters into the very core of the heroic genre. Critics have taken Pix to task for this anachronism, complaining that she reduces history to 'a quarrel over thwarted love,'[55] although more recent work seems to be reappraising this view, taking into account that its focus 'on an emotional dimension, an internal history, is part of a valuable feminist project.'[56] But, leaving aside the chronological inaccuracy of Queen Catharine's continued existence into the middle years of the century, Pix's play has left the basic participants and struggles of the War of the Roses pretty much untouched. The profiles of Edward IV and his two brothers, the Earl of Warwick's participation, as well as that of the Lancastrian champion, Owen Tudor, follow the pattern received through the English chroniclers. Moreover, stretching Katherine de Valois's lifespan was crucial to Pix's aims, insofar as it allowed her to set up a dramatic structure based on two love triangles: on the one hand, Catharine and her husband, Owen Tudor, vs. the scorned former suitor, Edward IV; on the other, Catharine's ward Isabella[57] and her lover the Duke of Clarence, vs. the rejected Sir James Thyrrold. Both love triangles are linked by the villainy of Richard, Duke of Gloucester, brother to Edward and Clarence, years before he would become Richard III.

Underlying the tight structure of the play is a critique of the masculinist bias of the heroic ethos that rests on the romanticization of the male lovers, Owen Tudor and the Duke of Clarence, while questioning the emotional callousness of their rivals, Edward and Thyrrold. Both Tudor and Clarence repeatedly manifest their rejection of ambition and the struggle for power in favor of a harmonious relationship with their loved ones. Warned that trying to visit his wife might cost him his life, Tudor replies that he 'had rather/ See the Queen tho' my life's the forfeit, than/ Be Edward or Henry or any happier King/ That you can think of;'

---

[55] Cotton, *Women Playwrights of England c. 1363–1750*, p. 115.

[56] Findlay et al., *Women and Dramatic Production*, p. 201.

[57] Pix's editor Anne Kelley believes that Isabella is an entirely fictitious character, although she does mention that the Duke of Clarence married Isabel Neville, the Earl of Warwick's elder daughter, in 1469 (*Eighteenth-Century Women Dramatists, vol. 2*, p. 287, n. 40). I agree with Luis-Martínez that Pix's Isabella is a fictionalized Isabel Neville ('Mary Pix's Queen Catharine and the Interruption of History,' p. 187), given her and her younger sister's Anne close relationship with the two Plantagenet brothers. Anne would marry Richard, Duke of Gloucester (later Richard III) in 1471.

and he then instructs his friend: 'If you out-live me,/ Report me as a Man that Catharine smil'd on.'[58] It is precisely his prioritizing the private realm over the public that brings about his death, since despite his wife's urgent entreaties to consider the danger he is in, he forgets all precautions and prefers to 'indulge the/ Pleasing ecstasie, nor wake, till we are/ Forced to wake.'[59] Similarly, the Duke of Clarence's pursuit of his love affair with Catharine's ward Isabella is fraught with danger from both parties. Whether the affair is discovered by Clarence's brothers or by the Lancastrians is equally threatening for the lovers. Yet, he ignores his brothers' warnings against the match, since he considers their philosophy is utterly misguided:

> Let my ambitious Brothers waste their time,
> In climbing up the Royal precipice;
> Let Casuists argue the injustice of the War,
> Whilst I retiring from the bustling Crowd,
> Find my sure Bliss in Isabella's eyes.[60]

In believing 'Possessing the dear object that's beloved,/ Superior to ambition, a sublime Joy,' as Isabella argues,[61] and in their determination to put their life on the balance to achieve that end, both male characters come to embody a different kind of hero and a new kind of masculinity. Although they are described as brave and accomplished warriors, even in the face of large numbers of their enemies, courage is only one of their virtues, and not the most defining one by far. While they are willing and indeed eager to enter into emotional bonds, their rivals are unable, and even afraid, to do so. Edward's thwarted love for Catharine[62] stunted his emotional growth, leaving in its place an endless supply of hatred for his more successful rival, Owen Tudor:

> Yes; by my wrongs I swear, by all the Racks
> Of disappointed Love, my abler Arm
> Shall for the weakness of my Youth atone.
> I'll hack this beauteous body, since even rage
> And envy must allow his Person lovely.
> Till doting Katharine shall not distinguish
> His mangl'd Carcass from the meanest Slave's.[63]

---

[58] *Queen Catharine*, Act III, p. 95.
[59] *Queen Catharine*, Act III, p. 98.
[60] *Queen Catharine*, Act II, p. 87.
[61] *Queen Catharine*, Act IV, p. 107.
[62] As Luis-Martínez rightly points out, this relationship is another anachronism, since Edward IV was born in 1442 and Katherine de Valois had died in 1437 ('Mary Pix's *Queen Catharine* and the Interruption of History,' p. 182).
[63] *Queen Catharine*, Act I, p. 81.

His inability to deal with emotions has turned Edward into the kind of womanizing man who, in Gloucester's malicious words, 'like the wanton Summer fly,/ [has] blown upon and tainted all our Beauties.'[64] As a matter of fact, Edward fears true love and tenderness as sure signs of weakness. In seeing Catharine sink on her knees over the dying Tudor, Edward asks Gloucester for help against the surging tide of feelings: 'Yet help me, Brother, for thou I find art steady,/ And tenderness struggles with revenge.'[65] Similarly, Thyrrold is unable to cope with Isabella's rejection, and his love gives way to 'Revenge, Rage, Spite, Envy and Ambition:/ Sure the damn'd medley must at least produce/ A perfect madness.'[66] This other scorned suitor, like Edward, is henceforth moved exclusively by his desire for revenge, using all means necessary to bring it about. He betrays Queen Catharine, who is in his keeping, and forces Isabella to marry him.

Like Morena in *Ibrahim* and Jacincta in *The Conquest of Spain*, Isabella must face male violence (this time even sanctioned by a priest) in one of the most pathetic scenes of the play. While she movingly begs and cries, Thyrrold insists he must have his way. Although saved in the nick of time by the arrival of Clarence, Isabella dies an accidental death, as punishment for having been guided by a passion that made her neglect her duties towards her tutor, Queen Catharine, thus bringing about the ruins of the title, 'the fatal/ Ruines which my head-long passion caus'd.'[67] As in Pix's other plays, young women are shown to be continually exposed to male violence and warned to protect themselves from it. Once more, their helplessness when deprived of the protection of a male relative is emphasized. Interestingly, Queen Catharine herself is also associated to the 'ruins' in the title, this time by Edward, who on leaving a distracted Catharine he has had his revenge on, remarks: 'Oh Catharine! Oh fatal Beauty, what ruins/ Thy love has made.'[68] Thus, the play contrasts two dissenting perspectives, male and female. For Edward, women are temptresses whose power over men is to be feared, since it is the harbinger of destruction. For Isabella, women have to learn to control their passions and not be ruled by their emotions, since that makes them into the targets of male violence.

However, Isabella is only one of the two main women characters in a play which 'accords value to the typically feminine realm of personal experience.'[69] One might expect Queen Catharine to be a *femme forte*, since she bears the play's title and is so clearly its protagonist. For Luis-Martínez, 'Catharine is Pix's highest achievement in this tragedy,' and he goes on to describe 'her independence of mind, her denunciation of political injustice, and her self-affirmation through the defence of her own passions.'[70] Although it is quite true that Catharine is full of

---

[64] *Queen Catharine*, Act II, p. 92.
[65] *Queen Catharine*, Act IV, p. 113.
[66] *Queen Catharine*, Act II, p. 87.
[67] *Queen Catharine*, Act V, p. 123.
[68] *Queen Catharine*, Act IV, p. 114.
[69] Findlay et al., *Women and Dramatic Production*, p. 201.
[70] Luis-Martínez, 'Mary Pix's *Queen Catharine* and the Interruption of History,' pp. 201 and 203.

dignity, she is essentially powerless. Pix has chosen to portray a queen in her lowest hours. When she tries to oppose Edward's invading forces, she finds that she has no army and that, though bearing the highest titles, she is ultimately helpless: 'am I not/ Daughter of France and England's Queen? Have I no/ Power? Where are my Guards? Alas, I had forgot, I've/ None.'[71] Likewise, when Isabella is being taken away by Thyrrold and cries for her assistance, Catharine sympathizes but is unable to help. With the murder of her husband Owen Tudor, Catharine retreats into despair and madness. Pix shows this descent into hell in terms powerfully reminiscent of Shakespeare's Ophelia:

> *Curtain rising, discovers Queen Catharine sitting on a Couch, with Herbs and Flowers by her, attended.*
>
> CATHARINE
> Here, give me more, more of the Cypress, and
> That grave shading yew, let the Carnations lose their colour,
> And display the blooming Rose in some black die,
> Till I have made my Garland
> Dark as my Woes, and Dismal as my Despair [!][72]

Although this fits well with tragedy's characteristic theme of the fall of the mighty, textual evidence reveals that Catharine's power is more figurative than real. Typically, characters including herself reminisce about her past role as Henry V's queen, rather than consider her current state as queen dowager in a kingdom torn by internal strife. Audiences would be particularly influenced (and thus, misled) by Edward IV's memories, in Act I, of Catharine at the peak of her beauty, depicting her as a goddess, a haughty queen whom Edward served 'with all the lowest marks of servile Courtship.'[73] Similarly, Catharine remembers 'the crowded Court of Paris/ Rheims, or Windsor, when scarce a passage/ Cou'd be made for gazing Princes, and for/ Kneeling Subjects.'[74] This remarkable mystification does not stop at Catharine but extends to her two husbands, Henry V and Owen Tudor. Henry was, in the words of his trusted chamberlain Lord Dacres, a conqueror comparable only to Alexander the Great, and for Owen Tudor, he was a hero whom later kings can only aspire to copy, while Tudor himself shares Henry's superior qualities when he is presented by Catharine as 'my Henry's Soul cast in purer mold.'[75]

---

[71] *Queen Catharine*, Act IV, p. 112.
[72] *Queen Catharine*, Act V, p. 125. Indeed, this is not the only Shakespearean trait Catharine displays. Her moment of premonition in Act IV, p. 109, when she thinks she sees 'a bloody hand that parts/ Our meeting arms,' is oddly reminiscent of *Macbeth*. The way others see her, as a lusty woman only too eager to marry a second time after her first husband's death (deriving perhaps from Holinshed), links her to *Hamlet*'s Queen Gertrude.
[73] *Queen Catharine*, Act I, p. 80.
[74] *Queen Catharine*, Act II, p. 85.
[75] *Queen Catharine*, Act II, p. 83.

Their eulogy is complete when Lord Dacres looks at the children of Catharine by Owen Tudor and foresees 'a noble stock of Princes, which must Bless/ And Wed, and intermixing, heal the distracted Land.'[76] Strikingly, Pix eulogizes the Lancastrian genealogy even while showing it during its direst times, with the triumph of the House of York. Her vision of history establishes a continuous line flowing from the House of Lancaster to the Tudors. Such continuity is rooted in an acknowledgement of the key role played by Queen Catharine, as grandmother to the future Henry VII. In such historical vision, the victory of the House of York with Edward IV and later Richard III is seen as an anomaly. Even though Edward speaks the final words of the play, they read as a critique of his own rule, since they markedly refuse to accept that a kingdom can be maintained by force: 'Kingdoms are given by the powers above,/ And the chief blessing is our peoples love:/ Whilst we are just, they ought and must be kind,/ No Cement does so fast as Justice mind.'[77] Instead, in true Whig fashion, Edward's last remarks insist on the importance of the contract between ruler and ruled, thus undermining the warrior ethos that on the surface appears to be triumphant.

Such warrior ethos in an extreme form is epitomized by Edward's brother Richard, Duke of Gloucester, who stands as Catharine's strongest opponent, both in character and in action. Richard is emotionally detached from everyone else, to the point that he considers his two older brothers as mere obstacles on his path to the crown. He is malevolent and uses rumor and deceit to bring about his goals, endlessly plotting very much like Iago in Shakespeare's *Othello*. His success is, however, undercut by Queen Catharine's feminine body, since it is the maternal body, her very womb, that holds the seeds for an alternative, more egalitarian future. Therefore, Pix's 'heavy English tale' is imbued with a feminized, Whig perspective that rewrites the history play's heroic discourse and 'writes back' to Shakespeare in his own realm.

Delarivier Manley's *Lucius, the First Christian King of Britain* (1717) is another play that looks back to the tradition of English historical drama, showing 'how "factual" materials could be adapted not only to comment on masculine politics and philosophy—a practice well established by Shakespeare and Dryden—but also to hypothesize a crucial feminine agent in the inception of British culture.'[78] The counterpart of Queen Catharine is Rosalinda, Queen of Albany and Aquitaine, held hostage by the combined armies of King Vortimer of Britain and King Honorius of Gallia after they have won a war to check Rosalinda's husband Otharius's expansionist ambitions. At the onset of the play, Rosalinda is a widow and the object of several men's competing desires. She is secretly loved by Lucius, Prince of Britain; by Vortimer himself; and by Arminius, Prince of Albany and

---

[76] *Queen Catharine*, Act V, p. 127.
[77] *Queen Catharine*, Act V, p. 128.
[78] Jack M. Armistead and Debbie K. Davis, Introduction to Delarivier Manley's *Lucius*, The Augustan Reprint Society (Los Angeles: William Andrews Clark Memorial Library, 1989), p. iii.

her kinsman. Lucius himself is the object of two women's affections: Emmelin, Princess of Gallia, and Alenia, Princess of Albany (sister to Arminius). These two sets of lovers establish a complex web of conspiracies, since most of them are dissemblers and double dealers. Thus, Arminius poses as helper to Vortimer, whom he hates for the tyrant he is and as his rival for Rosalinda's hand, while his sister Alenia cross-dresses as Rosalinda's page Sylvius, in order to assist her brother and also to thwart her beloved Lucius's chances with the queen. At the center of these intricate webs of deceit lie Lucius and Rosalinda, the only characters who remain constant and honest throughout the tragic events.

Manley's play deploys here theatrical resources closer to comedy than to tragedy, like the intricacy of the love plot or the woman cross-dressing for love, but she holds the constant threat of violence over the characters, particularly over Rosalinda, and she sets them against the background of the strained relations of several countries: Britain, Albany (Scotland), and Gallia (France). Although to modern readers the story of the virtuous Lucius, the usurper King Vortimer, and the Christianization of Britain may sound pseudo-mythical at best, it had some support in the historical knowledge of the period, as it was loosely based on accounts of the early history of Britain and its kings given by chroniclers such as Geoffrey of Monmouth or James Tyrrell.[79] As Pix did for the Shakespearean history play, so does Manley with these chronicles, setting up a love plot as the private cause of momentous historical events. It comes as no surprise, then, to learn that King Vortimer's thwarted passion for the then-betrothed Rosalinda led him to invade and conquer Albany and later to seek out an alliance with King Honorius of Gallia against Rosalinda's husband Otharius, very much as Edward's bitter disappointment over Catharine's preference for Owen Tudor had sparkled his thirst for revenge.[80] Vortimer's anger is boundless, and he would violently take what has been denied him for so long:

> May I not ravish her, I cou'd not win?
> May I not seize, what wou'd not be bestow'd?
> I dream of bless'd Enchantment in her Arms:
> I, restless, burn, and rave on furious Joy.
> And nothing but Possession may asswage
> The Love-sick, raging Fever of my Love.[81]

---

[79] Manley's editors, Armistead and Davis, mention several such sources for this play in their Introduction, p. vi. Nicholas Rowe had explored similar territory in *The Royal Convert* (pub. 1708), which features a virtuous Christian lady, Ethelinda, in the Saxon kingdom of Kent.

[80] Critics have also identified verbal echoes of Shakespeare's *Richard III* in Manley's *Lucius*, which forges one more link with Pix's *Queen Catharine* (Herman, *The Business of a Woman*, p. 203; Carnell, *A Political Biography*, p. 222).

[81] Delarivier Manley's *Lucius*, The Augustan Reprint Society (Los Angeles: William Andrews Clark Memorial Library, 1989), p. 36.

Unlike Queen Catharine, however, who is afforded at least the appearance of power, Queen Rosalinda is shown as a helpless victim from the beginning, with her very destiny hanging in the balance as she awaits the arrival of the victorious kings of Gallia and Britain: 'A Widow I, without a Dow'r or Name;/ No more the Queen of Albany or Aquitain,' as she sadly declaims at the beginning of Act II.[82] Even though she shows substantial dignity in hardship, Rosalinda lacks the stamina of previous women characters in Manley's dramatic oeuvre. Throughout the play she is hounded by Vortimer, deceived by Arminius and Alenia, and rescued from rape and death only in the nick of time, thus providing a spectacle of passive, distressed femininity. Her one act of agency is, as Canfield has remarked, to choose a new consort in Lucius and to secretly marry him, an action in itself quite revolutionary in the context of English serious drama, where women in similar circumstances are severely punished.[83]

Nevertheless, in setting up a scenario of conflict concerning those three nations, Manley's play has the power to invoke parallelisms with the current times that were altogether absent from Pix's earlier tragedy. The year 1707 had witnessed the Union of Scotland and England under the last Stuart monarch, Queen Anne, an event that at least in part originated in the fear of a Jacobite rebellion at her death. Moreover, James II's son by Mary of Modena, James Edward Stuart (known as the Pretender) continued to live in France and to enjoy the support of its king. A plot connecting those three nations was hardly free of associations, wittingly or not. Moreover, Manley's play touches on related issues of legitimacy and religion. Lucius is unaware for most of the play that he is not truly Vortimer's son, his biological father being the legitimate king of Britain whose crown and marriage bed Vortimer had usurped, a situation that takes on added layers of meaning in connection to the Hanoverian succession and to rumors surrounding the particulars of James Edward Stuart's own birth, whose legitimacy many doubted. Likewise, religion was a key issue in post-Revolutionary England, since it was the refusal of James II and his son to convert to Protestantism that barred them from a return to power. Like many Tories, Manley must have harbored a desire for the Pretender to be more flexible in religious matters than he proved to be. Such is the case of Lucius, who in the play converts out of love for the virtuous Rosalinda, thus bringing about a prosperous union of the English and Scottish crowns under the true heir.

However, the Jacobite resonances of Manley's play so soon after the first Jacobite Rebellion might have been dangerous for the author, despite the celebrity she enjoyed towards the end of her writing career. In addition, *Lucius* was produced by Sir Richard Steele, whose Whig partisanship was well known, and therefore

---

[82] *Lucius*, p. 9.

[83] J. Douglas Canfield, 'Shifting Tropes of Ideology in English Serious Drama, Late Stuart to Early Georgian,' in *Cultural Readings of Restoration and Eighteenth-Century English Theater*, ed. J. Douglas Canfield and Deborah C. Payne (Athens: The University of Georgia Press, 1995), pp. 200–201.

whose support for an obviously Jacobite play would have been rather doubtful. Furthermore, the play is reported to have been a huge box-office success, which indicates that it catered for a variety of theatre-goers, not necessarily Tories only. Manley skillfully contrived an ambiguous plot that might be constructed differently according to its audience's political allegiances. As Herman has explained, the play 'succeeded in being interpretable as offering a message of support to either side of the political divide.'[84] The triumph of a ruler with a hereditary birthright over an alliance of a usurping king and the king of France must have felt satisfactory for Whigs supporting the Hanover king, even though, in case the message was unclear, Steele took the liberty to highlight it in his prologue to the play's revival in 1720.[85]

Like her preceding play, *Almyna*, *Lucius* has a happy ending, with the male protagonist expressing his gratitude at having passed the test of fate:

> That I have pass'd the threat'ned Storms of Fate,
> Aveng'd my Parents, and preserv'd my Wife,
> Are Blessings first deriv'd to me from Beauty.
> Benighted, grov'ling on my Mother Earth,
> 'Till Beauty call'd, I unenlightened lay:
> By Beauty led, I fought eternal Day.
> I view those shining Realms of Light above,
> And gain immortal Happiness by Love.[86]

The triumph of love, birthright, and religion contribute to make this play a 'crowd-pleaser' that became a resonant stage success.[87] Despite Lucius's gallant declaration, however, Rosalinda's leading role in bringing about this happy state of affairs, beyond her independent action of marrying Lucius clandestinely, is rather questionable. In adapting historical sources for this final play, Manley's political partisanship took precedence over her feminism. History, however, continued to be of notable interest for other women playwrights of this period, as will be seen in the next chapter.

---

[84] *The Business of a Woman*, p. 200.
[85] *The Business of a Woman*, p. 202.
[86] *Lucius*, p. 54.
[87] The term is used by Carnell, *A Political Biography*, p. 222.

Chapter 6
Late Stuart Writers II: Catharine Trotter and the Historical Tragedy

Catharine Trotter: The Playwright and Her Critics

Like other women writers of her generation, Catharine Trotter (1674–1749) has received limited critical attention up to now. She started as an author of narrative with *Olinda's Adventures* (1693), but Trotter later tried her luck at writing for the stage with the tragedy *Agnes de Castro* (performed by Rich's Company, as stated in the previous chapter, in the season of 1695–96 and published in 1696). Although the more public side of her writing career ended when she married Reverend Patrick Cockburn in 1708, she managed to reinvent herself later as the author of philosophical treatises in support of John Locke.[1]

Catharine Trotter was rediscovered in the 1980s by several feminist critics who reprinted her work, first by Fidelis Morgan and Edna Steeves, later by Kathryn Kendall; more recently some of her plays have been the object of careful scholarly editions by Anne Kelley.[2] Criticism of her work has tended to read the relationships established by her women characters as erotic liaisons, and thus attempted to suggest Trotter's supposedly lesbian identity, in a trend first started by Kendall, who

---

[1] For a more detailed account of Trotter's life and her critical fortunes, see Anne Kelley, *Catherine Trotter: An Early Modern Writer in the Vanguard of Feminism* (Aldershot: Ashgate, 2002). On Trotter's early narrative work, see also Sonia Villegas-López, 'Devising a New Heroine: Catharine Trotter's *Olinda's Adventures* and the Rise of the Novel Reconsidered,' in *Re-shaping the Genres: Restoration Women Writers*, ed. Zenón Luis-Martínez and Jorge Figueroa-Dorrego (Bern: Peter Lang, 2003), pp. 261–78.

[2] Edna Steeves edited Trotter's plays together with Mary Pix's oeuvre in the already mentioned facsimile collection, *The Plays of Mary Pix and Catharine Trotter* (New York: Garland, 1982); Fidelis Morgan included Trotter's tragedy *Fatal Friendship* in a selection of Restoration plays by women entitled *The Female Wits: Women Playwrights of the Restoration* (London: Virago, 1981). Kendall selected Trotter's comedy for the collection *Love and Thunder: Plays by Women in the Age of Queen Anne* (London: Methuen, 1988). More recently, Anne Kelley included two of Trotter's plays, her one comedy, *Love at a Loss*, and her last tragedy, *The Revolution of Sweden*, in vol. 2 of *Eighteenth-Century Women Playwrights* (London: Pickering & Chatto, 2001). Finally, Kelley has also edited a selection of Trotter's works that includes facsimiles of *Agnes de Castro* and *Fatal Friendship* in *Catharine Trotter's The Adventures of a Young Lady and Other Works* (Aldershot: Ashgate, 2006).

hailed *Agnes de Castro* as 'the first lesbian play in English stage history,'[3] and later continued by writers such as Emma Donoghue, who reads the play in the context of 'the literature of passionate female friendship [describing] not spinsterhood but a double life, shared between a male lover/husband and a beloved woman.'[4] Other critics have been drawn to the philosophical underpinnings of her work, especially as perceived in her letters and essays.[5] Finally, others have dismissed her work as an irrelevant contribution to the history of literature, when not openly claiming that it is badly written. A recent article on her comedy *Love at a Loss* (1700), for instance, describes it as a 'dispirited, limp version of the clever games played by Restoration wits and coquettes.'[6] Other times, the critic appears to follow previous readings: 'The play [*Agnes de Castro*] need hardly detain us: it is, as Nancy Cotton wryly observes, "a Senecan tragedy a hundred years out of date."'[7]

Nevertheless, perhaps the most interesting question posed by Trotter's drama is her choice of tragedy over comedy as her dramatic genre. Only one of her five plays is a comedy, the above-mentioned *Love at a Loss* (1700). In the decade 1696–1706 she had four tragedies produced: *Agnes de Castro* (1696) was followed by *Fatal Friendship* (1698) and *The Unhappy Penitent* (1701), and she ended her stage career with *The Revolution of Sweden* (1706). Her consistent investment in tragedy may be puzzling when one considers Aphra Behn's preference for comedy, or the fact that other writers of her generation, for example Mary Pix, moved easily between comedy and tragedy. This does not seem to have been Trotter's case.

Moreover, Catharine Trotter was no doubt the female playwright of the period who gave tragedy the most careful thought, and in many ways, her agenda was at odds with that of male practitioners of the genre, even those who were most adept at writing she-tragedies.[8] Trotter articulately described her ideas about drama and tragedy halfway through her playwriting life, in the lengthy dedication of her tragedy *The Unhappy Penitent* (1701) to Lord Halifax, a Whig patron of the arts

---

[3] Kendall, ed, *Love and Thunder: Plays by Women in the Age of Queen Anne* (London: Methuen, 1988), p. 11.

[4] Emma Donoghue, *Passions Between Women: British Lesbian Culture 1668–1801* (London: Scarlet Press, 1993), p. 130.

[5] Such is the case of Trotter's editor and analyst Anne Kelley as well as of scholars from the field of Philosophy, such as Kathryn Ready. See Kelley's article '"In Search of Truths Sublime": Reason and the Body in the Writings of Catharine Trotter,' *Women's Writing* 8.2 (2001), pp. 235–50, as well as her monograph *Catharine Trotter* (2002) for further evidence of this approach.

[6] J. Karen Ray, 'Friendly Fire: the Oxymoron of Authority in Catherine Trotter's *Love at a Loss*,' *Restoration and Eighteenth-Century Theatre Research* 14.1 (1999), p. 75.

[7] Mary L. Williamson, *Raising Their Voices: British Women Writers, 1650–1750* (Detroit: Wayne State University Press, 1990), p. 189.

[8] See my essay, 'Issues of Gender and Genre in Two Tragedies of the Long Eighteenth Century,' for a contrastive reading of the politics and aesthetics of Trotter's *The Unhappy Penitent* (1701) and Nicholas Rowe's *The Fair Penitent* (1703).

and Congreve's protector.[9] In discussing the role models available to her, only Shakespeare appears to be above reproach, his work being, in Trotter's opinion, always true to nature. More contemporaneous writers she finds less worthy of imitation. Dryden 'commands our admiration of himself, but little moves our concern for those he represents.' Otway excelled only 'in the pathetic,' while Lee 'instead of being great he is extravagant.' What Trotter found less inspiring was the fact that the proper subject matter of tragedy was love, and this seemed to her 'not noble, not solemn enough for tragedy.' She further contends that

> The most that can be allow'd that passion is to be the noblest frailty of the mind, but 'tis a frailty, and becomes a vice, when cherish'd as an exalted virtue; a passion which contracts the mind, by fixing it entirely on one object, and sets all our happiness at stake on so great hazard as the caprice, or fidelity of another [...] yet this is made the shining virtue of our heroes; *we are to rejoice in their success, or pity their disappointments, as noble lovers, patterns for our imitation, not as instances of human frailty*. (my italics)[10]

Therefore, the purpose of her tragedy *The Unhappy Penitent,* and by extension, her concept of the whole genre, is none other than to enlighten her audience, male and female, on the inadvisability of love as a true guide for human behavior, or a suitable goal for which to strive. She chooses tragedy as a fit instrument to instruct people, but, interestingly enough, she is also seeking to elevate the moral tone of the average tragedy of her times.

In leaning very strongly towards moral principles and wholeheartedly supporting the rules of decorum, Trotter's dramatic theory and practice bring her closer to the French dramatists of the seventeenth century than to her contemporaries in England. As a matter of fact, in the aforementioned dedicatory letter, Trotter cites the French theorist Nicholas Boileau's *L'Art Poétique* (1674; translated in 1683 as *The Art of Poetry*) to support her idea that love may be a weakness rather than a virtue. Another influential codification of French dramatic theory, L'Abbé d'Aubignac's *La pratique du théâtre*, had been translated into English as *The Whole Art of the Stage* in 1686.[11] Trotter's rationalistic stress on the conflict between love and honor seems to owe much to these French theorists and to the drama of Corneille and Racine, most of all in her 'taste for austere minimalism.'[12] Through them, Trotter's drama reaches back to classical drama. Like her predecessors Mary Sidney or Elizabeth Cary, she is influenced by French renderings of Senecan drama, although these later formulations tend to de-emphasize its violence:

---

[9] Catharine Trotter, Epistle Dedicatory to *The Unhappy Penitent* (London: Printed for William Turner and John Nutt, 1701).

[10] Trotter, Epistle Dedicatory to *The Unhappy Penitent*.

[11] Maximilian E. Novak, 'Drama, 1660–1740,' in *The Cambridge History of Literary Criticism, vol. IV: the 18th Century*, ed. H. B. Nisbet and Claude Rawson (Cambridge: Cambridge University Press, 1997), pp. 167–8.

[12] Richard E. Goodkin, 'Neoclassical Dramatic Theory in Seventeenth-Century France,' in *A Companion to Tragedy*, ed. Rebecca Bushnell, p. 390.

As for the most important Latin model for French classical tragedy, Seneca's plays were quite widely read throughout the period. They were much admired for their rhetorical dexterity and their moral vigor, both of which traits would be central to the French classical aesthetic. The extreme, violent nature of Senecan tragedy also had a certain appeal in the period leading up to the beginnings of French classicism, although this element was to be increasingly frowned upon or at least driven underground as the classical aesthetic, which places a premium on propriety and decorum, developed.[13]

The connections of Trotter's plays to French aesthetic theories and her debt to a Senecan moral universe have been neglected so far, due perhaps to current critical preference for the two plays that deviate at least in part from her dramatic theories: her only comedy *Love at a Loss* and her tragedy *Fatal Friendship*.[14] The latter is rather exceptional among Trotter's plays, as it has drawn laudatory comments from theorists of Restoration tragedy such as J. Douglas Canfield, who places it alongside Nicholas Rowe's *The Fair Penitent* (1703) as a valuable example of the Revolutionary personal tragedies,[15] or Christopher J. Wheatley, who asserts that Trotter's play represents 'the completed movement to private tragedy.'[16]

Such views appear rather out of touch with the context of Trotter's work. The comedy was a one off. For reasons she did not expand upon, Trotter decided not to write any more comedies. She may have shared the French view that it was an inferior genre, and thus unsuitable for the high moral ground for which she generally strove. Thus, the interest generated by her comedy probably owes more to the general importance of this genre in the context of Restoration drama than to the relative value of Trotter's contribution. As for *Fatal Friendship*, it is the one tragedy she did not endow with a recognizable historical background and aristocratic characters, features to which she returned in subsequent works. Therefore, it might be argued that critics have been drawn to those plays which better fit ready-made theories about Restoration drama, even though they may add little to our knowledge of women playwrights in general or Catharine Trotter's work in particular.

A comprehensive view of Trotter's *oeuvre* shows the recurrence of certain features in her remaining three plays. They are all historical tragedies, displaying a similar pattern. As a backdrop for the action, she depicts a country experiencing the threat of national or international strife: a political takeover, an invasion, or a revolt. There she places the stories of women who face a moral dilemma, very much like Mariam in Cary's tragedy, and they must take a momentous decision. This involves choosing the good of the country over their personal feelings, or the other way round. Trotter's historical tragedies thus enact the dichotomy public vs. private, reason vs. passion, duty vs. Love; and in enacting such philosophical dilemmas her

---

[13] Goodkin, 'Neoclassical Dramatic Theory in Seventeenth-Century France,' p. 374.

[14] Anne Kelley is a notable exception in having chosen *The Revolution of Sweden* as Trotter's most representative tragedy for her 2001 edition.

[15] *Heroes and States*, p. 166.

[16] 'Tragedy,' p. 79.

characters attempt to meet the exacting demands of the author's concept of tragedy as a genre that is meant to elevate her audience's moral standing.

Catharine Trotter's Historical Tragedies: Feminism, Monarchy, Citizenship

Perhaps the one critic who has put forward a comprehensive view of Trotter's drama to date is Michel Adam, whose 1987 essay 'L'héroïne tragique dans le théâtre de Catherine Trotter' devised a descriptive analysis and categorization of Trotter's characters. Adam considered Trotter a unique woman writer in her generation for several reasons:

> L'œuvre dramatique nous frappe par trois constantes principales: son aspect réfléchi que nous avons déjà souligné; le souci qu'avait Catherine de se "démarquer" de ses rivals; l'élévation morale des ses pièces, qui s'accompagnait à la fois d'un éloge de la Vertu, et d'un féminisme de bon aloi, le tout à caractère didactique.[17]

Adam's taxonomy identified each woman character as belonging to one of three groups. First, those who, in imitating men's behavior, became the villains of the piece, like Elvira and Bianca in *Agnes de Castro*. Second, those whose very virtues (loyalty, sincerity, generosity) turned them into victims of others' wrongdoing, like Lamira in *Fatal Friendship* or Lesbia in *Love at a Loss*. Finally several characters who stand out as role models, like Anne of Brittany in *The Unhappy Penitent* and Constantia in *The Revolution of Sweden*.[18]

Even though Adam's analysis is sound on the whole, such a descriptive approach fails to tease out the nuances of Trotter's multifaceted philosophy of women's role in society, particularly in relation to Whig theories of citizenship and government. Moreover, by looking at all the plays together without taking into account their relative chronology or the differences stemming from different dramatic conventions (comedy vs. tragedy, for instance), we can miss important data concerning the evolution of Trotter's thought over the decade of her professional involvement in the theatre.

However, by looking at the three historical tragedies in the order they were written, we may indeed obtain some added insights, including the fact that, although Trotter consistently uses the same plot pattern, her resolution of the dilemma her characters face is never exactly the same. Thus, though the problem continued to plague her and worry her, over the years she envisioned different ways out of it,

---

[17] Michel Adam, 'L'héroïne tragique dans le théâtre de Catherine Trotter,' in *Aspects du théâtre anglais: 1594–1730*, ed. Nadia Rigaud(n.p.: Université de Provence, 1987), p. 98: 'Her dramatic oeuvre is striking for three recurrent features: its reflective quality, already described; Catherine's care to 'be different' from her rivals; the high moral ground of her plays, together with their praise of Virtue and their genuine feminism, always with a didactic purpose' (my translation).

[18] Adam, 'L'héroïne tragique,' 102ff.

as we will see by establishing for each play first the public and then the private conflicts at stake, and lastly the solution the playwright puts forth.

Catharine Trotter's first play, *Agnes de Castro* (pub. 1696), is set in early fourteenth-century Portugal, where Prince Don Pedro has married a Spaniard, Constantia. Aphra Behn's novel *Agnes de Castro* (1688) brings to the fore diplomatic relations between Spain and Portugal in the Middle Ages that occupy only the background in Aphra Behn's *Abdelazer*. England had maintained a strong link with Portugal since those very times, and they had strengthened with the marriage of Charles II to the Portuguese princess Catherine of Braganza. The setting had then a certain appeal for an English readership, and the tale itself was recommended by its seal of true historical romance as well as by the great number of writers of several nationalities who had circulated it in verse (such as the Portuguese Luis de Camoes), in drama (in Spanish works by Jerónimo Benjumea and Luis Vélez de Guevara), and in prose (Mme. de Brillac in France).

The story needs a historical contextualization of the strife going on between the neighboring kingdoms, which lasted approximately two centuries, from Portugal's initial independence from Spain around 1143 to the end of the fourteenth century, when the full victory of the Portuguese over the Castilians at the battle of Aljubarrota in 1385 put an end to the violent attempts of the Spanish to swallow up the smaller and weaker kingdom. However, Spanish rulers did not stop aspiring to incorporate Portugal; in fact, marriage alliances between both nations were a common practice, resulting in Philip II of Spain and his successors managing to become kings of Portugal too, even if only for a short period (1580–1640).

Behn's text glosses over the presence of diverse factions at court and their connections with international affairs, disguising them as jealousy and adultery. The only explicit mention of marriage politics appears near the beginning, when the narrator describes the marriage of Prince Dom Pedro to Bianca, the daughter of the king of Castile, another Pedro, to be followed by a second marriage to another Castilian princess, this time '*Constantia Manuel*, Daughter of *Don John Manuel*, a Prince of the Blood of *Castille*, and famous for the Enmity he had to his King.'[19] Thus both marriages are set squarely in the midst of the currents and tensions running through the neighbor kingdoms. Later on, Dom Pedro tries to evade his painful love for Agnes by going away, and his destination and motives are thus explained:

> After having, for a long time, combated with himself, he determin'd to do, what was impossible for him, to let *Agnes* go. His Courage reproach'd him with the Idleness, in which he past the most youthful, and vigorous of his Days; and making it appear to the King, that his Allyes, and even the Prince *Don John Emanuel*, his Father in Law, had concerns in the World, which demanded his presence on the Frontiers; he easily obtain'd liberty to make this Journey, to which the Princess wou'd put no obstacle.[20]

---

[19] Behn, 'Agnes de Castro,' in *The Works of Aphra Behn*, vol. 3, ed. Janet Todd, p. 128.
[20] Behn, 'Agnes de Castro,' p. 142.

Behn seems to be uninterested in describing who those allies, enemies, or borders might be, perhaps considering them irrelevant for the plot. Nevertheless, it would be helpful to know that at the time a civil war was taking place in Castile that would lead to a change of dynasty. Portugal's involvement was desired by some and feared by others, particularly since the reigning families of both countries were related by blood. Agnes herself was closely connected to a powerful aristocratic family, the Albuquerques, and therefore stood for a faction that wanted the prince to take sides in the Spanish conflict, even to the point perhaps of claiming the Castilian crown for himself. In the context of the novel, knowledge of these facts helps us see that Dom Alvaro and his sister Elvira are not just the villains of the piece, one a cruel favorite and the other a jilted lover but, beyond that, that they stand for a section of Portuguese public opinion that we might call 'nationalist' nowadays and that sought to steer clear of the dangers of getting involved in Spain's complex politics.

Further evidence of the political tapestry in the background of this tale can be found in Catharine Trotter's own dramatic adaptation of *Agnes de Castro*, which follows the outline and borrows a fair amount of the wording of Behn's novel. However, unlike Behn, who followed Brillac very closely, Trotter may have used other sources, succeeding in introducing more depth and complexity in the plot. Like Behn in *Abdelazer*, Trotter gives the opening scene to the villains, and she has Elvira voice her resentment for the heroines in much the same way that the Moor expressed his discontent, grounding it in the Spanish tyranny that they both suffer, one as a Portuguese woman, the other as a Moorish prince:

ELVIRA
Was it not an affront to all the court
To bring her [Agnes] here as in defiance to us;
As if she [Constantia] thought none of us worth her Love,
Not one in Portugal for her Converse.

BIANCA
Their being bred from Infancy together,
Might make it difficult to separate;
And then their near Relation.

ELVIRA
A Princess, must have none;
She came to wear the Crown of Portugal,
And then, shou'd have renounc'd all other Claims:
She'as now, new Friends, new Country, new Relations,
And shou'd forget the Old; not be a Spaniard here.[21]

---

[21] Catharine Trotter, *Agnes de Castro*, in *Catharine Trotter's The Adventures of a Young Lady and Other Works*, ed. Anne Kelley (Aldershot: Ashgate, 2006), p. 1.

Moreover, the prince alludes to his participation in the civil wars as 'parricidal.'[22] Although the focus of the plot remains the tragic love affair between Pedro, prince of Portugal, and his wife Constantia's close companion, the Castilian noblewoman Agnes de Castro, Trotter conveys a fuller picture of the times and the setting of her tale than Behn had managed to do before her, with a little touch here and there. Her play provides a fuller political context that fleshes out her characters and clarifies causes and effects for some behavior that otherwise might seem odd and arbitrary, such as the relentless hatred of the king for Agnes de Castro both before and after the death of Princess Constantia, hatred that would lead him to order her murder, or the resentment of the Portuguese party as expressed by Elvira in the quote above. Added to the discontent at court, there is a lurking rebellion that is only vaguely hinted at, but that seems contrived in order to explain away the prince's convenient absence from court in certain climatic episodes.[23]

In the private sphere, the domestic crisis springs from Don Pedro's having fallen in love with his wife's companion, Agnes, and the ensuing discovery of his passion. Agnes is too discreet to reveal her own feelings, and offers to leave Portugal in order to 'cure the prince's frenzy,'[24] but she hints that she is perhaps not completely indifferent to such feelings. Agnes is much more than the flat character of a virtuous young woman. Her virtue is not a stagnant given, but the result of careful introspection and a constant struggle against her passions. Her soul-searching is quite as exacting as Mariam's in Cary's tragedy. Like Cary, Trotter allows us frequent glimpses into the character's state of mind, particularly when Agnes realizes she is eager to see the prince again, but manages to check 'the sinful Tumult in my Breast.'[25] Nevertheless, when the prince suddenly becomes a widower and insists that she should remain close, she lets feelings guide her behavior:

> [To herself] Oh! How his Words prevail upon my Heart;
> It melts, 'twill yield I fear, why shou'd it not,
> Shou'd he who for my Freedom, Fame, and Life,
> Expos'd his own, receive his Death from me?
> Is treating thus the Man my Princess lov'd,
> The way to pay her Memory respect?
> And do I thus, obey her dying Charge?[26]

In letting her behavior be dictated by her feelings and not by rational thought, Agnes appears to have committed an irredeemable sin. Accordingly, in this first work the playwright accords a severe punishment, and Agnes is accidentally killed by the villain. The fact that it is an accidental death suggests Agnes's purity of mind and body. A true villainess (that is, a woman who has ambitiously sought out power or love for herself, like the villainess Elvira in this play) would be punished

---

[22] *Agnes de Castro*, p. 16.
[23] 'KING: Go, as my General, quell this rash Rebellion,' *Agnes de Castro*, p. 16.
[24] *Agnes de Castro*, p. 7.
[25] *Agnes de Castro*, p. 24.
[26] *Agnes de Castro*, p. 44.

with murder. But it is significant that Trotter does not allow for Agnes's happiness in this world; she is not completely without fault. With her death, proper order is reasserted both in the private and the public spheres. The reign of passion ends here, and the Spanish influence ceases too. The rebellion vaguely hinted at has likewise been quelled.

Trotter's next historical tragedy, *The Unhappy Penitent* (first staged by Rich's Company in February 1701), is set in the late fifteenth century in France, with the background of the marriage alliances of the French Bourbons with other continental kingdoms. The plot shows King Charles VIII reconsidering the wisdom of his engagement with Margarite of Austria. Suggested instead is an alliance with Brittany by means of an alternative marriage of state to Princess Anne of Brittany. This would successfully put an end to a whole generation of conflicts between both countries, but the king is worried about the moral implications of his breach of contract with Margarite. The public-private dilemma is described in the opening scene in two conversations: first between two courtiers waiting in the king's antechamber, and later between the king and two Privy Council members, Du Lau and Graville, both of them in favor of securing an everlasting peace with Brittany through marriage. The king's qualms over a breach of faith are put aside with Graville's comment that it was the king's father's promise, and not his own, and that, in any case, 'princes ought, in marriage, to consider/ Interest of state alone.'[27]

The public turmoil represented by the two alternative political alliances for the king of France has its private counterpart in the emotional upheaval Margarite of Austria is going through, since she is torn between her growing love for Lorrain and her duty to maintain her former engagement with France. In this play too, Trotter conveys women's virtue not as an innate trait but as a constant troubled negotiation between one's duties and inclinations, the demands made by the good of others vs. the impulse to gratify one's desires. At first, as the evidence of the king's breach of contract seems overwhelming, she foolishly thinks herself free, and accepts Lorrain's love:

> MARGARITE
> How oft (to silence this ungrateful Jealousy)
> Must I repeat, I never lov'd this Charles [the king]?
> Till I saw you [Lorrain] ne'er knew what 'twas to Love,
> But being bred from Infancy together,
> And looking on him as my destin'd Husband,
> I cherish'd what esteem he seem'd to merit,
> Which then (not knowing one I cou'd prefer,
> Nor having felt a stronger Passion) I
> Imagin'd Love;[28]

Later she is distressed when she finds out that the French king intends to keep his word to her after all, but by then she is unable to resist Lorrain's entreaties. Once

---
[27] *The Unhappy Penitent*, pp. 3–4.
[28] *The Unhappy Penitent*, p. 11.

Margarite has chosen the path of emotion, she cannot retrace her steps. She has left the realm of reason behind to embark on a journey of passion. She accepts his offer of marriage and marries him in secret at the end of Act III. This fall into passion can never be rewarded by the author. Instead, Margarite's new husband is tricked by a rival into believing that she is false and wanton, and she is publicly accused of dishonor. She then comes to understand that she has sinned by letting herself be guided by passion, and that she must do penitence:

> MARGARITE
> I have deserv'd it all!
> Lorrain's my crime, and 'tis but equal punishment
> To be depriv'd of that for which I sinn'd;
> I see the hand of Heav'n in it, and submit.[29]

Once more, the country's good takes precedence over the individual's. Order is restored by bringing about the marriage of France and Brittany. Although this may be read, in socio-historical terms, as the better political alliance, the fact remains that Ann of Brittany is also the better woman. Unlike Margarite's, her behavior is always ruled by reason and common sense. Interestingly, Ann's higher moral value is indicated here by the fact that she speaks the moral of the play:

> ANN OF BRITTANY
> Unhappy Pair! Let us correct ourselves
> By these Examples, seeing how vainly
> They sought happiness, in following
> Unruly passion, that blind, as rash, ever
> With inconsiderate haste, obstructs its own designs.[30]

Even more strikingly, the pairing of female characters in *The Unhappy Penitent* does not involve here a villainess and a heroine, like the Agnes-Elvira pairing in the earlier tragedy. Although the plot would appear to pitch the two women characters as rivals for the affection and the hand of the king, nothing could be farther from the truth. Trotter chooses to make the women good friends, and she often contrives to bring them together onstage. Margarite receives Ann as 'the truest friend, the perfectest/ Of all her sex,'[31] and asks for her advice, following it to the best of her ability. Ann too behaves with perfect selflessness, as she calmly points out that the king should honor his previous commitment and marry the woman he has been contracted to for years rather than marry her, arguing furthermore that she could not possibly love someone she could not value: 'Think not I cou'd be happy in possessing/ What I knew owing to the Faithlessness,/ And Infamy of him that shar'd it with me.'[32] The fact that Trotter devised the two characters not as a contrasting pair with diverging qualities but

---

[29] *The Unhappy Penitent*, p. 35.
[30] *The Unhappy Penitent*, pp. 47–8.
[31] *The Unhappy Penitent*, p. 13.
[32] *The Unhappy Penitent*, p. 14.

as a closely bonded pair with similar aims was also suggested by typecasting, because the actresses playing these two parts, Anne Oldfield (Ann of Brittany) and Jane Rogers (Margarite of Flanders), specialized in a similar type, that of young, virginal women. Furthermore, Margarite does not have to die in order to be purged of her sin. Rather, she is given the chance to recant and to do penitence by going away to a spiritual retreat. This punishment, though grave, is less severe than the one dealt to Agnes in the previous historical tragedy. Loneliness rather than death is the price to be paid for following one's heart's dictates.

Trotter's third and last historical tragedy, *The Revolution of Sweden* (premiered in February 1706 by the Queen's Company), is set in the early sixteenth century during the Danish invasion of Sweden. The Swedes have organized their resistance thanks to the leadership of Gustavus. One of their party, Erici, summarizes the invasion and the tyrannical rule of the Danes as he addresses the patriots in the opening scene, railing them to resist with reminders of 'That horrid Scene of Murders, Rapes, and Rapine,/ The Prelude to unparallell'd Barbarities/ Committed daily since in every Province!'[33] Clearly here Trotter goes further than ever before in spelling out the kind of conflict in which the realm is involved. The nation is endangered by a foreign invasion that deprives citizens of their rights, not by a vague rebellion or by an unwise political alliance. True merit, represented by Gustavus, must defeat tyranny, embodied by the Danish usurper. The play's dedicatee on this occasion is another leading member of the Whig faction, Harriet Godolphin, eldest daughter to the Duke of Marlborough, highly acclaimed for his victory at the battle of Blenheim a year earlier. A Whig conceptualization of citizenship lies at the heart of Trotter's last play. According to Anne Kelley, the source text was Mitchel's popular translation of Vertot's *Histoire des revolutions de Suede*, which in turn had been dedicated to one of the Whigs dignitaries involved in requesting William of Orange's presence in England in 1688.[34]

The private sphere also suffers here the impact of the violence overrunning the nation. Constantia, married to the patriot Count Arwide, is taken hostage by the Danes. During her captivity, she is tricked into believing that her husband has signed a treaty with them, betraying their country in exchange for her safety. Since she is a patriot too, she feels she must denounce her husband's treason:

CONSTANTIA
Oh Arwide, Arwide,
On what a Trial hast thou set my Virtue!
Thus to divide my Duty to my Country and my Husband.
At what an easie rate we keep our Virtue,
When it has no Affection to contest with,
But when oppos'd, how weak are our Resolves,
Or were they firm, how difficult it is

---

[33] Catharine Trotter, *The Revolution of Sweden*, in *Eighteenth-Century Women Playwrights, vol. II: Mary Pix and Catharine Trotter*, ed. Anne Kelley (London: Pickering and Chatto, 2001), p. 204.

[34] Kelley, *Catharine Trotter*, p. 135.

> To judge aright, on what we shou'd resolve;
> So liable are all things to receive a Colour
> From those Passions, through which our Reason views 'em;
> I fear 'tis that, the soft Reflection of my Love,
> That wou'd perswade, I ought not to reveal
> My Husband's guilt.
> [...]but cou'd I answer
> To my Conscience, my Country, or the sole
> Equitable Judge, and Framer of the whole,
> That to conceal the Treachery of one,
> I suffer'd the Destruction of a Nation?
> Is there a tye so Sacred to be held
> In competition with the Publick Safety?
> And yet—Oh! Can my Heart consent t'expose
> My Arwide, to the Mercy of an injur'd Enemy?[35]

Once more, the character's ambivalence and hesitations resonate with echoes of Mariam's plight, torn between public duty and private emotions. In this third attempt, Trotter offers a still more straightforward blueprint for women's behavior. In her consideration, women are, above all, citizens of their country, who must always put public duty before any other. Interestingly, while Agnes and Margarite were either unmarried or newly married, Constantia has been married for some time, and it is with the authority and experience of a wife, that is, of someone fully aware of the conditions of the marriage contract, that she describes her plight. Constantia finally decides to accuse her husband of treason in a public meeting, and yet she offers at the same time to continue to live with him 'in all respectful duty.' Thus she is discharging both duties, as a public citizen and as a private person.

Although the play remains a tragedy, there is partly a happy ending that ensues from such rational (though perhaps unlikely in practice) reconciliation of the private and public spheres. The restoration of order and both collective and individual happiness result from the discovery that it was all a plot of the Danes and their Swedish followers, and Arwide's innocence is proved. Here the rebellion against tyranny succeeds, and the couple is happily reunited. Collective satisfaction results from the destruction of tyranny, foreign rule, and injustice, and not from quelling a rebellion or from the foreseeable benefits of a marriage alliance. Private harmony springs from the union of two individuals who are fully aware of their public dues. Arwide and Constantia appear as virtuous human beings and capable citizens, equal in their full engagement with their society while enjoying a mutually agreeable partnership.

Of the main female characters examined in the plays so far, only Constantia is rewarded for her actions. She is the only one to never let passion guide her away from her public duty as a citizen. She is the only one to let reason reign supreme. In contrast, the female characters of previous historical tragedies were punished in various degrees when they let passion control their destiny. Death or loneliness

---

[35] *The Revolution of Sweden*, p. 254.

was the result: passion did not bring them closer to fulfillment but cut them off from their lovers and from themselves.

Constantia is rewarded as well because she does not forget that she has private duties to perform too, as a wife to her husband. This is emphasized in *The Revolution of Sweden* through the contrast with another female character, Christina, a patriot who is married to a traitor, a supporter of the Danish invader. She prioritizes her public duty and leaves her husband, joining the patriots in male disguise under the name Fredage.

> CHRISTINA
> When I behold this Vertuous Lord [Gustavus], consider him
> As our Deliverer, whose glorious Name
> Posterity will Bless,
> I feel a secret Joy for having been
> The destin'd Author of his Preservation:
> But when I view myself, driv'n like a Vagabond
> About the World, flying a Husbands Cruelty;
> A Wretch deni'd a Refuge by her nearest Friends,
> Wandring in a disguise that ill becomes
> Her Sex, to beg Protection from a Stranger;
> But most, Oh Laura, when I think how all
> May be interpreted to my dishonour
> I must lament my Fate! Was there no means but this?
> Why was I pointed out the Instrument?
> Had Sweden been less happy in Gustavus,
> If I had not been wretched for his Safety?[36]

Although she is portrayed sympathetically, as one who is forced by circumstances to follow a transgressive path, the fact remains that she has become masculinized, and her behavior is deemed inappropriate. She has crossed over to a dimension outside the borders of conventional femininity. Though she is a victim of the tragic situation of her country, her failure to perform her womanly or wifely duties is perceived in the tragedy as deviant and monstrous, and she eventually dies at the hand of her own husband.

Thus, in looking into the conflict between the public and the private spheres in the historical tragedies of Catharine Trotter, it becomes evident that this issue worried her consistently for at least a decade, and that she probed her way, time and again, into a solution that might satisfactorily reconcile both realms in a productive way for women. It seems obvious that she was not advocating radical changes in women's material or even psychological condition. Transgressing behavior was consistently punished in her writing. Trotter did not believe in an appropriation of the men's sphere that meant a "masculinization" of women. She appears to have believed that women should not give up on the duties of wife and mother, unlike polemical writers such as Mary Astell. Rather, she seems to have wanted to promote a rational approach to women's social role, and to encourage finding

---

[36] *The Revolution of Sweden*, p. 210.

rational answers to issues of love and passion that, to her mind, so threatened a woman's social status. In the dedication of her last play to Harriet Godolphin, Trotter invokes the example of French women: 'Numbers we know among them, have made a considerable Progress in the most difficult Sciences, several have gain'd the Prizes of Poesie from their Academies, and some have been chosen Members of their Societies.'[37] Trotter's concern was to bring about women's full citizenship, and such agenda was only possible, in her view, if the theatre became an instrument of virtue, so that 'our Pleasures shou'd be useful to our Morals, serve to correct our Vices, and animate the Mind to Virtue.'[38]

Fatal Friendship and Private Tragedy

In dedicating *Fatal Friendship*[39] (acted by Betterton's Company in May 1698) to the then Princess Anne of Denmark, Trotter voices once more her concern that the end of her play might be 'to discourage Vice, and recommend a firm unshaken Virtue.'[40] Although her aim here may be similar to that of her other plays, some of its features markedly depart from the standard ones described so far. In fact, the box-office and critical success of *Fatal Friendship*, as Kelley has argued, was 'possibly because it was the most conventional within the contemporary dramatic parameters, the emphasis being on the moral dilemmas of the principal male protagonist within a somewhat melodramatic plot.'[41]

The displacement of the moral dilemmas from the women characters of other plays onto the male protagonist is, as Kelley remarks, the most pointed of these departures. The title itself alludes to the friendship between the protagonist, Gramont, and the exiled Italian soldier Castalio, who has defended him at the cost of his own freedom. On visiting Castalio in prison, Gramont complains that he is unable to help him pay the fine that would set him free, and he despondently grumbles against his fate, pointing out that 'I alone have been/ Your evil Genius, that you have cause to curs;/ Your Fatal Friendship, the unlucky hour/ You sav'd my Life, or that which gave me Birth;/ O that it ne'er had been.'[42] Gramont is feminized by his helplessness in the face of adversity and by his situation of dependency on a powerful male figure, his father Count Roquelaure. Staves comments that 'Trotter explores Gramont's moral suffering to suggest fundamental difficulties posed by the aristocratic masculine code of morality. She is troubled by the level of violence

---

[37] *The Revolution of Sweden*, p. 197.

[38] *The Revolution of Sweden*, p. 197.

[39] Occasionally, this play has been erroneously identified as *The Fatal Friendship* in critical literature.

[40] Catharine Trotter, Epistle Dedicatory to *Fatal Friendship*, in *Catharine Trotter's The Adventures of a Young Lady and Other Works*, ed. Anne Kelley (Aldershot: Ashgate, 2006).

[41] Kelley, *Catharine Trotter*, p. 91.

[42] Trotter, *Fatal Friendship*, p. 19.

associated with the masculine defense of honor.'[43] Yet, this is not a particularly violent play. With the exception of an isolated allusion to a war between France and Spain in which the characters seem to have been involved and a duel in which Gramont unhappily killed a powerful general's son, there is no confrontation until the very end, and none of the wars, anarchy, or revolution that Trotter's other tragedies usually make much of.

Moreover, the aristocratic code of honor remains firmly in place, particularly as embodied in Castalio, whose qualities are praised by all other characters as being those of the exemplary cavalier. Rather, like the women characters examined above, Gramont's weakness is an excess of sentiment, which in Trotter's rationalistic universe usually condemns its owner to some heavy sentence. Pressed by the hard circumstances in which he is involved, he pushes aside all his punctiliousness and decides that 'to keep/ a little peace of mind, the pride of never straying' is less important than relieving his loved ones' suffering.[44] In abandoning the high moral ground that Trotter exacts from all her characters, Gramont's fate is decided, and he stabs himself in self-loathing just as the tide of adversity is finally turning.

However, Staves may be right when she points out that '*Fatal Friendship* continues concerns of seventeenth-century aristocratic romance, but re-imagines them in a more realistic bourgeois mode.'[45] This is the play that most emphasizes the corrupting power of money. Gramont fears the prospect of poverty for himself and for his secret wife Felicia, and he bitterly complains that he lacks the wherewithal to help others, either by buying Castalio's freedom or by ransoming his son, improbably kidnapped by pirates. This leads him to acquiesce to wed the rich widow Lamira despite already being married in secret to Felicia. Other characters use their wealth to assert their power and independence, to obtain what they lust for and to ensure their subordinates' obedience, like Felicia's brother or Gramont's father, who threaten to withdraw the means to succor them. Finally, money is the instrument of vengeance, as when Lamira discovers the existence of Felicia's marriage to Gramont and uses her wealth as a bribe to separate them.

Most of all, money is the ally of tyranny, for in that regard Trotter's philosophy remains consistent. Her critique targets a General who never appears onstage but whose power, reaching as high as the king, is exerted at several levels and is felt widely, as his animosity against Gramont extends to his friends and allies. This shadowy figure transmits the idea of the corruption of the system characteristic of Whig partisanship and found elsewhere in Trotter's tragedies. Secrecy is central to this corruption, as it contributes to the permanence of tyrannical power: 'The political agenda, therefore, is clearly that tyranny is corrupting and destructive, but that secret and unethical alliances are equally incompatible with social and political stability. In the end, secret plots are revealed to be merely the mirror image of tyranny, stemming from the same lack of integrity and right reason.'[46]

---

[43] *A Literary History*, p. 109.
[44] *Fatal Friendship*, p. 20.
[45] *A Literary History*, p. 109.
[46] Kelley, *Catharine Trotter*, p. 91.

Tyranny is felt also by the women characters, as their fate is decided by their kinsmen. Lamira's husband was 'a Tyrant/ Your Parents forc'd upon your tender years'[47] whose jealousy reaches from beyond the grave, so that if she marries again, she must forfeit most of her fortune. For this second marriage she lets herself be guided by her feelings and by her kinsman Bellgard, whose advice has a selfish motivation, and so she is deceived into a bigamous wedding and abused by Gramont, who has married her out of mercenary needs. Her articulate rage at being thus used, however, places her at a remove from the typical victim. Unlike Felicia, who has always been a dependent, Lamira is, after all, a woman proud of her ability to manage her own financial affairs.[48] In learning of their ill usage by Gramont, the reactions of these two women could not be more different;[49] Felicia collapses in grief, while Lamira confronts her abuser with accusations:

> Mistaken Man thou hast rous'd a Woman's Rage;
> In spite of all thy hardned Villany,
> Thou shalt repent thou dist provoke me thus;
> I'll haunt your Steps, and interrupt your Joys;
> Fright you with Reproaches, blast her Fame;
> I'll be the constant Bane of all your Plesaures,
> A Jarring, Clamorous, very Wife to thee,
> To her a greater Plague, than thou to me.[50]

In embodying female rage, Lamira thus runs the risk of turning into a villain, for female anger and outspokenness are conventionally constructed as signs of monstrosity. Yet, Trotter avoids demonizing Lamira by validating her grievance, and by having Gramont accept it as well.[51] The author also resists the pull of the plot that pits the two women against each other by emphasizing their common plight. In this respect, Lamira and Felicia stand mid-way between the contrastive pair heroine vs. villainess of the earlier play *Agnes de Castro* and the female bonding of the later tragedy *The Unhappy Penitent*. There is a strong current of tension between Gramont's two wives in their close encounters, most pointedly before Lamira understands that Felicia is not a lover but a legal though secret wife with an older claim over Gramont than hers. Yet Trotter manages to convey the common traits of their situation, particularly in how they are both dependent on male power. Felicia's case is even more striking, as her being bound by secrecy for so long has placed her into the yet harder position of having to reject the marriage proposal tendered by her secret husband's father—an incestuous match she cannot envision without horror—without daring to disclose her reasons. As a matter of

---

[47] *Fatal Friendship*, p. 12.
[48] Significantly, Lamira was acted by Mrs. Barry; Felicia, by Mrs. Bracegirdle.
[49] Findlay et al., *Women and Dramatic Production*, p. 192.
[50] *Fatal Friendship*, p. 26.
[51] Rebecca Merrens, 'Unmanned with Thy Words: Regendering Tragedy in Manley and Trotter,' in *Broken Boundaries: Women and Feminism in Restoration Drama*, ed. Katherine M. Quinsey (Lexington: The University Press of Kentucky, 1996), p. 47.

fact, Trotter's presentation of Felicia's situation in the opening scene has echoes of Aphra Behn's *The Rover*, which opened to Don Pedro pressing his sister Florinda to accept the marriage offer of the much older but wealthy Don Vincentio (or else the Viceroy's son) and forget the honorable but penniless Belvile. In *Fatal Friendship*, Bellgard reminds Felicia first of her dependency on his generosity as well as of the decreased family fortunes, in order to make her pliable to the prospect of an excelled rank and vast possessions, and finally he threatens her with poverty if she does not obey. Felicia's stoic acceptance of misfortune, however, elevates her over most other characters, including her husband, who instead of resignation opts to follow the path of least resistance and thus brings about the tragic ending. Lamira too strikes a dignified pose towards the end, announcing her intention to enter a convent and denouncing the deceitfulness of men and the 'Vicissitude of Miseries'[52] that makes up life. The play thus suggests that 'male matchmaking and a misplaced faith in the importance of homosocial bonds [are] a brutally destructive force.'[53]

While *Fatal Friendship* proved to be a successful theatrical venture, one should not forget that the author turned away from this more 'private' pattern and returned to historical tragedy in her later plays. One can only hypothesize that she was dissatisfied with a social framework that centered on the male figures while pushing women to the margins. Both Lamira and Felicia lack agency, though in differing degrees, and they are both largely contained within a domestic sphere. While Trotter succeeds in showing men as responsible for this unfair situation, she does not seem to be able to offer a more productive alternative. As Kelley contends: 'As in all Trotter's writing, the alternative to a corrupt and unworkable patriarchy is presented as a society in which the mediating influence of rational women restores an ethical framework.'[54] It seems indeed to have been this playwright's ambition to show women outside the domestic sphere, more fully participating in society. The turning point came with *The Unhappy Penitent*, a play for which she devised a woman character that transcended the limits of women's conventional roles, someone who might be a true leader and moral guidance for the whole country.[55] From then on, her efforts were directed towards showing that a woman's well-regulated life, based on high moral principles, might have an impact beyond her home.

---

[52] *Fatal Friendship*, p. 56.

[53] Findlay et al., *Women and Dramatic Production*, p. 193.

[54] Kelley, *Catharine Trotter*, pp. 131–2.

[55] As Michel Adam pointed out: 'Beaucoup moins émouvante qu'Agnes ou que Felicia, Anne n'est, au fond, qu'un "animal politique". Cést là justement que l'on découvre le changement d'orientation qui se produit dans la pensée de Catherine Trotter, dès 1701. Elle abandonne le plan sentimental pour glorifier la Raison d'État ce qu'elle fera à nouveau cinq ans plus tard dans *The Revolution of Sweden*' ('L'héroïne tragique,' p. 109). I do not completely agree with Adam's view that Trotter's ideas changed materially after 1701. She seems to me to be remarkably consistent in ends even if her means evolved over time, but he rightly pinpoints political aspirations as Ann's essential feature.

Chapter 7
The Last of the Stuarts: Jane Wiseman and Anne Finch

Jane Wiseman's *Antiochus the Great*

During Queen Anne's reign, the generation of the 1690s, who continued to have their plays produced, was joined by some new women playwrights. Susanna Centlivre would be the most successful of the newcomers, although she would prove to be much more adept with comedy than tragedy, particularly after her 1709 coup *The Busy Bodie* and its sequel *Marplot* the following year.[1] Stanton's data concerning the most successful women dramatists of the period 1660–1800 places her at the very top, above Aphra Behn and Elizabeth Inchbald, with nineteen plays both staged and published.[2] Interestingly, the second most popular tragedy of the whole period was *Antiochus the Great or, the False Relapse*, by an unknown young woman called Jane Wiseman.[3] *Antiochus the Great* was staged in the season of 1701 by Betterton's Company and published in 1702 with a dedicatory letter to John Jefferies, Baron of Wem, referring to the success of the play, which may have been owing, at least in part, to the skills of the experienced actors playing the lead characters, Mr. Powell and Mrs. Barry.[4] Of Wiseman herself, nothing is known with any certainty, except that she was close to playwrights such as Centlivre and Farquhar, and that she may have left the stage after getting married and setting up a tavern on the proceeds of her one play.[5] If *Antiochus the Great* was actually her

---

[1] For William J. Burling, Centlivre's most remarkable feat is the creation of 'three comedies that held the stage for more than a century, *The Busy Bodie* (1709), *The Wonder* (1714), and *A Bold Stroke for a Wife* (1718),' while her only serious play of note is *The Cruel Gift*, performed late in 1716 ('"Their Empire Disjoyn'd": Serious Plays by Women on the London Stage, 1660–1737,' in *Curtain Calls: British and American Women and the Theater, 1660–1820*, ed. Mary Anne Schofield and Cecilia Macheski (Athens: Ohio University Press, 1991), p. 320.

[2] Judith Phillips Stanton, '"This New-Found Path Attempting": Women Dramatists in England, 1660–1800,' in *Curtain Calls*, p. 336.

[3] Stanton, '"This New-Found Path Attempting,"' p. 334. Stanton ranks the plays on the grounds of the number of years they were produced. The most successful tragedy appears to have been Pix's *Ibrahim*, followed by *Antiochus the Great* and then Behn's *Abdelazer*.

[4] George Jefferies, father to John, was a Tory who served as Lord Chancellor to James II and died in the Tower of London after the Glorious Revolution. Little is known of his son, and the Tory partisanship of the father makes him an odd choice for Wiseman, who according to Kendall might have been a Whig (*Love and Thunder*, London: Methuen, 1988, p. 115).

[5] Kendall, *Love and Thunder*, p. 114.

first and only dramatic work, then it was certainly 'an astonishing achievement.'[6] Burling considers it 'unfortunately neglected [because] it ranks among the best love-triangle plots, and afforded Mrs. Barry and Mrs. Bracegirdle a vehicle for their special skills in portraying tormented women.'[7]

Wiseman spins a domestic tale of tyranny around the figure of the title king, Antiochus, originally one of the successors of Alexander the Great in Asia, who earned the name 'the Great' for his struggle to restore the empire to its former greatness. The Antiochus of Wiseman's tragedy, however, is described as a tyrant who has seduced the noble Leodice and has had a son by her but has later retracted his promises of marriage in favor of a marriage of state to Berenice, daughter to Philadelphus, king of Egypt, with whom he had been at war. The love plot thus pits Leodice and Berenice against each other in terms similar to those concerning Herod's cast-away first wife Doris and his second wife Mariam in Elizabeth Cary's tragedy. Leodice's rage at being abused by her lover is directed against him, but also against 'an Usurping Queen,/ Who by the Priviledge of all Empty Title/ Possesses all my Right.'[8]

In addition, Antiochus's marriage, like Herod's, alters the succession by making his son by Leodice illegitimate, while his ensuing progeny by Berenice would be next in line to the throne. This is one of the key issues in the play, just as it was in *The Tragedy of Mariam*, and Leodice, like Doris, draws much of her strong will against the tyrant from deep concerns regarding her son's future. However, instead of encouraging the child to plan for revenge, Leodice uses him affectively, by sending him close to his father with instructions to influence Antiochus's emotions in their favor. Accordingly, one of the most pathetic scenes in the play sets father and son face to face, the child innocently asking 'What have I done to anger you?/ You never send to bring me to your sight,/ Nor take me in your Arms now I am come,/ As you were us'd to do.'[9] The emotional impact of this confrontation on the audience was doubtlessly high. Likewise, Antiochus declares he is overcome by the boy's entreaties, calls himself 'a faithless, perjur'd king' and states his regret at having so mistreated mother and son.

Yet, the king exhibits most of the worst traits derided by Whig partisans, including a hedonistic lifestyle, sexual promiscuity, and whimsical behavior, and eventually he dies a victim to Leodice's rage, who justifies her actions thus:

> Inconstant Monarch, what cou'd I do less?
> Was I not scorn'd when Banish'd? Now a Prisoner.
> I Lov'd you, and was treated ill.
> In private, and by stealth oblig'd;
> But openly Dejected and Disgrac'd.[10]

---

[6] Kendall, *Love and Thunder*, p. 115.

[7] Burling, 'Their Empire Disjoyn'd,' p. 321. However, the published play lists Mrs. Barry and Mrs. Bowman (not Mrs. Bracegirdle) in the cast.

[8] Jane Wiseman, *Antiochus the Great*, in Kendall, *Love and Thunder*, p. 119.

[9] *Antiochus the Great*, p. 134.

[10] *Antiochus the Great*, p. 149.

Like Lamira in Trotter's *Fatal Friendship*, also acted by Mrs. Barry, Leodice is given voice to loudly complain against her mistreatment by those who allegedly should have protected her, and in that respect she departs from the stereotype of the villainess. Yet, like other seduced women in the period's tragedies, namely Jacincta in *The Conquest of Spain*, she is not allowed to survive her fall from innocence, and she too drinks of the poison that allows her to fulfill her vengeance against her seducer.

Leodice's rival Berenice closely meets the standards of female virtue and survives a false accusation of unfaithfulness with her former suitor Ormades, who has followed her to Antiochus's court. Although she is very much in love with him, she prepares thoroughly in order to send him on his way with a cold good-bye, distancing her private self from her state persona: 'I come, Ormades, but I come the Queen,'[11] she says on her way to their meeting. However, like Leodice, she is a complex character who refuses to take virtuous behavior to its last consequences by meekly accepting a husband she loathes and who has wrongly distrusted her, so in being offered a chance for reconciliation, she instead replies with abhorrence:

> Restor'd to thee! To thy loath'd Arms!
> Stand off thou Tyrant! I detest thee now.
> See where my dear Ormades bleeding lies,
> The untimely Sacrifice to thy curst Jealousie.[12]

While the contrasting pair Leodice/Berenice affords Wiseman an already conventional exploration of the nuances of female virtue and deviancy, Ormades helps Wiseman set up a comparison between the relative qualities of birth and merit. Unlike Antiochus, whose right of birth is not balanced by the right traits, Ormades is described as bearing the characteristics of the warrior hero, for 'All Egypt lately wonder'd at his Actions./ Fame had no leasure but to sound his Praise:/ Still he was foremost to the bloody Field,/ And Fought, and Conquer'd like a Demi-God.'[13] Ormades is also an honest, selfless, and considerate friend, and a faithful lover, all of them traits Antiochus fails to display. Using staple elements of early eighteenth-century serious drama, Wiseman manages to produce an interesting, consistent play that raises within a domestic framework already familiar questions about the power and responsibilities of the monarchy from a Whig perspective.

Anne Finch and Jacobite Aesthetics

Perhaps one of the best examples of how Tory-Whig tensions in England concerning the Stuart monarchy persisted in English drama well into the eighteenth century is Anne Finch's work. Finch (née Kingsmill) was Maid of Honor to James II's

---

[11] *Antiochus the Great*, p. 140.
[12] *Antiochus the Great*, p. 144.
[13] *Antiochus the Great*, p. 137.

second wife, Mary of Modena, and thus part of an entourage of young women who read in several languages, watched and performed plays, sang, and even painted. For Barash,

> Like many of the major women writers of the later seventeenth and early eighteenth centuries—Anne Killigrew, Aphra Behn, Jane Barker, Delarivier Manley, and Sarah Churchill—Anne Finch wrote her earliest poetry in response to the female community and mythic female authority engendered by James II's second and Catholic wife, Mary of Modena.[14]

She seems to have taken up writing more seriously after her marriage to Heneage Finch in 1684.[15] Although she is best known for her poetry, she authored two plays, the tragicomedy *The Triumphs of Love and Innocence*, written around this period, and the tragedy *Aristomenes: or, the Royal Shepherd*, which seems to have been penned in 1690. In a foreword to *The Triumphs*, however, Finch expressed her total opposition to having her work performed, stating that 'a more terrible injury cannot be offer'd me, then to occasion, or permit them ever to be represented.'[16] She was also very critical of her own work, so much so that only *Aristomenes* would find its way to publication in the folio edition of 1713 (*Miscellany Poems on Several Occasions*), while her tragicomedy remained in manuscript form. She dedicates *Aristomenes* to her husband, emphasizing once more that she prefers and fears his judgment over that of the pit and boxes, and claims that her work is 'plain, and homely fare' meant not for court entertainment but to enjoy in the country 'by a good winter's fire.'[17] However, both plays are closer to court preoccupations than Finch would care to acknowledge, since they engage with such topics as legitimate rule, kingship, and exile, and thus convey Finch's anxieties concerning the Stuart succession, the exile of James II, and her own—personal and familial—Jacobite sympathies.

Aristomenes seems to have been written at an extremely taxing time, in the aftermath of the Glorious Revolution, as she awaited the trial against her husband, who had tried to join the royal family in France. After his release, they retired to the countryside, to the property in Eastwell (Kent) of their kinsman the Earl of Winchilsea, from whom they would inherit the title in 1712. As non-jurors, their social and economic situation remained precarious, and they seldom left their exile, although contact and visits with writers such as Congreve and Pope seem to have been fairly regular.

---

[14] Carol Barash, 'The Political Origins of Anne Finch's Poetry,' *The Huntington Library Quarterly* 54.4 (1991), pp. 329–30.

[15] Barbara McGovern, *Anne Finch and Her Poetry: A Critical Biography* (Athens: The University of Georgia Press, 1992), p. 53.

[16] Myra Reynolds, *The Poems of Anne Countess of Winchilsea*, Chicago: The University of Chicago Press, 1903, p. 271.

[17] Reynolds, *The Poems of Anne Countess of Winchilsea*, p. 337.

Like Margaret Cavendish before her, Finch portrays a kingdom torn by war and threatened by foreign invasion, where aristocratic values continue to offer hope for survival and prosperity. Although Hellenistic motifs and topics never actually disappeared from the English stage, renewed interest in the classical pastoral world would seem to be particularly in tune with Augustan stylistic concerns while reaching backwards to the aesthetics of seventeenth-century royalism. Finch's tragedy is inspired by the Greek historian Pausanias, who describes the wars of Messenians and Spartans in book IV of his *Guide to Greece*. Pausanias recounts several pseudo-mythical stories concerning the Messenian leader Aristomenes, how he once escaped by following a vixen, and how on a separate occasion he was rescued from imprisonment by a young maid whom he rewarded by giving her his son Gorgon in marriage.[18]

These stories found their way into Finch's plot. Demagetus, Prince of Rhodes, roams the Messenian countryside disguised as a shepherd called Climander. His purpose is to find the woman the Oracle has determined he must marry in order to bring peace to his kingdom. Since the only information given by the Oracle is that she will be 'the Beauteous Daughter of the Best of Men,' he estimates she is most likely to be found among 'simple Swains,' for 'perfect Innocence, and Virtue/ Was to be found but in their lowly Rank.'[19] During his stay, however, he finds not the idyllic fields, woods, and groves characteristic of the pastoral world, but lands overrun by wars between the Messenians and the invading Lacedemonians from which their inhabitants run in fright: 'For all the Lawns, that lie beyond the Hill, / Where still our Flocks were us'd to feed in peace, Are fill'd with War, and dark with flying Arrows.'[20] Constrained as he is by the Oracle's predictions, Demagetus/Climander finds it hard not to join the Messenians' party and their leader Aristomenes, and as the heroic resistance of the Messenians weakens with the news of their leader's capture, Demagetus enters the battle against the Lacedemonians. Finch thus shows the fall from grace that Messenia (that is, England) has experienced from the vantage point of an outsider, who also manages to introduce an admiring account of the leader's many qualities.

Finch successfully interweaves the love conventions of the (disrupted) pastoral world with the heroic plot. Among the fleeing Messenians is Aristomenes' daughter Herminia disguised as a shepherdess, whom Demagetus succors while he is still wearing Climander's name and appearance. On hearing that her father was declared by an Oracle 'of all the Grecian Race to be the Best,'[21] Demagetus declares his love, claiming that fate has joined them, but Herminia is wary of their difference in rank, and events delay the disclosure of their true identities until the end of

---

[18] Pausanias, *Guide to Greece: Southern Greece*, trans. Peter Levi (Harmondsworth: Penguin Classics, 1971), pp. 146–7.
[19] Anne Finch, *Aristomenes: or, The Royal Shepherd*, in Reynolds, *The Poems of Anne Countess of Winchilsea*, p. 340.
[20] *Aristomenes*, p. 342.
[21] *Aristomenes*, p. 364.

the play. A second love affair develops between Amalintha, daughter to the king of the Lacedemonians, Anaxander, and Aristomenes's son Aristor, who had met during a hunt when he saved her life. Now the Messenian father and son are on the run, and Amalintha helps them both as much as she can. Here Finch draws from Pausanias's account, by contriving to have Amalintha meet Aristomenes, who has managed to escape his dungeon cell by following a fox and, on recognizing him, helps him with directions to leave the palace grounds, as well as with a dagger. His return is acclaimed by the humble countryside people, who rejoice:

> He is return'd, and stands, like Fate, amongt 'em,
> The Plain's Protector, and the Army's Genius,
> The Virgin's Refuge, when the Town's in Flames,
> And Shield to those whom Fortune makes his Vassals.[22]

Aristomenes's arrival restores the happy cycle of the natural world, celebrated gaily by its inhabitants:

> To Laugh, to Sing, to Dance, to Play,
> To rise with new appearing Day;
> And ere the Sun has kiss'd 'em dry,
> With various Rubans Nosegays tye.
> Deckt with Flow'rs and cloath'd in Green,
> Ev'ry Shepherdess be seen:
> Ev'ry Swain with Heart and Voice
> Meet him, meet him, and rejoice:
> With redoubl'd Paeans sing him,
> To the Plains, in Triumph to bring him:
> And let Pan and Mars agree,
> That none's son kind and brave as He.[23]

The happy conclusion of Act III, however, is short lived, as are the reunions of the two young couples in Act IV, since the war with the Lacedemonians rages on. Finch brings the play to a climactic end in the final battle, during which some Lacedemonians infiltrate the Messenian camp in order to punish Amalintha for her betrayal, and they seriously wound both her and Aristor, who came to her assistance. With these materials Finch constructs a most effectively moving scene in which the two lovers take their parting while trying to keep from the other the fact that they are dying, and they expire in each others' arms, pledging their eternal love. But the spotlight remains on Aristomenes' dignified pain as he surveys the cost of his victory—'Defeated Armies, slaughter'd Friends are here;/ Disgraceful Bonds, and Cities laid in Ashes'—and he stoically accepts his fate: 'By Fortune favoured now, and now oprrest,/ And not, 'till Death, secure of Fame, or Rest.'[24]

---

[22] *Aristomenes*, p. 378.
[23] *Aristomenes*, p. 379–80.
[24] *Aristomenes*, p. 410.

Finch's tragedy thus evinces clear marks of the author's hardship in the aftermath of the Glorious Revolution and, most of all, attests to the strength of her Jacobite partisanship, remarkably in the portrayal of Aristomenes as a stand-in for James II. Moreover, her decision to include it among those writings she selected for publication in the folio edition of 1713, when Queen Anne's death was imminent, notably suggests that she never stopped wishing for a second Stuart Restoration. Although James II had long been dead, Finch may have thought that the publication of this play might remind readers of the qualities of the Catholic Stuarts and help turn public opinion against the Hanoverian succession, strengthening the claim of his son to the crown. Her hopes, like those of other Tory non-jurors, would be dashed by the failure of the Jacobite Rebellion of 1715.

Aristomenes also allows us to close this examination of Stuart women playwrights' works by providing further evidence of the power of the tragic genre as a vehicle for the partisan and domestic concerns of their authors. All in all, through shifting patterns of characterization, plotting, and socio-historical backgrounds, the tragedies under analysis here display outstanding commonalities running through the seventeenth century and well into the eighteenth. Gender and genre, as we suggested at the beginning of our study, establish challenging and thought-provoking links that have so far been neglected and that deserve to be teased out further.

Works Cited

Primary Sources

Behn, Aphra, *Abdelazer, or the Moor's Revenge*, in *The Works of Aphra Behn, vol. 5*, ed. Janet Todd, London: William Pickering, 1996, pp. 239–315.
———, *Agnes de Castro*, in *The Works of Aphra Behn, vol. 3*, ed. Janet Todd, London: William Pickering, 1996, pp. 121–61.
———, *The Forc'd Marriage, or the Jealous Bridegroom*, in *The Works of Aphra Behn, vol. 5*, ed. Janet Todd, London: William Pickering, 1996, pp. 1–81.
———, *The Luckey Chance*, in *The Works of Aphra Behn, vol. 7*, ed. Janet Todd, London: Pickering, 1996, pp. 209–84.
———, *The Widdow Ranter or, the History of Bacon in Virginia*, in *The Works of Aphra Behn, vol. 7*, ed. Janet Todd, London: William Pickering, 1996, pp. 285–354.
———, *The Young King, or the Mistake*, in *The Works of Aphra Behn, vol. 7*, ed. Janet Todd, London: William Pickering, 1996, pp. 79–151.
Boothby, Frances, *Marcelia, or the Treacherous Friend*, in *The Early Modern Englishwoman: A Facsimile Library of Essential Works, series II. Printed Writings, 1641–1700: Part 1, vol.7: Miscellaneous Plays*, gen. eds. Betty S. Travitsky and Patrick Cullen, Aldershot: Ashgate, 2000.
Cary, Elizabeth, *The Tragedy of Mariam, the Fair Queen of Jewry, with The Lady Falkland: Her Life, by One of her Daughters*, ed. Barry Weller and Margaret W. Ferguson, Berkeley: University of California Press, 1994.
Cavendish, Margaret, *Bell in Campo, Parts I and II*, in *Margaret Cavendish, Duchess of Newcastle: The Convent of Pleasure and Other Plays*, ed. Anne Shaver, Baltimore: The Johns Hopkins University Press, 1999, pp. 107–69.
———, *The Lady Contemplation, Parts I & II*, in *Playes Written by the Thrice Noble, Illustrious and Excellent Princess, the Lady Marchiones of Newcastle*, London: Printed by A. Warren, for John Martyn, James Allestry, and Tho. Dicas, 1662, pp. 181–246.
———, *Loves Adventures, Parts I and II*, in *Margaret Cavendish, Duchess of Newcastle: The Convent of Pleasure and Other Plays*, ed. Anne Shaver, Baltimore: The Johns Hopkins University Press, 1999, pp. 21–106.
———, *The Unnatural Tragedie*, in *Playes Written by the Thrice Noble, Illustrious and Excellent Princess, the Lady Marchiones of Newcastle*, London: Printed by A. Warren, for John Martyn, James Allestry, and Tho. Dicas, 1662, pp. 323–66.
———, *Youths Glory and Deaths Banquet, Parts I & II*, in *Playes Written by the Thrice Noble, Illustrious and Excellent Princess, the Lady Marchiones of Newcastle*, London: Printed by A. Warren, for John Martyn, James Allestry, and Tho. Dicas, 1662, pp. 122–80.

Finch, Anne, *Aristomenes: or, The Royal Shepherd*, in *The Poems of Anne Countess of Winchilsea*, ed. Myra Reynolds, Chicago: University of Chicago Press, pp. 337–411.
Manley, Delarivier, *Almyna: or, the Arabian Vow*. London: Printed for William Turner, 1707.
―――, *Lucius, the First Christian King of Britain*, ed. Jack M. Armistead and Debbie K. Davies, The Augustan Reprint Society, Los Angeles: William Clark Memorial Library, 1989.
―――, *The Royal Mischief*, in *Eighteenth-Century Women Playwrights, vol. 1: Delarivier Manley and Eliza Haywood*, ed. Margarete Rubik and Eva Mueller-Zettelmann, London: Pickering & Chatto, 2001, pp. 43–104.
Pix, Mary, *The Conquest of Spain*, in *The Plays of Mary Pix and Catharine Trotter, vol. 1*, ed. Edna Steeves, New York: Garland, 1982.
―――, *Ibrahim, the Thirteenth Emperour of the Turks*, in *The Plays of Mary Pix and Catharine Trotter, vol. 1*, ed. Edna Steeves, New York: Garland, 1982.
―――, *Queen Catharine: or, the Ruines of Love*, in *Eighteenth-Century Women Playwrights, vol. 2: Mary Pix and Catharine Trotter*, ed. Anne Kelley, London: Pickering and Chatto, 2001, pp. 67–128.
Purkiss, Diane, ed., *Three Tragedies by Renaissance Women*, London: Penguin, 1998.
Sidney, Sir Philip, 'The Defence of Poesy,' in *Selected Writings*, ed. Richard Dutton, Manchester: Carcanet, 1987, pp. 102–48.
Trotter, Catharine, *Agnes de Castro*, in *Catharine Trotter's* The Adventures of a Young Lady and Other Works, ed. Anne Kelley, Aldershot: Ashgate, 2006, pp. 1–48.
―――, *Fatal Friendship*, in *Catharine Trotter's* The Adventures of a Young Lady and Other Works, ed. Anne Kelley, Aldershot: Ashgate, 2006, pp. 210–289.
―――, *The Revolution of Sweden*, in *Eighteenth-Century Women Playwrights*, vol. 2, ed. Anne Kelley, London: Pickering & Chatto, 2001, pp. 193–276.
―――, *The Unhappy Penitent*, London: Printed for William Turner and John Nutt, 1701.
Wiseman, Jane, *Antiochus the Great or, The Fatal Relapse*, in *Love and Thunder: Plays by Women in the Age of Queen Anne*, ed. Kendall, London: Methuen, 1988, pp. 113–53.

Secondary Sources

Adam, Michel, 'L'héroïne tragique dans le théâtre de Catherine Trotter,' *Aspects du théâtre anglais: 1594–1730*, ed. Nadia Rigaud, n.p.: Université de Provence, 1987, pp. 97–115.
Altaba-Artal, Dolors, *Aphra Behn's English Feminism: Wit and Satire*, London: Associated University Presses, 1999.
Andrea, Bernadette, *Women and Islam in Early Modern English Literature*, Cambridge: Cambridge University Press, 2007.

Backscheider, Paula, *Spectacular Politics: Theatrical Power and Mass Culture in Early Modern England*, Baltimore: The Johns Hopkins University Press, 1993.
Ballaster, Ros, *Fabulous Orients: Fictions of the East in England, 1662–1785*, Oxford: Oxford University Press, 2005.
Barash, Carol, 'The Political Origins of Anne Finch's Poetry,' *The Huntington Library Quarterly* 54.4 (1991), pp. 327–51.
Battigelli, Anna, *Margaret Cavendish and the Exiles of the Mind*, Lexington: The University Press of Kentucky, 1998.
Beilin, Elaine V., *Redeeming Eve: Women Writers of the English Renaissance*, Princeton: Princeton University Press, 1987.
Belsey, Catherine, *The Subject of Tragedy: Identity and Difference in Renaissance Drama*, London: Routledge, 1985.
Bennett, Alexandra G., 'Female Performativity in *The Tragedy of Mariam*,' *Studies in English Literature* 40.2 (2000), 293–309.
———, 'Margaret Cavendish and the Theatre of War,' *In-Between: Essays and Studies in Literary Criticism* 9:1 & 2 (2000), pp. 263–73.
———, 'Testifying in the Court of Public Opinion: Margaret Cavendish Reworks *The Winter's Tale*,' in *Cavendish and Shakespeare, Interconnections*, ed. Katherine Romack and James Fitzmaurice, Aldershot: Ashgate, 2006, pp. 85–102.
———, ed., *Margaret Cavendish:* Bell in Campo *and* The Sociable Companions, Peterborough: Broadview Press, 2002.
Birchwood, Matthew, *Staging Islam in England, Drama and Culture, 1640–1685*, Cambridge: D.S. Brewer, 2007.
Boehrer, Bruce Thomas, *Monarchy and Incest in Renaissance England*, Philadelphia: University of Pennsylvania Press 1992.
Bonin, Erin Lang, 'Margaret Cavendish's Dramatic Utopias and the Politics of Gender,' *Studies in English Literature* 40.2 (2000), pp. 339–54.
Bowerbank, Sylvia, "The Spider's Delight: Margaret Cavendish and the "Female Imagination,"' *English Literary Renaissance* 14.3 (1984), pp. 392–408.
Braden, Gordon, *Renaissance Tragedy and the Senecan Tradition: Anger's Privilege*, New Haven: Yale University Press, 1985.
Brant, Clare and Diane Purkiss, eds., *Women, Texts and Histories 1575–1760*, London: Routledge, 1992.
Breitenberg, Mark, *Anxious Masculinity in Early Modern England*, Cambridge: Cambridge University Press, 1996.
Bridges, Liz, '"We were somebody in England": Identity, Gender, and Status in *The Widdow Ranter*,' in *Aphra Behn (1640–1689). Identity, Alterity, Ambiguity*, ed. Mary Anne O'Donnell, Bernhard Dhuicq, and Guy Leduc, Paris: L'Harmattan, 2000, pp. 75–80.
Brown, Laura, 'The Defenseless Woman and the Development of English Tragedy,' *Studies in English Literature, 1500–1900*, 22.3 (1982), pp. 429–43.
———, *English Dramatic Form, 1660–1760*, New Haven: Yale University Press, 1981.

Burks, Deborah G., *Horrid Spectacle: Violation in the Theater of Early Modern England*, Pittsburgh: Duquesne University Press, 2003.

Burling, William J., '"Their Empire Disjoyn'd": Serious Plays by Women on the London Stage, 1660–1737,' in *Curtain Calls: British and American Women and the Theater, 1660–1820*, ed. Mary Anne Schofield and Cecilia Macheski, Athens: Ohio University Press, 1991, pp. 311–24.

Bushnell, Rebecca, 'The Fall of Princes: the Classical and Medieval Roots of English Renaissance Tragedy,' in *A Companion to Tragedy*, ed. Rebecca Bushnell, Oxford: Blackwell, 2005, pp. 289–306.

Callaghan, Dympna, 'Re-Reading Elizabeth Cary's *The Tragedy of Mariam, Faire Queene of Jewry*,' in *Women, "Race," and Writing in the Early Modern Period*, ed. Margo Hendricks and Patricia Parker, London: Routledge, 1994, pp. 163–77.

———, *Woman and Gender in Renaissance Tragedy*, New York: Harvester Wheatsheaf, 1989.

Canfield, J. Douglas, *Heroes and States: On the Ideology of Restoration Tragedy*, Lexington: The University Press of Kentucky, 2000.

———, 'Shifting Tropes of Ideology in English Serious Drama, Late Stuart to Early Georgian,' in *Cultural Readings of Restoration and 18th-Century English Theater*, ed. J. Douglas Canfield and Deborah C. Payne, Atlanta: University of Georgia Press, 1995, pp. 195–227.

Carnell, Rachel K., *A Political Biography of Delarivier Manley*, London: Pickering and Chatto, 2008.

———, 'Subverting Tragic Conventions: Aphra Behn's Turn to the Novel,' *Studies in the Novel* 31.2 (1999), pp. 133–51.

Cartwright, Kent, *Theatre and Humanism*, Cambridge: Cambridge University Press, 1999.

Chalmers, Hero, 'Dismantling the Myth of "Mad Madge": the Cultural Context of Margaret Cavendish's Authorial Self-Presentation,' *Women's Writing* 4.3 (1997), pp. 323–39.

———, 'The Politics of Feminine Retreat in Margaret Cavendish's *The Female Academy* and *The Convent of Pleasure*,' *Women's Writing* 6.1 (1999), pp. 81–94.

———, *Royalist Women Writers 1650–1689*, Oxford: Clarendon Press, 2004.

Clarke, Danielle, *The Politics of Early Modern Women's Writing*, Harlow: Pearson Education, 2001.

Clucas, Stephen, ed., *A Princely Brave Woman: Essays on Margaret Cavendish, Duchess of Newcastle*, Aldershot: Ashgate, 2003.

Cohen, Walter, 'Prerevolutionary Drama,' in *The Politics of Tragicomedy: Shakespeare and After*, ed. Gordon McMullan and Jonathan Hope, London: Routledge, 1992, pp. 122–50.

Corporaal, Marguérite, 'An Empowering Wit and an "Unnatural" Tragedy: Margaret Cavendish's Representation of the Tragic Female Voice,' *Early Modern Literary Studies* Special Issue 14 (2004.), pp. 12.1–26 <URL: http://purl.oclc.org/emls/si-14/corpempo.html>.

Cottegnies, Line, and Nancy Weitz, eds., *Authorial Conquests: Essays on Genre in the Writings of Margaret Cavendish*, Madison: Fairleigh Dickinson University Press, 2003.

Cotton, Nancy, *Women Playwrights in England, c. 1363–1750*, Lewisburg: Bucknell University Press, 1980.

Cuder-Domínguez, Pilar, 'Iberian State Politics in Aphra Behn's Writing,' in *Aphra Behn (1640–1689): Le modèle européen*, ed. Mary Ann O'Donnell and Bernard Dhuicq, Paris: Bilingua GA Editions, 2005, pp. 45–51.

———, 'The Islamization of Spain in William Rowley and Mary Pix: The Politics of Gender and Nation,' *Comparative Drama* 36.3–4 (2002–03), pp. 321–36.

D'Monté, Rebecca, '"Making a Spectacle": Margaret Cavendish and the Staging of the Self,' in *A Princely Brave Woman: Essays on Margaret Cavendish, Duchess of Newcastle*, ed. Stephen Clucas, Aldershot: Ashgate, 2003, pp. 109–26.

Dobrée, Bonamy, *Restoration Tragedy, 1660–1720*, Oxford: Clarendon Press, 1929.

Dolan, Frances E., '"Gentlemen, I Have One Thing More To Say": Women on Scaffolds in England, 1563–1680,' *Modern Philology* 92.2 (1994), pp. 157–78.

Donoghue, Emma, *Passions Between Women: British Lesbian Culture 1668–1801*, London: Scarlet Press, 1993.

Ezell, Margaret J. M., *Writing Women's Literary History*, Baltimore: The Johns Hopkins University Press, 1993.

Felski, Rita, ed., *Rethinking Tragedy*, Baltimore: The Johns Hopkins University Press, 2008.

Ferguson, Margaret W., 'The Spectre of Resistance: *The Tragedy of Mariam* (1613),' in *Staging the Renaissance: Essays on Elizabethan and Jacobean Drama*, ed. David Scott Kastan and Peter Stallybrass, London: Routledge, 1991, pp. 235–50.

Ferguson, Moira, '"A wise, wittie and learned lady": Margaret Cavendish,' in *Women Writers of the 17th Century*, ed. Katharina M. Wilson and Frank J. Warnke, Athens: University of Georgia Press, 1989, pp. 305–40.

Figueroa Dorrego, Jorge, 'Cultural Confrontations in Aphra Behn's *Oroonoko* and *The Widow Ranter*,' in *Culture and Power IV: Cultural Confrontations*, ed. Chantal Cornut-Gentille D'Arcy, Zaragoza: Universidad de Zaragoza, 1999, pp. 193–201.

Findlay, Alison, *A Feminist Perspective on Renaissance Drama*, Oxford: Blackwell, 1999.

Findlay, Alison, and Stephanie Hodgson-Wright with Gweno Williams, *Women and Dramatic Production 1550–1700*, Harlow: Pearson, 2000.

Findlay, Alison, Gweno Williams, and Stephanie J. Hodgson-Wright, '"The Play is ready to be Acted": Women and Dramatic Production, 1570–1670,' *Women's Writing* 6.1 (1999), pp. 129–48.

Fitzmaurice, James, 'Shakespeare, Cavendish, and Reading Aloud in Seventeenth-Century England,' in *Cavendish and Shakespeare, Interconnections*, ed. Katherine Romack and James Fitzmaurice, Aldershot: Ashgate, 2006, pp. 29–46.

Foster, Verna A., *The Name and Nature of Tragicomedy*, Aldershot: Ashgate, 2004.

Gómez-Lara, Manuel José, 'The Politics of Modesty: The Collier Controversy and the Societies for the Reformation of Manners,' in *The Female Wits: Women and Gender in Restoration Literature and Culture*, ed. Pilar Cuder-Domínguez, Zenón Luis-Martínez, and Juan A. Prieto-Pablos, Huelva: Servicio de Publicaciones de la Universidad de Huelva, 2006.

Goodkin, Richard E. 'Neoclassical Dramatic Theory in Seventeenth-Century France,' in *A Companion to Tragedy*, ed. Rebecca Bushnell, Oxford: Blackwell, 2005, pp. 374–90.

Green, Reina, '"Ears Prejudicate" in *Mariam* and *Duchess of Malfi*,' *Studies in English Literature* 43.2 (2003), pp. 459–74.

Gruber, Elizabeth, 'Insurgent Flesh: Epistemology and Violence in *Othello* and *Mariam*,' *Women's Studies* 32 (2003), pp. 393–410.

Grundy, Isobel, and Susan Wiseman, eds., *Women, Writing, History 1640–1740*, Athens: University of Georgia Press, 1992.

Hannay, Margaret P. 'Patronesse of the Muses,' in *Readings in Renaissance Women's Drama. Criticism, History and Performance 1594–1998*, ed. S. P. Cerasano and Marion Wynne-Davies, London: Routledge, 1998, pp. 142–55.

Heller, Jennifer L., 'Space, Violence, and Bodies in Middleton and Cary,' *Studies in English Literature* 45.2 (2005), pp. 425–41.

Herman, Ruth, *The Business of a Woman. The Political Writings of Delarivier Manley*, Newark: University of Delaware Press, 2003.

Hiscock, Andrew, 'The Hateful Cuckoo: Elizabeth Cary's *Tragedie of Mariam*, a Renaissance Drama of Dispossession,' *Forum for Modern Language Studies* 33.2 (1997), pp. 97–114.

———, '"Here's no design, no plot, nor any ground": the Drama of Margaret Cavendish and the Disorderly Woman,' *Women's Writing* 4.3 (1997), pp. 401–20.

Hobby, Elaine, *Virtue of Necessity: English Women's Writing 1646–1688*, London: Virago, 1988.

Hodgson-Wright, Stephanie, 'Jane Lumley's *Iphigenia at Aulis. Multum in parvo*, or less is more,' in *Readings in Renaissance Women's Drama. Criticism, History and Performance 1594–1998*, ed. S. P. Cerasano and Marion Wynne-Davies, London: Routledge, 1998, pp. 129–41.

Hopkins, Lisa, *The Female Hero in English Renaissance Tragedy*. London: Macmillan Palgrave, 2002.

Howe, Elizabeth, *The First English Actresses*, Cambridge: Cambridge University Press, 1992.

Hughes, Derek, and Janet Todd, eds., *The Cambridge Companion to Aphra Behn*, Cambridge: Cambridge University Press, 2004.

Hughes, Derek, *English Drama, 1660–1700*, Oxford: Clarendon, 1996.

———, 'Frances Boothby,' *Oxford Dictionary of National Biography*, Oxford University Press, 2004–09, online edition.

———, *The Theatre of Aphra Behn*, London: Palgrave, 2001.

Hutner, Heidi, *Colonial Women: Race and Culture in Stuart Drama*, Oxford: Oxford University Press, 2001.

———, ed., *Rereading Aphra Behn; History, Theory, and Criticism*, Charlottesville: University Press of Virginia, 1993.

Kelley, Anne, *Catharine Trotter: An Early Modern Writer in the Vanguard of Feminism*, Aldershot: Ashgate, 2002.

———, '"In Search of Truths Sublime": Reason and the Body in the Writings of Catharine Trotter,' *Women's Writing* 8.2 (2001), pp. 235–50.

Kelly, Erin E., 'Mariam and Discourses of Martyrdom,' in *The Literary Career and Legacy of Elizabeth Cary, 1613–1680*, ed. Heather Wolfe, London: Palgrave Macmillan, 2007, pp. 35–52.

Kendall, ed., *Love and Thunder: Plays by Women in the Age of Queen Anne*, London: Methuen, 1988.

King, Heather, '"Be Mistress of Your Self, and Firm to Virtue": Female Friendship in Catharine Trotter's *The Unhappy Penitent* (1701),' *Eighteenth-Century Women* 3 (2003), pp. 1–23.

King, Kathryn P., 'Essay Review: Female Agency and Feminocentric Romance,' *The Eighteenth Century* 41.1 (2000), pp. 56–65.

Kroll, Richard, *Restoration Drama and the 'Circle of Commerce': Tragicomedy, Politics, and Trade in the Seventeenth Century*, Cambridge: Cambridge University Press, 2007.

Krontiris, Tina, 'Mary Herbert. Englishing a purified Cleopatra,' in *Readings in Renaissance Women's Drama. Criticism, History and Performance 1594–1998*, ed. S. P. Cerasano and Marion Wynne-Davies, London: Routledge, 1998, pp. 156–66.

Lamb, Mary Ellen, *Gender and Authorship in the Sidney Circle*, Madison: University of Wisconsin Press, 1990.

Lennep, William van, ed., *The London Stage 1660–1800. Part I: 1660–1700*, Carbondale: Southern Illinois University Press, 1965.

Lewalski, Barbara K., *Writing Women in Jacobean England*, Cambridge, Mass: Harvard University Press, 1993.

Loftis, John, *The Spanish Plays of Neoclassical England*, New Haven: Yale University Press, 1973.

Loomba, Ania, *Gender, Race, Renaissance Tragedy*, Oxford: Oxford University Press, 1989.

López-Peláez Casellas, Jesús, 'The Enemy Within: Otherness in Thomas Dekker's *Lust's Dominion*,' *Sederi* 9 (1998), pp. 203–07.

———, '"Race" and the Construction of English National Identity: Spaniards and North Africans in English Seventeenth-Century Drama,' *Studies in Philology* 106 (2009), pp. 32–51.

Lowenthal, Cynthia, *Performing Identities on the Restoration Stage*, Carbondale: Southern Illinois University Press, 2003.

Luis-Martínez, Zenón, '"Human Eyes Dazed by Woman's Wit": Gendering Bodies and Minds in English Renaissance Poetry and Drama' in *La mujer del texto al contexto*, ed. Laura P. Alonso, Pilar Cuder, and Zenón Luis, Huelva: Servicio de Publicaciones de la Universidad de Huelva, 1996, pp. 69–89.

———, 'Mary Pix's *Queen Catharine* and the Interruption of History,' in *Reshaping the Genres: Restoration Women Writers*, ed. Zenón Luis-Martínez and Jorge Figueroa-Dorrego, Bern: Peter Lang, 2003, pp. 175–209.

———, *In Words and Deeds: The Spectacle of Incest in English Renaissance Drama*, Amsterdam: Rodopi, 2002.

MacDonald, Joyce Green, *Women and Race in Early Modern Texts*, Cambridge: Cambridge University Press, 2002.

Maguire, Nancy Klein, *Regicide and Restoration: English Tragicomedy, 1660–1671*, Cambridge: Cambridge University Press, 1992.

———, 'Tragicomedy,' in *The Cambridge Companion to English Restoration Theatre*, ed. Deborah Payne Fisk, Cambridge: Cambridge University Press, 2000, pp. 86–106.

———, '"The Whole Truth" of Restoration Tragicomedy,' in *Renaissance Tragicomedy: Explorations in Genre and Politics*, ed. Nancy Klein Maguire, New York: AMS Press, 1987, pp. 218–39.

Marsden, Jean I., *Fatal Desire. Women, Sexuality, and the English Stage, 1660–1720*, Ithaca: Cornell University Press, 2006.

———, 'Mary Pix's *Ibrahim*: the Woman Writer as Commercial Playwright,' *Studies in the Literary Imagination* 32.2 (1999), pp. 33–44.

———, 'Rape, Voyeurism, and the Restoration Stage,' in *Broken Boundaries: Women and Feminism in Restoration Drama*, ed. Katherine M. Quinsey, Lexington: The University Press of Kentucky, 1996, pp. 185–200.

———, 'Tragedy and Varieties of Serious Drama,' in *A Companion to Restoration Drama*, ed. Susan J. Owen, Oxford: Blackwell, 2001, pp. 228–42.

Masten, Jeffrey, *Textual Intercourse: Collaboration, Authorship, and Sexualities in Renaissance Drama*, Cambridge: Cambridge University Press, 1997.

Matar, Nabil, *Turks, Moors, and Englishmen in the Age of Discovery*, New York: Columbia University Press, 1999.

McCabe, Richard A., *Incest, Drama and Nature's Law 1550–1700*, Cambridge: Cambridge UP, 1993.

McGovern, Barbara, *Anne Finch and Her Poetry: A Critical Biography*, Athens: University of Georgia Press, 1992.

McGrath, Lynette, *Subjectivity and Women's Poetry in Early Modern England*, Aldershot: Ashgate, 2002.

McMullan, Gordon, and Jonathan Hope, eds., *The Politics of Tragicomedy: Shakespeare and After*, London: Routledge, 1992.

Mendelson, Sara Heller, *The Mental World of Stuart Women: Three Case Studies*, Brighton: Harvester, 1987.

———, 'Playing Games with Gender and Genre: the Dramatic Self-Fashioning of Margaret Cavendish,' in *Authorial Conquests: Essays on Genre in the Writings* of *Margaret Cavendish*, ed. Line Cottegnies and Nancy Weitz, Madison: Fairleigh Dickinson University Press, 2003, pp. 195–212.

Merrens, Rebecca, 'Unmanned with Thy Words: Regendering Tragedy in Manley and Trotter,' in *Broken Boundaries: Women and Feminism in Restoration Drama*, ed. Katherine M. Quinsey, Lexington: The University Press of Kentucky, 1996, pp. 31–53.

Milhous, Judith, *Thomas Betterton and the Management of Lincoln's Inn Fields, 1698–2001*, Carbondale: Southern Illinois University Press, 1979.

Milling, Jane, '"In the Female Coasts of Fame": Women's Dramatic Writing on the Public Stage, 1669–71,' *Women's Writing* 7.2 (2000), pp. 267–93.

Mora, María José, Manuel J. Gómez-Lara, Rafael Portillo, and Juan A. Prieto-Pablos, eds., *The Woman Turned Bully*, Barcelona: Edicions Universitat de Barcelona, 2007, pp. 34–6.

Morgan, Fidelis, ed., *The Female Wits: Women Playwrights of the Restoration*, London: Virago, 1981.

Nelson, T. G. A., 'The Ambivalence of Nature's Law: Representations of Incest in Dryden and His English Contemporaries,' in *Incest and the Literary Imagination*, ed. Elizabeth Barnes, Gainesville: University Press of Florida, 2002, pp. 117–37.

Novak, Maximilian E., 'Drama, 1660–1740,' in *The Cambridge History of Literary Criticism, v. IV: the 18th Century*, ed. H. B. Nisbet and Claude Rawson, Cambridge: Cambridge University Press, 1997, pp. 167–83.

Orr, Bridget, *Empire on the English Stage, 1660–1714*, Cambridge: Cambridge University Press, 2001.

Owen, Susan J., *Restoration Theatre and Crisis*, Oxford: Clarendon Press, 1996.

Pausanias, *Guide to Greece: Southern Greece*, trans. Peter Levi, Harmondsworth: Penguin Classics, 1971.

Payne, Linda R, 'Dramatic Dreamscape: Women's Dreams and Utopian Vision in the Works of Margaret Cavendish, Duchess of Newcastle,' in *Curtain Calls: British and American Women and the Theater, 1660–1820*, ed. Mary Anne Schofield and Cecilia Macheski, Athens: Ohio University Press, 1991, pp. 18–33.

Peacock, Judith, '"Writing for the Brain and Writing for the Boards: the Producibility of Margaret Cavendish's Dramatic Texts,' in *A Princely Brave Woman: Essays on Margaret Cavendish, Duchess of Newcastle*, ed. Stephen Clucas, Aldershot: Ashgate, 2003, pp. 87–108.

Pearson, Jacqueline, 'Blacker than Hell Creates: Pix Rewrites Othello,' in *Broken Boundaries: Women and Feminism in Restoration Drama*, ed. Katherine M. Quinsey, Lexington: The University Press of Kentucky, 1996, pp. 13–30.

———, *The Prostituted Muse: Images of Women and Women Dramatists, 1642–1737*, New York: St. Martin's Press, 1988.

———, '"Women may discourse ... as well as men": Speaking and Silent Women in the Plays of Margaret Cavendish, Duchess of Newcastle,' *Tulsa Studies in Women's Literature* 4.1 (1985), pp. 33–45.

Potter, Lois, '"True Tragicomedies" of the Civil War and Commonwealth,' in *Renaissance Tragicomedy: Explorations in Genre and Politics*, ed. Nancy Klein Maguire, New York: AMS Press, 1987, pp. 196–217.

Pulsipher, Jenny Hale, '*The Widow Ranter* and Royalist Culture in Colonial Virginia,' *Early American Literature* 39.1 (2004), pp. 41–66.

Purkiss, Diane, 'Blood, Sacrifice Marriage: why Iphigenia and Mariam have to die,' *Women's Writing* 6.1 (1999), 27–45.

———, *Literature, Gender and Politics during the English Civil War*, Cambridge: Cambridge University Press, 2005.

Quinsey, Katherine M., ed., *Broken Boundaries: Women and Feminism in Restoration Drama*, Lexington: The University Press of Kentucky, 1996.

Raber, Karen L., *Dramatic Difference: Gender, Class, and Genre in the Early Modern Closet Drama*, Newark: University of Delaware Press, 2001.

———, 'Gender and the Political Subject in *The Tragedy of Mariam*,' *Studies in English Literature* 35 (1995), 321–43.

———, 'Warrior Women in the Plays of Cavendish and Killigrew,' *Studies in English Literature* 40.3 (2000), pp. 413–33.

Randall, Dale B. J., *Winter Fruit: English Drama 1642–1660*, Lexington: The University Press of Kentucky,1995.

Ray, J. Karen, 'Friendly fire: the Oxymoron of Authority in Catherine Trotter's *Love at a Loss*,' *Restoration and 18th Century Theatre Research* 14:1 (1999), pp. 74–82.

Ready, Kathryn J., 'Damaris Cudworth Masham, Catharine Trotter Cockburn, and the Feminist Legacy of Locke's Theory of Personal Identity,' *Eighteenth-Century Studies* 35.4 (2002), pp. 563–76.

Rees, Emma L. E., *Margaret Cavendish: Gender, Genre, Exile*, Manchester: Manchester University Press, 2003.

———, guest ed., special issue on Margaret Cavendish, *Women's Writing* 4.3 (1999).

Reiss, Timothy J., 'Renaissance Theatre and the Theory of Tragedy' in *The Cambridge History of Literary Criticism vol. 3: the Renaissance*, ed. Glyn P. Norton, Cambridge: Cambridge University Press, 1999, pp. 229–47.

Reynolds, Myra, ed., *The Poems of Anne Countess of Winchilsea*, Chicago: University of Chicago Press, 1903.

Righter, Ann, 'Heroic Tragedy,' in *Restoration Theatre*, ed. John Russell Brown and Bernard Harris, New York: Capricorn Books, 1967, pp. 134–57.

Roberts, Jeanne Addison, 'Sex and the Female Hero,' in *The Female Tragic Hero in English Renaissance Drama*, ed. Naomi Conn Liebler, New York: Palgrave, 2002, pp. 199–215.

Roberts, David, *The Ladies: Female Patronage of Restoration Drama*, Oxford: Clarendon, 1989.

Romack, Katherine, and James Fitzmaurice, eds., *Cavendish and Shakespeare, Interconnections*, Aldershot: Ashgate, 2006.

Ross, Shannon, '*The Widdow Ranter*: Old World, New World—Exploring an Era's Authority Paradigms,' in *Aphra Behn (1640–1689): Identity, Alterity,*

Ambiguity, ed. Mary Anne O'Donnell, Bernhard Dhuicq, and Guy Leduc, Paris: L'Harmattan, 2000, pp. 81–90.

Rubik, Margarete, *Early Women Dramatists, 1550–1800*, London: Macmillan, 1998.

———, 'Estranging the Familiar, Familiarizing the Strange: Self and Other in *Oroonoko* and *The Widdow Ranter*,' in *Aphra Behn (1640–1689): Identity, Alterity, Ambiguity*, ed. Mary Anne O'Donnell, Bernhard Dhuicq, and Guy Leduc, Paris: L'Harmattan, 2000, pp. 33–41.

Salzman, Paul, *Reading Early Modern Women's Writing*, Oxford: Oxford University Press, 2006.

Sanders, Julie, '"A woman write a play!": Jonsonian Strategies and the Dramatic Writings of Margaret Cavendish; or, Did the Duchess Feel the Anxiety of Influence?' in *Readings in Renaissance Women's Drama. Criticism, History and Performance 1594–1998*, ed. S. P. Cerasano and Marion Wynne-Davies, London: Routledge, 1998, pp. 293–305.

Scott-Douglass, Amy, 'Enlarging Margaret: Cavendish, Shakespeare, and French Women Warriors and Writers,' in *Cavendish and Shakespeare, Interconnections*, ed. Katherine Romack and James Fitzmaurice, Aldershot: Ashgate, 2006, pp. 147–78.

Shaver, Anne, ed., *Margaret Cavendish, Duchess of Newcastle:* The Convent of Pleasure *and Other Plays*, Baltimore: The Johns Hopkins University Press, 1999.

Shell, Alison, *Catholicism, Controversy, and the English Literary Imagination, 1558–1660*, Cambridge: Cambridge University Press, 1999.

———, 'Elizabeth Cary's Historical Conscience: *The Tragedy of Mariam* and Thomas Lodge's *Josephus*,' in *The Literary Career and Legacy of Elizabeth Cary, 1613–1680*, ed. Heather Wolfe, London: Palgrave Macmillan, 2007, pp. 52–67.

Shell, Marc, *The End of Kinship*, Stanford: Stanford University Press, 1988.

Stanton, Judith Phillips, '"This New-Found Path Attempting": Women Dramatists in England, 1660–1800,' in *Curtain Calls: British and American Women and the Theater, 1660–1820*, ed. Mary Anne Schofield and Cecilia Macheski, Athens: Ohio University Press, 1991, pp. 325–54.

Staves, Susan, *A Literary History of Women's Writing in Britain, 1660–1789*, Cambridge: Cambridge University Press, 2006.

Steeves, Edna, ed., *The Plays of Mary Pix and Catharine Trotter*, New York: Garland, 1982.

Straznicky, Marta, *Privacy, Playreading, and Women's Closet Drama, 1550–1700*, Cambridge: Cambridge University Press, 2004.

Suzuki, Mihoko, 'Gender, the Political Subject, and Dramatic Authorship: Margaret Cavendish's *Loves Adventures* and the Shakespearean Example,' in *Cavendish and Shakespeare, Interconnections*, ed. Katherine Romack and James Fitzmaurice, Aldershot: Ashgate, 2006, pp. 103–20.

Thomas, Susie, 'This Thing of Darkness I Acknowledge Mine: Aphra Behn's *Abdelazer, or, The Moor's Revenge*,' *Restoration* 22 (1998), pp. 18–39.

Todd, Janet, and Derek Hughes, 'Tragedy and Tragicomedy,' in *The Cambridge Companion to Aphra Behn*, ed. Janet Todd and Derek Hughes, Cambridge: Cambridge University Press, 2004, pp. 83–97.

Todd, Janet, ed., *Aphra Behn Studies*, Cambridge: Cambridge University Press, 1996.

———, *The Works of Aphra Behn*, London: Pickering, 1996.

Tomlinson, Sophie, '"My brain the stage": Margaret Cavendish and the Fantasy of Female Performance,' in *Women, Texts and Histories 1575–1760*, ed. Clare Brant and Diane Purkiss, London: Routledge, 1992, pp. 134–63.

———, *Women on Stage in Stuart Drama*, Cambridge: Cambridge University Press, 2005.

Vaughan, Virginia Mason, *Performing Blackness on English Stages, 1500–1800*, Cambridge: Cambridge University Press, 2005.

Velissariou, Aspasia, '"Tis pity that when laws are faulty they should not be mended or abolish": Authority, Legitimation, and Honor in Aphra Behn's *The Widdow Ranter*,' *Papers on Language and Literature* 38.2 (2002), pp. 137–66.

Venet, Gisèle, 'Margaret Cavendish's Drama: An Aesthetic of Fragmentation,' in *Authorial Conquests: Essays on Genre in the Writings of Margaret Cavendish*, ed. Line Cottegnies and Nancy Weitz, Madison: Fairleigh Dickinson University Press, 2003, pp. 213–28.

Villegas-López, Sonia, 'Devising a New Heroine: Catharine Trotter's *Olinda's Adventures* and the Rise of the Novel Reconsidered,' in *Re-shaping the Genres: Restoration Women Writers*, ed. Zenón Luis-Martínez and Jorge Figueroa-Dorrego, Bern: Peter Lang, 2003, pp. 261–78.

Vitkus, Daniel, *Turning Turk: English Theater and the Multicultural Mediterranean, 1570–1630*, London: Palgrave Macmillan, 2003.

Waith, Eugene, *The Pattern of Tragicomedy in Beaumont and Fletcher*, North Haven: Archon Books, 1969.

Ward, Wilbur Henry, 'Mrs. Behn's *The Widow Ranter*: Historical Sources,' *South Atlantic Bulletin* 41.4 (1976), pp. 94–8.

Wheatley, Christopher J., 'Tragedy,' in *The Cambridge Companion to English Restoration Theatre*, ed. Deborah Payne Fisk, Cambridge: Cambridge University Press, 2000, pp. 70–85.

Wilcox, Helen, ed., *Women and Literature in Britain 1500–1700*, Cambridge: Cambridge University Press, 1996.

Williams, Gweno, '"No *Silent Woman*": The Plays of Margaret Cavendish, Duchess of Newcastle,' in *Women and Dramatic Production, 1550–1700*, ed. Alison Findlay and Stephanie Hodgson-Wright with Gweno Williams, Harlow: Longman, 2000, pp. 95–122.

———, 'Translating the Text, Performing the Self,' in *Women and Dramatic Production 1550–1700*, ed. Alison Findlay and Stephanie Hodgson-Wright with Gweno Williams, Harlow: Pearson Education, 2000, pp. 15–41.

Williamson, Mary L., *Raising Their Voices: British Women Writers, 1650–1750*, Detroit: Wayne State University Press, 1990.

Wiseman Susan, *Drama and Politics in the English Civil War*, Cambridge: Cambridge University Press, 1998.

———, 'Gender and Status in Dramatic Discourse: Margaret Cavendish, Duchess of Newcastle,' in *Women, Writing, History 1640–1740*, ed. Isobel Grundy and Susan Wiseman, Athens: The University of Georgia Press, 1992, pp. 159–77.

Wolfe, Heather, ed., *The Literary Career and Legacy of Elizabeth Cary, 1613–1680*, ed. Heather Wolfe, London: Palgrave Macmillan, 2007.

Yeazell, Ruth Bernard, *Harems of the Mind: Passages of Western Art and Literature*, New Haven: Yale University Press, 2000.

Index

Adam, Michel 107, 119, 130
Alexander the Great 97, 122
Altaba–Artal, Dolors 65, 130
Andrea, Bernardette 87–9, 93, 130
Anne, Queen 103, 104, 121, 127, 130, 135
Ariadne 81
   She Ventures and He Wins 81
Armistead, Jack 98, 99, 130
Astell, Mary 48, 115
Aubignac, Abbé d' 105
   Pratique du théâtre, La 105

Backscheider, Paula 81, 131
Ballaster, Ros 90, 131
Barash, Carol 124, 131
Barker, Jane 124
Barnes, Elizabeth 41, 137
Barry, Elizabeth 68, 82–3, 86, 88, 118, 121–2, 123
Battigelli, Anna 1, 35, 131
Beaumont, Francis 7–8, 36, 140
Behn, Aphra 1–2, 8, 11–12, 41, 55–6, 58, 60–80, 81–2, 84, 85, 87, 90–91, 92, 104, 108–10, 119, 121, 124, 129, 130, 131, 132, 133, 134, 135, 138, 139, 140
   Abdelazer 11, 12, 60, 68–75, 76, 84, 90, 108, 109, 121, 129, 139
   Agnes de Castro (Behn) 108, 129
   Forc'd Marriage, The 56, 60–65, 67, 129
   Love Letters between a Nobleman and his Sister 41
   Luckey Chance, The 56, 129
   Nun, The 82
   Oroonoko 1, 72, 76, 77, 133, 139
   Rover, The 2, 119
   Widdow Ranter, The 67, 76–80, 129, 131, 133, 138, 139, 140
   Young King, The 60, 65–8, 129
Beilin, Elaine, V. 16, 18, 26, 131
Belsey, Catherine 2, 19, 131

Bennett, Alexandra G. 19, 36, 46–8, 52, 131
Betterton, Mary 68
Betterton, Thomas 56, 68, 81, 86, 137
Birchwood, Matthew 84, 131
Boehrer, Bruce Thomas 41, 131
Boileau, Nicholas 105
   Art Poetique, L' 105
Bonin, Erin Lang 47, 131
Boothby, Frances 8, 11, 55–60, 61, 81, 129, 134
   Marcelia 55, 57–60, 62, 129
Bowerbank, Sylvia 36, 131
Bowman, Elizabeth 122
Bracegirdle, Anne 76, 78, 82–3, 85, 86, 88, 90, 118, 122
Braden, Gordon 27, 131
Brant, Clare 5, 48, 131, 140
Breitenberg, Mark 31, 131
Bridges, Liz 79–80, 131
Brillac, Mme. de 108, 109
Brown, John Russell 4, 138
Brown, Laura 5–6, 82, 131
Buckingham, George Villiers, Duke of 82
   Rehearsal, The 82
Burks, Deborah G. 85, 132
Burling, William J. 121, 122, 132
Bushnell, Rebecca 3–4, 7, 105, 132, 134

Calderón de la Barca, Pedro 65
   Vida es Sueño, La 65
Callaghan, Dympna 4, 22, 24, 32–3, 80, 92, 132
Calprenède, La 65
   Cléopâtre 65
Camoes, Luis de 108
Canfield, J. Douglas 6, 74–5, 100, 106, 132
Carnell, Rachel K. 76, 87, 99, 101, 132
Cartwright, Kent 16, 132
Cary, Elizabeth 2, 9, 11, 15, 18–34, 36, 40, 58, 73, 85, 88, 105, 106, 110, 122, 129, 132, 134, 135, 139, 141

History of the Life, Reign and Death of Edward II 18
Lady Falkland, Her Life, The 18, 21, 129
Tragedy of Mariam, The ix, 2, 9, 11, 15–34, 58, 73, 88, 106, 110, 114, 122, 129, 131, 132, 133, 134, 135, 138, 139
Cary, Henry, Viscount Falkland 20
Catholic Faith 18–20, 68, 124, 127, 139
Cavendish, Margaret, Duchess of Newcastle 1, 8, 11, 12, 35–53, 55, 66, 67, 125, 129, 131, 132, 133, 134, 136, 137, 138, 139, 140, 141
Bell in Campo 37, 47–53, 129, 131
Blazing World, The 1
Convent of Pleasure, The 37, 39, 47, 48, 129, 132
Female Academy, The 37, 48, 132
Lady Contemplation, The, Parts I & II 39–40, 48, 53, 129
Loves Adventures, Parts I & II 37, 47, 52–3, 67, 129, 139
Playes Written by the ... Marchiones of Newcastle 35–6, 40, 129
Plays, Never Before Printed 36
Sociable Companions, The 131
Unnatural Tragedie, The 40–44, 66, 129, 132
Youths Glory and Deaths Banquet, Parts I & II 38, 40, 44–6, 51, 129
Cavendish, William, Duke of Newcastle 35
Centlivre, Susanna 121
Bold Stroke for a Wife, A, 121
Busy Bodie, The 121
Cruel Gift, The 121
Marplot 121
Wonder, The 121
Cerasano, S. P. 17, 18, 37, 134, 135, 139
Chalmers, Hero 8, 36, 37, 48, 49, 132
Charles II 65, 72, 81, 108
Churchill, Sarah 124
Cibber, Colley 93
Richard III 93
Clarke, Danielle 15–17, 21, 25, 132
closet drama 10, 15, 18, 20–21, 37, 138, 139
Clucas, Stephen 1, 35, 37, 45, 132, 133, 137
Cockburn, Patrick 103
Cohen, Walter 7–8, 132
comedy 12, 39, 40, 47, 52, 55, 58, 61, 78, 99, 104, 107, 121

Congreve, William 105, 124
Corneille, Pierre 2, 4, 55, 105
Horace 2
Cornut–Gentille D'Arcy, Chantal 76, 133
Corporaal, Marguérite 41, 132
Cottegnies, Line 1, 35, 39, 133, 137, 140
Cotton, Nancy 82, 94, 104, 133
Crown, John 1
Calisto 1
Cuder–Domínguez, Pilar 19, 83, 91, 104, 133, 134, 136
Cullen, Patrick 57, 129

D'Monté, Rebecca 45, 133
Daniel, Samuel 17, 20
Davenant, Sir William 7, 55, 83
Siege of Rhodes, The 7, 83
Davies, John 18
Muses Sacrifice, The 18
Davis, Debbie K. 98, 99
Dekker, Thomas 72, 135
Lust's Dominion 72–3, 75, 135
Dhuicq, Bernard 77, 78, 79, 131, 133, 139
Dobrée, Bonamy 4, 133
Dolan, Frances 27, 133
Donoghue, Emma 104, 133
dramatic theory 8, 12, 105–6, 134
dramatic unities 21, 39
Dryden, John 4, 5, 41, 61, 69, 76, 77, 82, 83, 98, 105, 137
Conquest of Granada, The 69, 83
Don Sebastian 41
Dutton, Richard 3, 130

Exclusion Crisis, the 61, 65, 69, 72
Ezell, Margaret J. 13, 133

Farquhar, George 121
Felski, Rita 3, 133
Ferguson, Margaret W. 19, 21, 26, 129, 133
Ferguson, Moira 35, 133
Figueroa Dorrego, Jorge 76, 93, 103, 133, 136, 140
Finch, Anne, Countess of Winchilsea 9, 12, 121, 123–7, 130, 131, 136, 138
Aristomenes 9, 12, 124–7, 130
Triumphs of Love and Innocence, The 124
Finch, Heneage 124

Findlay, Alison 2, 16, 24, 37, 47, 94, 96, 118–19, 133, 140, 141
Fisk, Deborah Payne 6, 7, 100, 132, 136, 140
Fitzmaurice, James 1, 35, 37, 41, 46, 48, 53, 131, 133, 138, 139, 140
Fletcher, John 7–8, 36, 140
  Faithful Shepherdess, The 7
  Loyal Subject, The 7
Ford, John 41
  'Tis Pity She's a Whore 41
Foster, Verna A. 7, 134
Foxe, John 27
  Acts and Monuments 27

Garnier, Robert 2, 3, 17, 20
gender 1, 15, 19, 73, 75, 79–80, 127, 131, 132, 133, 134, 135, 136, 137, 138, 140
  and cross–dressing 47, 52–3, 67, 78, 79, 99
  and drama 4–6, 9–12
  and heroic code 47–53
  and race 32–4, 40–46, 77, 92–3
  roles 22–31, 58–60, 79–80, 87–8
  and violence 63–5, 85–6, 91–2
Glorious Revolution, the 6, 81, 113, 121, 124, 127
Godolphin, Harriet 113, 116
Gómez–Lara, Manuel J. 83, 134, 137
Goodkin, Richard E. 105–6, 134
Green, Reina 22, 134
Gruber, Elizabeth 22, 30, 134
Grundy, Isobel 5, 50, 134, 141
Guarini, Giambattista 7
  Pastor Fido, Il 7

Hannay, Margaret 17–18, 134
Harris, Bernard 4, 138
Harris, Henry 68
Heller, Jennifer L. 22, 134
Hendrick, Margo 24, 132
Henrietta Maria, Queen 48
Herbert, Mary 17, 135
Herman, Ruth 86–8, 90, 99, 101, 134
Hiscock, Andrew 20, 53, 134
Hobby, Elaine 1, 134
Hodgson–Wright, Stephanie J. 2, 17, 37, 47, 133, 134, 140
Hope, Jonathan 7–8, 132, 136

Hopkins, Lisa 4, 134
Horace 3
  Pompey 2, 55
Howard, Frances 25
Howe, Elizabeth 55, 83, 85, 86, 134
Hughes, Derek 1, 55, 57, 60–61, 63, 70, 73, 75, 93, 134, 140
Humanism 16, 20, 132
Hutner, Heidi 1, 76–7, 80, 135

ideology
  Jacobitism 12, 88, 90, 100–101, 123–4, 127
  Royalist 8, 36, 38, 48–52, 74–5, 76–7, 87, 132, 138
  Tory 57, 61, 64, 87, 90, 121, 123, 127
  Whig 85, 98, 100–101, 104–5, 107, 113, 117, 122, 123
incest 41–2, 66, 87, 118, 131, 136, 137
Inchbald, Elizabeth 121
Interregnum, the 8, 9, 11, 35, 78

James II 12, 65, 72, 88, 100, 121, 123, 124, 127
Jonson, Ben 36, 37, 39, 139
Josephus 20–21, 139

Kastan, David Scott 19, 133
Kelley, Anne 93, 94, 103–4, 106, 109, 113, 116–17, 119, 130, 135
Kelly, Erin E. 21, 135
Kendall, Kathryn 103–4, 121–22, 130, 135
Killigrew, Anne 36, 38, 48, 124, 138
Killigrew, Thomas 38, 55
King, Kathryn P. 8–9, 135
Knight, Frances 82
Kroll, Richard 60–61, 135
Krontiris, Tina 17, 135

Lamb, Mary Ellen 17, 26–7, 135
Leduc, Guy 77, 78, 79, 131, 139
Lee, Mary 61, 68
Lee, Nathaniel 5, 105
Lennep, William van 56, 68, 76, 93, 135
Levi, Peter 96, 125, 137
Lewalski, Barbara K. 18, 21–2, 135
Liebler, Naomi Conn 25, 138
Locke, John 103, 138
Lodge, Thomas 20–21, 139

Loftis, John 68, 135
Loomba, Ania 4, 11, 30, 135
López–Peláez Casellas, Jesús 72, 84, 135
Lowenthal, Cynthia 85, 92, 135
Luis–Martínez, Zenón 19, 41, 83, 93–4, 95, 96, 103, 134, 136, 140
Lumley, Jane 2, 10, 15–18, 20, 134
   Iphigenia at Aulis 2, 16–17, 134, 138

McCabe, Richard A. 41, 136
MacDonald, Joyce Green, 33, 73, 75, 136
McGovern, Barbara 124, 136
McGrath, Lynette 19, 136
Macheski, Cecilia 37, 121, 132, 137, 139
McMullan, Gordon 7, 8, 132, 136
Maguire, Nancy Klein 7–8, 55, 136, 138
Manley, Mary Delarivier 2, 6, 12, 81–90, 92–4, 98–101, 118, 124, 130, 132, 134, 137
   Almyna 88–90, 92, 101, 130
   Lost Lover, The 81
   Lucius 6, 93, 98–101, 130
   Royal Mischief, The 81, 82, 84, 86–8, 130
Marlborough, Duke of 113
Marsden, Jean I. 5, 82, 85, 86, 88, 136
Mary of Modena 100, 124
masculinity 10, 11, 22, 28–31, 63, 131
   anxious masculinity 31, 131
   critique of 94, 95, 98, 116
   hegemonic masculinity 28–31, 47
   in women 66, 79, 85
Masten, Jeffrey 36, 136
Matar, Nabil 84, 136
Mendelson, Sara Heller 35, 38–9, 45, 136
Merrens, Rebecca 118, 137
Middleton, Thomas 4, 22, 134
Milhous, Judith 81, 86, 137
Milling, Jane 55, 56, 60, 137
Mora, María José 80, 137
Morgan, Fidelis 103, 137
Mueller–Zettelmann, Eva 82, 130
Nelson, T. G. A. 41, 137
Nisbet, H. B. 105, 137
Norton, Glyn P. 3, 138
Novak, Maximilian E. 105, 137

O'Donnell, Mary Anne 77, 78, 79, 131, 133, 139
orientalism 83, 84, 87, 88, 93

Orr, Bridget 68, 76, 83–5, 86, 90, 91, 137
Otway, Thomas 5, 61, 82, 105
Owen, Susan J. 61, 69, 71, 82, 136, 137

Parker, Patricia 24, 132
pastoral 8, 12, 67–8, 125
Pausanias 125–6, 137
   Guide to Greece 125, 137
Payne, Deborah C., *see* Fisk, Deborah Payne
Payne, Linda R. 37, 39, 45, 137
Peacock, Judith 37, 137
Pearson, Jacqueline 5, 12, 46, 51, 59, 92–3, 137
Pembroke, Countess of, *see* Sidney, Mary
Philips, Katherine 55, 56, 82
   Pompey 55, 56
Pix, Mary 2, 5, 12, 81–7, 90–100, 103, 104, 113, 121, 130, 133, 136, 137, 139
   Conquest of Spain, The 90–92, 96, 123, 130
   Ibrahim 5, 81, 84–8, 91–2, 96, 121, 130, 136
   Queen Catharine 93–100, 130, 136
Polwhele, Elizabeth 56
   Faithful Virgins, The 56
   Frolicks, The 56
Pope, Alexander 124
Portillo, Rafael 83, 137
Portugal 69, 70, 108–10
Potter, Lois 8, 138
Powell, George 84, 86, 121
Prieto–Pablos, Juan A. 83, 134, 137
Pulsipher, Jenny Hale 76, 138
Purkiss, Diane 2, 5, 15–16, 19, 20, 47, 48, 130, 131, 138, 140

Quinsey, Katherine M. 5, 12, 86, 118, 136, 137, 138

Raber, Karen L. 19, 36, 38, 41, 47, 138
race 4, 11, 15, 22, 32–4, 72, 73, 75, 77–8, 132, 135, 136
Racine, Jean 88, 105
   Bajazet 88
Randall, Dale 36, 138
Rawson, Claude 105, 137
Ray, J. Karen 104, 138
Rees, Emma L. E. 1, 35, 36, 39, 138

Reiss, Timothy 3, 138
Reynolds, Myra 124, 125, 130, 138
Righter, Ann 4, 138
Roberts, David 1, 138
Roberts, Jeanne Addison 25, 138
Rogers, Jane 82, 84, 113
Romack, Katherine 1, 35, 37, 41, 46, 48, 53, 131, 133, 138, 139
Ross, Shannon 78, 139
Rowe, Nicholas 99, 104, 106
   Fair Penitent, The 105, 106
   Royal Convert, The 99
Rowley, William 91, 133
   All's Lost by Lust 91
Rubik, Margarete 5, 77, 82, 130, 139

Salzman, Paul 10, 55, 60, 139
Sanders, Julie 37, 139
Schofield, Mary Anne 37, 121, 132, 137, 139
Scott–Douglas, Amy 48, 139
Seneca 9, 15, 18, 20, 27, 104, 105, 106, 131
Settle, Elkanah 83
   Empress of Morocco, The 83
Shakespeare, William 1, 3, 4, 7, 8, 17–18, 30, 35, 36, 37, 41, 46, 48, 53, 63, 85, 93–4, 97–9, 105, 131, 132, 133, 136, 138, 139
   Antony and Cleopatra 17
   Hamlet 70, 73, 97
   Macbeth 97
   Measure for Measure 41, 85
   Merchant of Venice, The 53, 62
   Much Ado About Nothing 63
   Othello 12, 22, 30–31, 32, 53, 62, 93, 97, 98, 134, 137
   Richard III 99
   Titus Andronicus 85
   Twelfth Night 53
   Winter's Tale, The 46, 63, 131
Shaver, Anne 38, 39, 47, 129, 139
Shell, Alison 19–20, 139
Shell, Marc 41, 139
Shirley, James 37, 41
Sidney, Mary, Countess of Pembroke 2, 10, 15, 16–18, 20, 105
   Tragedie of Antonie, The 2, 17
Sidney, Sir Philip 3, 130
Smith, William 68
Southerne, Thomas 82
   Fatal Marriage, The 82
Spain 12, 68, 69, 70, 72, 75, 91–2, 108–9, 111, 117
Stallybrass, Peter 19, 133
Stanton, Judith Phillips 121, 139
Staves, Susan 58, 83, 116–17, 139
Steele Richard 100–101
Steeves, Edna 84, 103, 130, 139
Stoicism 9, 26–7, 29, 34, 119, 126
Straznicky, Marta 20–21, 139
Suzuki, Mihoko 53, 139

theatre companies
   Betterton's, 81, 83, 86, 116, 121
   Duke's, the 55, 56, 61, 68, 81
   King's, the 55, 81
   Queen's, the 88, 90, 113
   Rich's 68, 84, 86, 103, 111
   United, the 81
theatres
   Dorset Garden 55
   Drury Lane 82, 90–91
   Lincoln's Inn Fields 81, 82, 137
Thomas, Susie 72–3, 75, 140
Todd, Janet 1, 56, 60–61, 65, 108, 129, 134, 140
Tomlinson, Sophie 8, 38, 48, 49, 140
Tragedy 1–11, 15, 19, 40–44, 58, 76, 77, 92, 97, 104–7
   Affective tragedy 4–5
   Heroic tragedy 4, 69, 138
   Historical tragedy 12, 18, 76, 80, 93, 98–9, 103, 106–8, 111–15, 119
   Revenge tragedy 63, 68, 84
   Senecan tragedy 9, 15, 18, 20, 27, 104, 105–6, 131
   She–tragedy 4–6, 82, 104
   of state 4
Tragicomedy 2, 7–9, 12–13, 40, 47, 55–6, 58, 60–62, 67–8, 76, 132, 134, 135, 136, 138, 140
Travitsky, Betty S. 57, 129
Trotter, Catharine 2, 5–6, 9, 12, 81–2, 84, 86, 91, 93, 103–19, 123, 130, 135, 137, 138, 139, 140
   Agnes de Castro 81, 82, 103–4, 108–10, 118, 130
   Fatal Friendship 6, 103, 106–7, 116–19, 123, 130

Love at a Loss 103, 104, 106, 107, 138
Olinda's Adventures 103, 140
Revolution of Sweden, The 103, 104, 106, 107, 113–16, 119, 130
Unhappy Penitent, The 104–5, 107, 111–13, 118–19, 130, 135

Vaughan, Virginia Mason 75, 140
Vélez de Guevara, Luis 108
Velissariou, Aspasia 76, 140
Venet, Gisèle 39, 140
Villegas–López, Sonia 103, 140
Vitkus, Daniel 84, 140
Vives, Juan Luis 16

Waith, Eugene 7, 140
Ward, Wilbur Henry 76, 140
Warnke, Frank J. 35, 133
Webster, John 4, 21
  Duchess of Malfi, The 21–2, 134
Weitz, Nancy 1, 35, 39, 133, 137, 140
Weller, Barry 21, 129
Wheatley, Christopher J. 5–6, 106, 140
Wilcox, Helen 5, 140
Williams, Gweno 2, 16, 17, 37, 47, 133, 140

Williamson, Mary L. 104, 141
Wilson, Katharina M. 35, 133
Winchilsea, Countess of, *see* Finch, Anne
Wiseman, Jane 12, 121–3, 130
  Antiochus the Great 12, 121–3, 130
Wiseman, Susan 5, 9, 35, 36, 38, 50, 53, 134, 141
Wolfe, Heather 18, 20, 21, 135, 139, 141
women
  agency 8, 27, 58–9, 68, 72–5, 78, 85, 87, 92, 96, 100, 119, 135
  authorship 55–6
  deviancy 27, 73, 85, 92, 115, 123
  heroism 4, 25, 34, 50, 80, 85, 134
  female rebellion 22, 24, 28, 32, 85, 87
  lesbian identity 103–4, 133
  sacrificial death 16, 26, 88
  self–fashioning 20, 38, 136
  suffering 17, 27, 34, 42, 59, 89, 116–17
Wycherley, William 61
  Love in a Wood 61
Wynne–Davies, Marion 17, 18, 37, 134, 135, 139

Yeazel, Ruth Bernard 83, 88, 90, 141